THE
EARLY TUDOR THEORY
OF KINGSHIP

THE
EARLY TUDOR THEORY
OF KINGSHIP

BY

FRANKLIN LE VAN BAUMER

NEW YORK / RUSSELL & RUSSELL

1966

TO
MY WIFE

PREFACE

NEVER in English history has the king played a more important rôle than during the first half of the sixteenth century. The early Tudor era marked the king's acquisition of greater powers, temporal and spiritual, than he has ever wielded indisputably before or since. During the reigns of Henry VII and Henry VIII the crown became, as never before, the focal point, the nerve center of the nation's religious, political, and economic life. By dint of the Reformation the king was regaled with the title of Supreme Head of the Church of England, thus acceding to the absolute sovereignty over the Church in England formerly exercised by the pope. In consequence of the growth of the New Monarchy, he similarly became the near-absolute ruler in the temporal sphere, supreme above rival jurisdictions within the state. Parliament, allied for the moment with the king against the pope and English clergy, was not prepared as yet to challenge seriously the king's newly-acquired sovereignty.

An especial importance attaches therefore to the theory of kingship propounded by English political writers during the early Reformation. What powers did Englishmen attribute to their king during one of the most revolutionary periods of their history? To what extent did the early Tudor publicists elaborate a new political creed to fit the facts of the new political actuality? To what degree were they still dominated by medieval ideas of kingship? Only in the answers to these questions can the significance of the English Reformation and the essential content of the Tudor political mentality be fully comprehended. It is the purpose of this

book to answer these questions with particular reference to
the reign of Henry VIII.

I have come to the conclusion that in the Henrician theory
of kingship there was much that was new—though perhaps
nothing that was new in the strictly chronological sense—
and much that was old. The Henricians stood on the threshold of a brave new world, but only on the threshold. They
preached a revolutionary theory of Royal Supremacy to
justify the great anti-ecclesiastical statutes of the Reformation Parliament. They advocated a doctrine of absolute non-
resistance to preserve intact the advances made by the New
Monarchy in the secular sphere. More often than not, however, they employed medieval phraseology to elucidate the
new point of view. And their attitude toward other problems of kingship was, for the most part, entirely in the medieval tradition. They taught, for example, that the Law,
natural and positive, is supreme within the state, not the
king. They believed that the king must share his rule with
parliament. They taught afresh and with vehemence the
king's moral responsibility to God to rule for the good of society as a whole, and not for his own selfish advantage. Their
political outlook was thus wholly alien to the new-fangled
theory of absolute monarchy and unlimited sovereignty being
propounded currently on the continent by some of the civil
lawyers.

There were good reasons, of course, why the Henrician
political writers were not prepared to throw overboard all
the traditional ideas of kingship. Although most of them
approved of the New Monarchy whole-heartedly, some of
them, foreseeing the Stuart era in a glass darkly, were apprehensive lest the king become too powerful. Hence, their emphasis on the ultimate sovereignty of Law and the king's
moral responsibility. Some of them, too, did not perceive
the newness of the New Monarchy, and saw no reason therefore to abandon the old concepts. Moreover, where there

was no immediate issue at stake, the Henricians as a whole were wisely content to let sleeping dogs lie. Their main job, after all, was to provide a theoretical basis for the king's authority in the realm at large, in both the spiritual and temporal spheres—to banish papal "pretensions" from the "empire" of England, to excoriate feudal disorders and the pointless riotings of the great unwashed, to exalt therefore the power of the crown. Why discuss prematurely the problems of the king *vs.* parliament, or of the king *vs.* the law? King and parliament were temporarily in alliance, and the royal prerogative courts were, for the moment, less of an evil than the "whore of Babylon," the White Rose Party, and the *canaille*. Why not keep the medieval doctrine of the king and the law, and allow the questions begged therein to go unanswered until a later day?

In advancing these views and others, I do not lay claim to entire originality. My principal purpose has been to bring together within one compass ideas which have hitherto been scattered in various places. In some of the chapters I believe that I have used new materials, and that I have suggested fresh lines of thought. But to anyone familiar with the field of Tudor political theory it will be evident at once that I owe a great debt to the works of J. W. Allen, W. S. Holdsworth, P. Janelle, C. H. McIlwain, and A. F. Pollard.

Moreover, I do not pretend that my work by any means exhausts the subject. It is a general sketch only, albeit a detailed one, and there is room for any number of supplementary monographs. For example, no adequate study has yet been made of the Henrician judges and their attitude toward the royal prerogative. In the pages below, I have emphasized the pamphlet, printed or in manuscript, rather than the legal decision, because it was the pamphlet which circulated among the people, and which therefore gave them what ideas of kingship they had. But I am by no means blind to the importance of the judges.

In conclusion, I wish to thank the following for generous assistance and advice in the preparation of this volume: Prof. Wallace Notestein of Yale University who has counselled and aided me on all scores more than I can tell during the past five years; Prof. J. E. Neale of the University of London who encouraged and guided me during the year when this book was first conceived; Prof. Cecil Driver of Yale University whose advice on style and organization has proved invaluable, and who had the infinite patience to criticize the rough drafts of this book when it was first being written as a dissertation for the degree of doctor of philosophy at Yale University; Prof. W. H. Dunham of Yale University who read the manuscript several times and who has given me many valuable suggestions; Prof. G. H. Sabine of Cornell University who kindly read the manuscript and saved me from several pitfalls; Prof. L. W. Labaree of Yale University who has helped no end in improving the book's physical appearance and general organization; and, last but not least, my wife who has been my severest critic, and who has been indefatigable in helping to prepare the manuscript and in reading proof.

F. Le V. B.

New Haven, Connecticut
  July 23, 1939

CONTENTS

Preface vii

I. The Theory of Kingship in Retrospect . . 1

II. The King and the Church: The Henrician
Statutes 21

III. The King and the Church: The Henrician
Pamphlets 35

IV. The Cult of Authority 85

V. The King and the Law 120

VI. The King's Moral Responsibility 192

Appendices:

A. Henry VIII's Propagandist Campaign 213

B. Bibliography of Early Tudor Literature on Political Theory 225

Bibliographical Note 239

Index 245

THE EARLY TUDOR THEORY
OF KINGSHIP

I

THE THEORY OF KINGSHIP IN
RETROSPECT

For we have taught that all the decrees of the royal law, when they are in error, ought to be corrected by the rules of the law of nature. Thus also we have proved that the rules of the political law, and the sanctions of customs and constitutions ought to be made null and void, so often as they depart from the institutes of nature's law, which we have above defined as the mother and mistress of all human laws. FORTESCUE, *De Natura Legis Naturae*, I, Chap. 29.

IN January, 1533, Henry VIII was secretly united in matrimony with Anne Boleyn. On June first of the same year, Archbishop Cranmer openly crowned Anne Queen of England in Westminster Abbey. By these acts the English Reformation was set in full swing. Henry VIII, anxious to secure the legitimacy of his eagerly expected son, had taken his "divorce" case out of the pope's hands, and had himself repudiated Catherine of Aragon. By so doing, he committed England to a course the every advance of which was unprecedented, illegal, and momentous. A bloodless revolution ensued, in which king and parliament united to throw off the papal yoke, to subjugate the newly created Church of England to the State, and to make the king the practical ruler of that State. Never before perhaps had a king of England enjoyed such plenary powers. Never again was he to enjoy them so indisputably.

This revolution in practical politics was accompanied by a revolution in political ideas, particularly in regard to those involving kingship. It is only natural that the salient features of a new political order should in large part be reflected in, and justified by, the political literature of the day. Thus, Tudor political theorists produced a doctrine of Royal Supremacy to lend weight to the title of Supreme Head of the English Church with which the Reformation Parliament regaled Henry VIII. They set up a veritable cult of royal authority, and proclaimed the essential sinfulness of resistance to the king under any circumstances. They asserted the superiority of the king in parliament over canon, statute, municipal, and even at times customary law. They fell short of enunciating a theory of unlimited royal sovereignty, it is true. Nevertheless, the king, in consequence of their labors, emerged from the conflict with Rome with a prestige greatly enhanced, and with an aureole of sanctity around him reminiscent of the Roman Emperors.

To look back to the fifteenth century is to discover an entirely different political psychology. There is, perhaps, no more striking contrast in English history than the disparity between the political ideas of the early English Reformation, and those of the fifteenth century. The contrast is between an era of rapid change, during which men were afire with new ideas, and a century of comparative inactivity, during which men clung largely to their traditional notions. Whereas the crucial years of Henry VIII's "triumphant" reign called forth political tracts in abundance, and overtaxed the printing establishments of Thomas Berthelet, Thomas Godfray, and others, the age of Sir John Fortescue could boast of few formal political treatises, much less of political pamphleteering on a wide scale.[1] Whereas the Reformation political writers produced a revolutionary theory of kingship, the fifteenth-century lawyers and churchmen stood staunchly by the medieval tradition, only occasionally making a concession to the order of the day.[2]

1. It is significant that information on fifteenth-century political ideas must be gleaned for the most part from Year Book reports, sermons, and speeches before parliament—and not from formal political treatises.

2. The only book available on fifteenth-century English political theory as a whole is S.B.Chrimes' *English Constitutional Ideas in the Fifteenth Century* (Cambridge, 1936).

The explanation for the essential conservatism of fifteenth-century political thought, as well as for the literary inertia of the period, is not far to seek. In the first place, prior to the introduction of the printing press, the public to which political writers could appeal was strictly limited.[3] Political speculation was discouraged at the outset by the mere physical handicap of having to circulate in manuscript. But of far greater importance was the fact that, in contradistinction to the years 1529–1540, the fifteenth century experienced no large-scale political revolution. The Reformation and the growth of centralized monarchy under the early Tudors, literally forced men to rearrange their ideas of kingship. But the fifteenth century was productive of no political tendency apparent enough to the public eye, or of sufficient scope, to warrant an ebullition of political speculation.

To be sure, the fifteenth century saw an increase of parliamentary activity and initiative under Henry IV and Henry V, following on Richard II's unsuccessful attempt to rule by prerogative. It also witnessed the spectacle of the Wars of the Roses. But neither Lancastrian parliamentary activity nor the Wars of the Roses can be said to have constituted a political movement of any scope or permanency. The attempt on the part of the Lancastrian parliaments to curb the expenses of the royal household, and to control the membership of the king's council, can hardly be dubbed a "constitutional experiment." For parliaments later in the century abandoned the novel position assumed by the parliaments of 1404 and 1406, and at no time during the century did either crown or commons advance claims of exclusive sovereignty.[4] The Wars of the

3. Printing was not introduced into England until 1477.
4. As J.E.A.Jolliffe aptly puts it in his *Constitutional History of Medieval England* (London, 1937), p. 431: "The older feudal dissension between crown and magnates has been fought out and finished; the final clash between crown and commons will not come until the seventeenth century. [The fifteenth century] is a time when there are few *fundamental* [italics mine] differences as to the constitution, when king and commons, and the lords also in some measure, proceed upon the assumption of common interest, and can meet without friction in parliament, accepting each other's advice and consent as useful elements in a

Roses, it may be thought, were for the most part dynastic quarrels, and the defeat or victory of Lancastrian or Yorkist claimants to the throne involved no fundamental constitutional issue.

Moreover, it was not until the end of the century that England turned definitely toward modern, absolute monarchy. Fifteenth-century kings were too absorbed in French campaigns, in fighting off fits of insanity, in maintaining themselves on the throne, to establish a strong, centralized government. The royal prerogative courts, it may be noted, had not yet reached that dizzy pinnacle to which they were later to be raised by Henry VIII and Cardinal Wolsey. And there was nothing very unusual in the relations between the English *regnum* and *sacerdotium* from 1399 to 1509. It is true that the monarchs beginning with Edward IV set to work to lay the foundations for the New Monarchy, in which the king was to assume new and sovereign powers. But this transition from centrifugal to centripetal government was at first so imperceptible, and its significance to contemporaries so little apparent, that its philosophical interpretation was not as yet forthcoming.

It is true that the political anarchy obtaining in England in consequence of the Wars of the Roses did give rise, in the case of Sir John Fortescue, to a plea for a monarchy stronger than any of its parts; and that the foundation of a centralized government under Henry VII influenced Edmund Dudley, one of the king's financial commissioners, to express some opinions more akin to the spirit of the New Monarchy than to the medieval tradition. But these views were exceptions to the rule, mere ripples on the surface of an otherwise placid sea. Significant as adumbrations of the future, they were as atypical of the general tenets of Fortescue and Dudley themselves, as of the political philosophy of the fifteenth century as a whole.

The theory of kingship normally espoused by the fif-

common decision, without deeply questioning the right from which they proceed."

teenth century was for the most part a time-honored one, reflecting scrupulously the comparatively static, sometimes reactionary character of the political events of the day. Inspired largely by the medieval tradition, the pre-Tudor publicists (such as there were) taught that the king, either *solus* or in parliament, is subject to "fundamental" law which he has the power to declare, but not to change or violate. They asserted that in the declaration of common law and in the levy of extraordinary taxation, the king must work in conjunction with lords and commons. They stressed the king's moral responsibilities toward society, emphasizing the fact that the king is responsible to God for the well-being of his subjects. True, they pointed toward the doctrine of non-resistance soon to become so popular under the New Monarchy, but they were not emphatic about it. And the sphere of spiritual sovereignty they reserved entirely for the Church, as of yore.

It may be concluded that the fifteenth-century lawyers and churchmen had no more to do with unlimited sovereignty,[5] or, for that matter, with sovereignty of any sort, than had the feudal society of the middle ages. Nor had they much to do with king-worship, for to have erected a

5. By "unlimited sovereignty" I understand throughout this work the power to legislate (1) without reference to an eternal law, or code of ideal principles; (2) without interference from any authority external to the state; and (3) without restriction by any other person, group, or constitutional body within the state. According to this definition, the king of England in no sense possessed unlimited sovereignty during the middle ages. He was checked on all three scores. He was legally bound, as will appear below, to derive positive law, whether in the form of statutes or royal proclamations, from natural and customary law. Theoretically, he possessed no legislative power whatever in the spiritual sphere where international canon and papal law reigned supreme. And within the English realm he was to some extent checked by the lords and commons in parliament.

Some are of the opinion that the present-day English Parliament possesses unlimited sovereignty. But the American Congress certainly wields no such power. It is checked by both the President and the Supreme Court, and behind the Supreme Court, by the Constitution and the Bill of Rights.

The theory of unlimited sovereignty, or "what has come to be known as the orthodox doctrine of sovereignty," finds its fullest expression in Thomas Hobbes, and in the works of John Austin and the German jurists of the late nineteenth century (see *Encyclopaedia of the Social Sciences*, article, "Sovereignty," by F.W.Coker).

cult of royal authority, or to have lingered long over the divinity which hedges a king, would have seemed strange indeed to men some of whom had witnessed the degrading spectacle of three monarchs being driven from the throne. The conception of "absolute monarchy" [6] was as alien to their tastes as it had been to the ecclesiastics and barons of a former day who had combined to resist the encroachments of an aggressive crown.

The prevalence of the idea of natural or "fundamental" law in fifteenth-century England is clearest indication of the fact that pre-Tudor England boasted no theory of absolute monarchy. For where there is fundamental law, there cannot be absolute monarchy—a fact which the medieval civilians, canonists, and feudal lawyers had well understood in their discussions of the powers of royalty. *Jus,* the medieval civilians and canonists had maintained, is neither the will of the prince, nor the enactment of some institution or assembly within secular society. It is, on the contrary, an eternal principle, or body of principles, emanating from the reason or will of God, unchangeable and ever-binding on the social animal. Man apprehends it through his reason and applies it by positive law to the mundane society in which he finds himself. This fundamental law of nature or reason may therefore be "interpreted" and "declared" by the rulers of the people, but never "made" or "enacted" in the modern legislative sense. The

6. By "absolute monarchy" I understand throughout this work a monarchy in which the king possesses unlimited sovereignty (see above, note 5). I am referring, in other words, to the extreme doctrine of absolutism propounded by Machiavelli, Hobbes, and the eighteenth-century theorists—"the doctrine of the absolute right of the ruler, i.e. the affirmation that the ruler is bound neither by the laws of nature nor by any kind of moral or legal limitation" (see *Encyclopaedia of the Social Sciences,* article, "Absolutism," by A.D.Lindsay). The *N.E.D.* definition of the "absolute" king is, to my mind, somewhat ambiguous. The "absolute" king is therein described as "having absolute power, governing absolutely; unlimited by a constitution or the concurrent authority of a parliament; arbitrary, despotic." For purposes of clarity, the definition might have added the phrase "unlimited by law, natural or positive," or *legibus solutus;* for no ruler living in a society dominated by natural and feudal law can truly be said to possess unlimited sovereignty, and hence to be absolute.

king, like all other human beings, is subject to its dictates.[7]

Translated into English terms, this conception of *Jus* had generally meant the superiority of the common law to other forms of human law. It is true that in the fifteenth and sixteenth centuries, English publicists begin to differentiate between natural and customary law, and to argue that natural law is ever immutable, but that customary law is sometimes transitory. But during the middle ages the ultimate identity of the two laws was assumed,[8] and the superiority of the common law to the king could be asserted with the knowledge that behind it lay the fundamental authority of God's immutable law of nature. That this conception of a fundamental law was generally accepted in medieval England cannot be doubted. Mc-Ilwain has shown conclusively that the kings themselves, in addition to the lawyers and ecclesiastics, recognized the principle that "there is a fundamental law which binds a king and beyond which he may not go"; and that consequently the king's laws must ultimately be derived from, and accord with, the common law.[9] Thus, William the Conqueror professed to restore the ancient laws of Edward

7. For the supreme medieval expression of the conception of natural law, see St. Thomas Aquinas, *Summa Theologica*, Part II (1st Part), Quaestio 91. According to St. Thomas, there are four kinds of law, all closely interrelated. There is the Eternal Law, identical with God's reason and beyond human comprehension. There is Natural Law, an imperfect reflection of the Eternal Law in man's nature, enjoining man, among other things, to seek good and to avoid evil, and to approximate the perfect life. There is Divine Law, another reflection of the Eternal Law, and manifested in the Scriptures. And fourthly, there is Human Law, which is Natural Law rendered specific in human law codes. Human Law is accordingly derived entirely from Natural Law, and "if in any point it deflects from the law of nature, it is no longer a law but a perversion of law."

8. According to McIlwain, "the law of nature . . . appears [in England] remarkably late, and when it first appears it comes largely as an attempt, born of the curiosity of the Renaissance, to account for a body of customary law which has long been in existence, and whose binding character is unquestioned, though its beginnings are lost in antiquity" (*The High Court of Parliament and its Supremacy*, New Haven, 1910, p. 97).

9. See *ibid.*, Chap. 2. This chapter, entitled "The Fundamental Law," is an admirable summary of the reverence with which medieval Englishmen regarded the common law.

the Confessor, and not to enact new laws. Magna Carta enunciated the principle that the king cannot demand more than the usual feudal dues, that he cannot violate the feudal contract, *i.e.*, the fundamental law of the realm. Parliament arraigned Richard II on the charge of having attempted "to maintain and defend those statutes and ordinances which are erroneous and unjust and repugnant to all law and reason."

This conception of a natural or fundamental law eminently superior to all forms of positive law, whether royal or otherwise, the fifteenth century inherited from its medieval past, and adapted to its own circumstances. Sir John Fortescue's political treatises, various learned speeches delivered before parliament by the lord chancellors from Stillington to Morton, law-court decisions, all these amply testify to the fact that the natural-law idiom with all its implications was still in constant use in the fifteenth century.[10]

Sir John Fortescue was perhaps the supreme exponent of the natural-law philosophy in fifteenth-century England. In his *De Natura Legis Naturae* especially, and in other books as well, Fortescue expounds the principles of natural law at length, following scrupulously the definitions laid down by the medieval political theorists. From these principles Fortescue drew the usual conclusions: (1) that the king, either *solus* or in parliament, is subordinate to natural law; (2) that in declaring and giving specific form to the law of nature, the king must work in conjunction with parliament—at least where it is a question of changing the customary law of the realm, or of levying extraordinary taxation; and (3) that the king must observe the law once promulgated.

10. See, for example, Bishop Stillington's speech to the parliament of 1468 (*Rotuli Parliamentorum*, V, 622); Cardinal Morton's discourse before the parliament of 1489 (printed in A.F.Pollard, *Reign of Henry VII from Contemporary Sources*, London, 1913, I, no. 45); and Year Books, 8 Ed.IV, Mich. pl. 35; 13 Ed.IV, Pas. pl. 5 (printed in Chrimes, *English Constitutional Ideas in the Fifteenth Century*, App., nos. 50, 58).

To Fortescue it was self-evident that the king, either *solus* or in parliament, is subordinate to natural law. All *human law*, he says, whether it be custom, the *jus gentium*, statute law, civil law, or the law of the king, is derived from, and is auxiliary to, the law of nature.[11] This is especially evident where the *jus regis*, the law issued by the king of his own authority, is concerned. Kings have their rights "as it were on loan, not from the prince's authority, but solely from the force of this law [*i.e.*, the law of nature], which proclaims itself common to all the powers of the world." [12] The *jus regis* can no more be compared to the law of nature than a fly to an eagle, or a blind mole to a lynx. "Let therefore the Law of the King give place to [the law of nature], as to its mistress and elder, nor presume any more by comparisons to make itself her equal." [13]

Fortescue adds that the king in parliament, no less than the king *solus*, is subordinate to the fundamental law. Statutes and constitutions are nothing more than the law of nature and custom reduced to writing.[14] Parliament is thus a judicial, not a legislative body. It renders decisions, it does not create law. It is a high court whose duty it is to declare the fundamental law, to give it practical application. It cannot create *novel ley* since all law is implicit in the fundamental law promulgated by God at the beginning of time. Conversely, positive law contrary to fundamental law is no law at all. "What things soever are either recorded in customs or comprehended in writings," says Fortescue, quoting canon law, "if they be adverse to natural law, are to be held null and void."[15] The king in parliament has not the right to reverse the fundamental

---

11. *De Natura Legis Naturae* (hereafter referred to as *De Natura*), printed in *The Works of Sir John Fortescue, Knight*, edited by Thomas (Fortescue) Lord Clermont (London, 1869), I, Cap. 5.

12. *Ibid.*, pp. 67–68.

13. *Ibid.*, p. 91.

14. *De Laudibus Legum Angliae*, printed in *The Works of Sir John Fortescue, Knight*, Cap. 15.

15. *De Natura*, p. 67.

property laws,[16] or the rule excluding women from the throne,[17] or, presumably, Magna Carta, for these are grounded on the law of nature. Clearly, the king in parliament, according to this view, no more possesses unlimited sovereignty than does the king *solus*.

Fortescue also held that the king is restricted in the process of promulgating positive law, and that he is bound to observe positive law once promulgated. He did not doubt, in fact no fifteenth-century common lawyer doubted, that the king has a prerogative by means of which he can legally suspend the operation of certain laws, and himself declare law by proclamation and by letters patent, and by adding to bills provisos which do not require the consent either of lords or commons. He did not doubt, to borrow Chrimes' expression, that "the king [is] absolute, even though limited,"[18] that is, that the king possesses a prerogative of wide national as well as feudal proportions. But neither did he doubt that in matters involving extraordinary taxation or a change in customary law, the king is bound to seek his subjects' consent. There are two kinds of kingdoms, he stated bluntly in the first chapter of his *Governance of England,* the *dominium regale* and the *dominium politicum et regale.* The second only is applicable to England. A king of England cannot at his pleasure make alterations in the law of the land, for the nature

16. Property, Fortescue says (*De Natura,* p. 82), originated in the law of nature before nations were established. In this respect, Fortescue disagreed with medievalists like Aquinas and Ockham who had taught that the institution of property was introduced into human society only after original sin, and that it is therefore grounded on the *jus gentium,* not the *jus naturale.* As Max Shepard points out ("The Political and Constitutional Theory of Sir John Fortescue," *Essays in History and Political Theory in honor of C.H.McIlwain,* Cambridge, 1936), Fortescue anticipated Locke's view that governments exist to perpetuate, not to take away private property. In this respect he may be regarded as the champion of the landed gentry of fifteenth-century England.

17. Fortescue's main contention in the *De Natura* is to prove that by the law of nature women and their descendants are excluded from the throne (see *De Natura,* especially II, Cap. 3). Edward IV had descended in the female line from Lionel, Duke of Clarence, Edward III's second son, whereas Henry VI, Fortescue's client, traced his lineage in the male line from John of Gaunt, Edward III's third son.

18. *English Constitutional Ideas in the Fifteenth Century,* p. 322.

of the government in England is political as well as regal. If the government were regal alone, the king could do anything he pleased according to the maxim of the civil law, *quod principi placuit legis habet vigorem*. But if the government is regal *and* political, as in England, the king can make no alterations in the laws of the realm, nor burden his subjects with strange impositions "without their own assent."[19] The statutes of England, Fortescue said in another place, are good because "not enacted by the sole will of the prince, but with the concurrent consent of the whole kingdom." [20]

It was, then, the general belief in pre-Tudor England that "the king is under God and the law, for it is the law which makes the king"; that the king, both *solus* and in parliament, is subject to the law, both natural and positive. But in several other respects as well, the temper of fifteenth-century England was alien to absolute monarchy. In the first place, the doctrine of the moral responsibility of the ruler was just as lusty in the fifteenth century as it had been in the preceding centuries.[21] The medieval political theorists had taught without exception that not only has a king to rule according to the law, according to certain prescribed rules and formulae, but that he is also

19. I do not mean to imply in this passage that Fortescue was in any sense advancing a theory of modern constitutional monarchy. His conception, as Chrimes has conclusively shown (pp. 319-322), was typically medieval. The king, except for the fact that he cannot alter the fundamental law of the land, or confiscate his subjects' property without their consent, is for all purposes absolute. All I am trying to say is that whenever the subject of positive or statute law was broached in the fifteenth century, it often implied the joint product of king and parliament working in co-operation.

20. *De Laudibus Legum Angliae*, p. 350.

21. I am well aware of the fact that the doctrine of the moral responsibility of the ruler does not of itself constitute an argument against absolute monarchy. Tyndale and James I, for example, were both vehement advocates of absolute monarchy (at least part of the time), and yet they could write at length concerning the king's moral obligations. But when the doctrine of the moral responsibility of the ruler is *combined with* the thesis of the king's subordination to the law, and when it receives an especial emphasis, then it can be used to no little advantage against absolute monarchs and tyrants. It was so used during the middle ages, and during the fifteenth and sixteenth centuries in England too, for that matter.

obliged by his very position to play a more positive rôle in society. God established the institution of government in human society for one reason only—to provide a check for man's vices and a remedy for his sins. It is the monarch's duty therefore, indeed his *raison d'être*, to administer justice, and to lead his subjects back to the rule of that pristine natural law from which, in consequence of original sin, they have been apostates.[22] The king then is God's representative on earth for a specific purpose, and after death he will be required to give account to God for the administration of his earthly kingdom. The idea that the king can rule according to his pleasure, provided he observes certain legal forms, was wholly alien to the medieval political mentality.

This doctrine of the moral responsibility of the ruler was no less emphasized in fifteenth-century England. Did not the coronation oath itself enjoin the king not only to uphold the laws and customs of the realm, but also to keep the peace, and to cause justice and mercy to be exercised in all his judgments as well? Fortescue wrote that a king's office stands in two things, one to defend his realm by the sword against external enemies, the other to defend his people by justice against wrongdoers at home.[23] The kingly office, he explained, originated in natural law. This means that after the introduction of sin into the world, the king was given the function of disposing men to virtue and of preventing anarchy by applying the rules of justice.[24] Fortescue drove home his point by quoting St. Thomas Aquinas—*"Rex datur propter regnum, et non regnum propter regem."* [25]

22. Thomas Aquinas was typical of medieval political thinkers on this score. "Quia igitur vitae, qua in presenti bene vivimus, finis est beatitudo coelestis," he says in the *De Regimine Principum*, I, Chap. 15, *"ad regis officium pertinet* [italics mine] ea ratione vitam multitudinis bonam procurare secundum quod congruit ad coelestem beatitudinem consequendam, ut scilicet ea praecipiat, quae ad coelestem beatitudinem ducant, et eorum contraria secundum quod fuerit possibile inderdicat."
23. *Governance of England*, edited by Charles Plummer (Oxford, 1885), p. 116.
24. *De Natura*, I, Cap. 10, 18.
25. *Governance of England*, p. 127.

The fifteenth century reflected the medieval aversion to absolute monarchy in a second respect. During the high middle ages when feudal barons and ecclesiastics had been at the zenith of their powers, the political theorists had taught almost to a man the lawfulness of resisting the tyrant. With the exception of Gregory the Great, Wiclif, and a few others, they had believed firmly in the enforcement by arms, if necessary, of the prince's legal and moral obligations. Of this prevailing mood, St. Thomas Aquinas' *Summa Theologica* is typical. The Schoolman admits therein that "sedition" is a mortal sin. But to revolt against a tyrant, he says, is not "sedition" because a revolt of this nature is dedicated to the common good.[26] Moreover, since the king is elected by the people, it is evident that he can be deposed by the same if he violates the *pactum* under the terms of which he was elevated to the throne.[27] The feudal element of medieval society had buttressed the theologian's argument by asserting that the people are absolved from their oath of allegiance to a king who violates the terms of the coronation oath, and who refuses to abide by the findings of the feudal court of which he is a member. The medieval tradition of resistance in England is epitomized in the ringing phrases of Richard II's deposition in 1399. Deposition is amply justified, the *Rolls of Parliament* for that year read, when the terms of the coronation oath are disregarded, and when a king like Richard II sets aside the laws of the kingdom in favor of his own will.[28]

The fifteenth century, it is true, did not altogether hold with this tradition. Already the rumblings of the Tudor doctrine of non-resistance are to be heard, albeit faintly, in the mouths of Bishop Russell[29] and zealous Lancastrians

26. *Summa Theologica*, Part II (2nd Part), Quaestio 42.
27. *De Regimine Principum*, I, Chap. 6.
28. *Rotuli Parliamentorum*, III, 416–424.
29. See the third draft of Bishop Russell's sermon for the parliament of Richard III (printed in Chrimes, *English Constitutional Ideas in the Fifteenth Century*, Chap. 2, Excursus 6, especially pp. 189–190).

like Fortescue[30] and the anonymous author of the tract *Somnium Vigilantis: A Defence of the Proscription of the Yorkists in 1459.*[31] No doubt the protracted political anarchy to which England was subjected during the Wars of the Roses, and the growth of the New Monarchy from Edward IV on, caused some writers to appreciate the value of stable government, and to regard the fruits of rebellion as more poisonous than tyranny itself. But it is equally true that the fifteenth century did not break entirely with the medieval tradition of resistance, and certainly its writers did not establish a cult of royal authority, or propound a theory of non-resistance similar to the thoroughgoing doctrine soon to be advanced under the Tudors. What the fifteenth century left unsaid, what it failed to emphasize, is the important point in this connection. It is well to remember, too, that despite his reverence for hereditary monarchy in general and the Lancastrian dynasty in particular, Fortescue had no love for tyrants and intimated, if he did not say it outright, that rebellion against tyrants is sometimes justified. The only thing which keeps Frenchmen from rising at the present time against their king, he says, is lack of courage, "which no Frenchman hath like unto an Englishman."[32]

The fifteenth-century political temper was hostile to absolute monarchy in one other important respect. The king, it was believed, has no right to spiritual sovereignty of any sort. Though master in the secular sphere subject to certain legal limitations, he is by no means master of his whole house. For in purely "spiritual" affairs—the definition of religious doctrine, the administration of Church government, the jurisdiction of Church courts—the *sacerdotium*, not the *regnum*, is supreme.

---

30. Fortescue remarks (*De Natura*, p. 70) that it is not lawful for subjects to kill a tyrant, although they have often done so in the past, for example, in the case of Nero. For God often appoints wicked kings expressly for the purpose of punishing people for their sins.

31. Printed in *Eng. Hist. Rev.*, XXVI (see especially, p. 520).

32. *Governance of England*, p. 141.

This was the orthodox view of the middle ages in respect
to temporal and spiritual sovereignty—the doctrine of the
two swords or Gelasian dualism.[33] Medieval papalists and
imperialists alike, however much they had differed as to
the precise limits of their respective spheres of influence,
had clearly recognized a dual rulership of human society.[34] The spiritual sword they had held to be the peculiar
weapon of the ecclesiastical hierarchy, and after the elev-
enth century, more especially of the pope; the temporal
sword that of emperor and king. Thus, the secular sovereign has no right to interfere in a realm which God has
assigned exclusively to the jurisdiction of his pastors.

From very early times English kings, no less than continental monarchs, had recognized the authority of the
Church within the spiritual sphere. The *ecclesia Anglicana*, like the *ecclesia Gallicana* and the *ecclesia Scoticana*,
they had admitted to be part of the universal Church of
which the pope was the head.[35] From time to time during
the middle ages, the crown had, of course, attempted to
safeguard its interests by occasionally refusing to admit a
papal legate into England, or by restricting the jurisdiction of certain papal bulls whose matter they considered
to be prejudicial to the royal prerogative or the law of
the land. But from the end of the twelfth century they had
conceded the right to make appeals to Rome without a
royal license, the validity of benefit of clergy, the prerog-

33. So called because in the fifth century Pope Gelasius I expounded the
theory of dualism authoritatively.

34. As G.H.Sabine says, however (*History of Political Theory*, New York,
1937, pp. 225–226): "Within this circle of ideas, there was, properly speaking,
neither church nor state in the modern meaning of those terms. There was not
one body of men who formed the state and one which formed the church, for all
men were included in both. There was only a single Christian society. . . .
Under God this society had two heads, the pope and the emperor, two principles
of authority, the spiritual rule of priests and the temporal rule of kings, and two
hierarchies of governing officials, but there was no division between two bodies
or societies."

35. There can be little doubt that during the middle ages the term *ecclesia
Anglicana* meant the Church *in* England, and not a separate organization more
or less independent of the papacy. On this point, see the statement of Z.N.
Brooke, *The English Church and the Papacy* (Cambridge, 1931), Chap. 1.

ative of the *ecclesia Anglicana* to issue laws and to judge cases in its own courts.[36] They had conceded, in other words, that the *ecclesia Anglicana* is a sovereign institution in its own sphere, independent of the king in theory, if not always in practice.

During the fifteenth century, Englishmen adhered faithfully to this view because as yet there was nothing sufficiently discordant in the relations between the English *regnum* and *sacerdotium* to warrant throwing it over. True, Henry IV's parliaments, and later parliaments too, evinced considerable anti-ecclesiastical feeling. There were also frequent attacks on the corruption of the Church. But that the relations between the English *regnum* and *sacerdotium* were on the whole amicable is proved by Henry VII's attitude toward the Church on the eve of the Reformation. As Bacon notes, Henry's attitude was entirely traditional. He took care to obtain papal recognition of his title to the throne, and he invariably filled the chancellorship with churchmen. His personal relations with the pope were extremely felicitous. He admitted into England the papal legate sent to sell indulgences for the crusade against the Turks and carefully abstained from attacking ecclesiastical wealth; while the pope on his side complied with Henry's wishes about appointments to bishoprics and abetted the king's reforms in the matter of sanctuaries and benefit of clergy.

With such conditions obtaining in the sphere of practical politics, it was only natural that contemporary political thought on the subject of the *regnum* and *sacerdotium* should have been likewise conservative. Not so long before, John Wiclif had brazenly proclaimed that the king is of greater dignity in this world than are bishops, and that, in fact, bishops derive their power from kings. But the association of the Lollards with the Peasants' Revolt and Oldcastle's rebellion had brought Wiclif's views into disrepute among the upper classes, and they accordingly en-

36. See Felix Makower, *Constitutional History and Constitution of the Church of England* (English trans., London, 1895), pp. 228–229, 357–359, 392, 399–404.

joyed no vogue during the fifteenth century. It was the law courts,[37] and the writings of Bishop Pecock and Fortescue, which reflected, far more accurately than Wiclif, English opinion on the subject of the *regnum* and *sacerdotium* just prior to the Reformation.

Bishop Pecock, however unorthodox his views in respect to the relative merits of natural law and the Scriptures, was entirely orthodox in his attitude toward the temporal and spiritual powers. In his much-maligned *Repressor of over much Blaming of the Clergy*, he attacks the Lollards bitterly, defending the medieval assumptions that the clergy might possess property, that the pope is the head of the universal Church, and that the ecclesiastical power of legislation is divinely ordained. It is just as lawful, he says, for the "overers" of the Church, with the consent of the "netherers," to make laws relating to spiritual matters and the government of Church officials, as it is for princes "with their commonalty" to make "politic and civil laws."[38] The assumption throughout the *Repressor* is that of Gelasian dualism, *i.e.*, that the king has no authority over the *sacerdotium* and its servants, that he is master of the temporal sphere only.

Fortescue's views were even more conservative. In both his *De titulo Edwardi Comitis Marchiae* and his *Declaration made upon certain writings against the king's title to the realm of England*—the one attacking Edward IV's title, the other defending it—Fortescue expounds the extreme ultramontane position typified by such writings as Innocent IV's *Commentaries on the Decretals* and Augustinus Triumphus' *Summa de Potestate Ecclesiastica*. One of the four primary requisites for the legitimization of a

37. The theory enunciated in the law courts was Gelasian dualism. The courts disallowed any papal action in derogation of the king's prerogative or the law of the land. On the other hand, they ruled that no layman can exercise spiritual jurisdiction (see, for example, Year Books, 11 Hen. IV, Mich. pl. 67, Pas. pl. 10, and 1 Hen. VII, Hil. pl. 10, printed in Chrimes, *English Constitutional Ideas in the Fifteenth Century*, App., nos. 19(i), 77.

38. *Repressor of over much Blaming of the Clergy*, edited by C. Babington (London, 1860), II, 454. For Pecock's views on ecclesiastical property and the headship of the pope, see *ibid.*, Parts III and IV.

king, says Fortescue, is papal recognition. Every king, whether male or female, is subject to the pope from the mere fact of being a member of Holy Church.[39] Holy Church is the kingdom of all Christian men, and accordingly just as David once held sway over the kingdom of Israel, so now the pope, the head of Holy Church and Christ's vicar, rules universally. All kings and princes of the Church are therefore subject to the pope in their persons and temporalities, as well as in their spiritualities, just as were David's subjects in the days of the prophets. This is not to say that the pope may seize a king's possessions without cause, but it does mean that Rome may interfere in the event that emperors and kings misrule their subjects. Christ, the King of all Kings, has delegated both swords to his vicar, the pope, who is therefore called *Rex et Sacerdos,* and who may compel temporal as well as spiritual princes to come to his councils.[40] Could a more unequivocal statement of the pope's universal authority be discovered anywhere?

It may be concluded that on the eve of the Reformation there was no belief in absolute monarchy among English publicists—in fact, quite the contrary. The current theory envisaged a king strictly limited in both the temporal and spiritual spheres, and by no flight of the imagination supreme above rival jurisdictions, or possessing unlimited sovereign power.

There were, however, two books written before the advent of the Reformation which definitely pointed toward the new order soon to be inaugurated by Henry VIII. Those books are Fortescue's *Governance of England,* and Edmund Dudley's *Tree of Commonwealth.* Both books are medieval in many respects, predominantly so perhaps. Yet they seem to stand more at the crossroads, looking back

39. *De titulo Edwardi Comitis Marchiae,* printed in *The Works of Sir John Fortescue, Knight,* Cap. 10.

40. *The Declaracion made by John Fortescu, Knyght, upon certayn wrytinges sent oute of Scotteland ayenst the kinges title to the roialme of Englond,* printed in *The Works of Sir John Fortescue, Knight,* p. 535. See also *De Natura,* Cap. 46.

frequently, but also adumbrating somewhat the political ideas of the revolution.

The first three chapters of Fortescue's *Governance of England* are medieval in inspiration—the king of England cannot change the common law or levy extraordinary taxes without the consent of his subjects since England is a *dominium politicum et regale*. The succeeding chapters, however, are inspired by a new sentiment. Fortescue demands therein a monarchy greater than any of its parts. He had observed the lawlessness and confusion resulting from the Wars of the Roses, and had himself been forced into exile in 1463, along with Henry VI and Queen Margaret. To prevent a repetition of St. Alban's and Tewkesbury, he urges therefore that the king be so endowed financially as to obviate the necessity of asking parliament for much money; and that his income over and above the revenues assigned for the ordinary expenses of government, "be greater than the livelihood of the greatest lord in England."[41] He insists that the king's council be composed of the wisest men in the kingdom, and not of factious noblemen, as of old.[42] He asserts that this same council ought to be given the power to amend the laws, and thus to guide the members of parliament by presenting bills "riped to their hands."[43] Many of Fortescue's practical suggestions were put into practice under Henry VII and Henry VIII.[44] And his theory that the king is superior to the jurisdiction of over-mighty subjects was the theory soon to be espoused by the advocates of the New Monarchy.

Edmund Dudley's *Tree of Commonwealth*[45] presages to

41. *Governance of England*, Chaps. 8–13.
42. *Ibid.*, Chap. 15.
43. *Ibid.*, p. 148.
44. For parallels between Fortescue's ideal state and Henry VII's government, see Caroline A.J.Skeel, "The Influence of the Writings of Sir John Fortescue," *Transactions of the Royal Hist. Soc.*, 3rd series, X, 84–88.
45. This book was written by Dudley in 1509 and 1510 during his imprisonment in the Tower, presumably in order to gain the favor of his new master, Henry VIII.

some extent the powers shortly to be given to the king over the *ecclesia Anglicana.* The king, Dudley says, must not only assume his traditional rôle as protector of the Church. He must also act as its overseer. The reformation of the Church, which Dudley, like Dean Colet, seems to have considered an urgent necessity, ought to be accomplished under royal guidance. It is the prince, and not the bishops, who has charge of the principal root which supports the tree of commonwealth; namely, the love of God. For it is he who appoints the bishops, and whose duty it is to see to it that the objects of his choice are virtuous and indefatigable in punishing misdoers in their dioceses.[46] Moreover, the king can foster the third root of concord or unity by settling disputes between clergy and laity. "If there be any manner of grudge between his subjects of the spirituality and his subjects of the temporality for privilege or liberties," says Dudley, "it were a great help to this noble root of concord, to have it established and reformed. *And no man can do it but the Prince. . . .*"[47]

46. *The Tree of Common Wealth: A Treatise by Edmonde Dudlay, Esq.* (Manchester, 1859), p. 9.
47. *Ibid.*, p. 16 (italics mine). Probably Dudley did not imply by this statement what Christopher St. German implied twenty-five years later. Unlike St. German, Dudley probably would have admitted the right of the Church to define doctrine and to have its own courts. But to give to the king the sole power of determining the precise boundary between the spiritual and temporal jurisdictions was to take the first great step toward the Act of Supremacy.

II

THE KING AND THE CHURCH:
THE HENRICIAN STATUTES

Be it enacted by authority of this present Parliament that the King our Sovereign Lord, his heirs and successors kings of this realm, shall be taken, accepted, and reputed the only Supreme Head in earth of the Church of England called *Anglicana Ecclesia.* . . . ACT OF SUPREMACY, 1534.

THE New Monarchy which Fortescue and Dudley had envisaged dimly in their writings became an established fact in the England of the first half of the sixteenth century. The creation of the strong monarchy supreme above feudal and ecclesiastical jurisdictions was, in fact, the outstanding political achievement of Europe as a whole during the Renaissance and Reformation. Throughout the fifteenth and early sixteenth centuries the reigning monarchs of France, Spain, Scandinavia, and Russia steadily increased their powers at the expense of rival medieval jurisdictions. In Italy and the Holy Roman Empire the petty potentates likewise currently consolidated their territorial principalities. England was no exception to the rule. Under Henry VII and Henry VIII the sovereignty of the English state became a reality, and the king, both *solus* and in parliament, acceded to powers which he had never heretofore enjoyed.

The fundamental reasons for the growth of state sovereignty in England are not far to seek. The political anarchy of the Wars of the Roses, and the confiscation and absorption into the royal domain of feudal estates by Henry VII, engendered both the desire and the means for the establishment of a monarchy greater than any of its parts. The rising middle class, yearning for an ordered society in which it could ply its trade more aggressively, supported centralized government wholeheartedly. The lust for ecclesiastical wealth and power which crown and laity shared in common, coupled with the growth of national feeling, was too powerful to permit the Church long to maintain an independent existence. Neither baronial stronghold, municipal law, local franchise, nor the privileges of the Church were sufficiently strong to ward off the onslaught of a monarchy impelled by such motives.

Perhaps the most conspicuous and revolutionary act in the creation of the strong monarchy during the Renaissance and Reformation was the absorption by the secular ruler of powers hitherto wielded by the *sacerdotium*. During the middle ages monarchs had admittedly possessed no power whatever in the spiritual realm, and had at times been hard put to it to resist ecclesiastical encroachments on their own secular preserve. They now proceeded to make themselves masters of their entire house—to a greater or lesser degree, depending on the peculiar conditions of their respective countries. Without actually repudiating papal hegemony, the fifteenth- and sixteenth-century French and Spanish sovereigns succeeded in establishing a thorough control over ecclesiastical appointments, in limiting appeals and the flow of money to Rome, and in encroaching to some extent on the jurisdiction of the ecclesiastical courts. Swimming with the Protestant tide, Scandinavia, the North German principalities, and many Swiss towns broke away from papal control altogether, and accomplished almost overnight the identification of Church and State within their territories, with king, duke, or city council in effective control.

England followed the example of Sweden, Brandenburg, and Zurich, rather than of France and Spain. The Reformation Parliament, piloted skilfully by Henry VIII and that "vicarius Satanae,"[1] Thomas Cromwell, swept away the traditional scheme of *regnum* and *sacerdotium* entirely, and introduced a new ecclesiastical order. Parliament made the king, in lieu of the pope, the *Supremum Caput* of a new Church *of* England, and transferred to him entire the legislative and judicial powers of the medi-

1. So Cardinal Pole calls Cromwell in his *Apologia ad Carolum Quintum*.

eval clergy. The term *ecclesia Anglicana* thus came to have a connotation altogether different from that which it had had in Fortescue's England. It now implied a *national* Church free of Roman control, and with the king, not the English clergy, as its absolute master. The revolutionary significance of the Reformation Parliament's work in this respect can clearly be ascertained by a comparison of the phraseology of one of Henry VIII's earlier statutes with one enacted twenty-four years later. In 1512 parliament granted to the king a subsidy to wage war on Louis XII because the French king, so the subsidy statute reads, was essaying to effect a schism in the Church of Christ. Among other blasphemies, Louis XII had had the audacity to demand the appearance of "our holy Father the Pope" before a council of his own calling "contrary to the laws of God and all holy Church . . . to the intent to have the whole Rule and governance of all holy Church under his dominion." And without cause or authority, he had at the same council decreed "that our said holy Father should from henceforth be sequestered . . . from all Jurisdiction and administration Papal."[2] This was, in 1512, considered a legitimate excuse for war. In 1536, the statute book was playing a different tune. It stated that the power of the Bishop of Rome, "by some called the Pope," was "pretended" and "usurped," and that anyone upholding Rome's jurisdiction in England shall incur the penalties of *praemunire*.[3]

The delimitation of papal and ecclesiastical powers in France and Spain, and their complete absorption by the secular power in England, Scandinavia, North Germany, and parts of Switzerland, naturally wrought a revolution in political theory as well as in practical politics. In every great period of transition the displacement of an old order by a new necessitates the repudiation of an antiquated philosophy and the formation of a new creed cal-

---

2. 4 Hen. VIII, c. 19 (All references to Henrician statutes are taken from the *Statutes of the Realm*, Vol. III).
3. 28 Hen. VIII, c. 10.

culated to justify, and to fit the facts of, political actuality.[4] In this the Reformation was like every other age. With the exception of Calvin, who denounced the authority of the Catholic *sacerdotium* only to advocate an even more thoroughgoing consistorial theocracy at Geneva, the leading continental religious and political reformers lost no time in denouncing Gelasian dualism, and in demanding the control of the Church everywhere by the omnipotent State. Luther asserted, albeit somewhat reluctantly, that the visible Church is a temporal thing, and that therefore it is the duty of the prince, not the clergy, who are but subjects like everyone else, to reform, organize, and manage the Church in his own particular community. According to Zwingli, the government of the Church—extending even to the definition of doctrine, which Luther maintained was beyond the competence of the prince—is theoretically the prerogative of the people as a whole, and practically of the people's "representatives," the secular rulers. This type of government, said Zwingli, most accurately reproduces the primitive Christian communities in which a Council of Ancients presided over the life of the community in all its aspects.[5] In France, especially toward the end of the century, extreme Gallicans like Servin and Barclay defended Henry IV against Pope Sixtus V's claim to determine the succession to the French throne. The "liberties" of the Gallican Church, they asserted, permit

4. I do not mean by this statement that books enunciating a new political creed always necessarily follow *after* the actual change has been made in the political structure. Obviously, in some cases they do not. Martin Luther's treatises, *An den christlichen Adel* and *Von Weltlicher Uberkeyt*, were written *before* North German princes like Joachim II of Brandenburg turned Lutheran and seized control of the Church organization within their principalities. And Christopher St. German, as we shall see below (pp. 66, 71), anticipated in his writings some of the features of statutes passed by the Reformation Parliament. Nevertheless, Luther and St. German were both giving expression to an order which seemed imminent, and which had been prefaced by such experiments as the Pragmatic Sanction of Bourges and the Concordat of 1516 in France, the Statutes of Provisors and Praemunire in England, and similar devices in Spain.

5. See Georges de Lagarde, *Recherches sur l'esprit politique de la Réforme* (Douai, 1926), pp. 308–320.

the French clergy to obey the king in all things, spiritual or temporal.

The appearance of a new intellectual creed justifying the king's right to ecclesiastical as well as secular power is perhaps more noticeable in England than in any of the continental countries. In the fifteenth century, as we have seen, the relations between the English *regnum* and *sacerdotium* had been, on the whole, reasonably amicable. English publicists had consequently not seen fit to question the clergy's divine right to spiritual jurisdiction.[6] During the momentous days of the Reformation Parliament, however, it was found that Pecock's Gelasianism and Fortescue's Ultramontanism would not do. The English mind required a philosophy more in keeping with the political revolution of the moment. Accordingly, the government employed the printing press to turn out in rapid succession pamphlets which sought to prove that neither the pope nor the English clergy had any right to spiritual, much less to temporal, power within England, and that the king was, and always had been, the rightful head of the *ecclesia Anglicana*.

Over one hundred years after the smoke had cleared from the battlefield of the early English Reformation, an eminent English political theorist was to state the royal supremacy in ecclesiastical matters in the following words: "All Pastors, except the Supreme, execute their charges in the Right, that is by the Authority of the Civil Sovereign, that is, *Jure Civili*. But the King, and every other Sovereign, executeth his Office of Supreme Pastor, by immediate Authority from God, that is to say, *in God's Right*, or *Jure Divino*."[7] It is the purpose of this and the succeeding chapter to discover the source from which Thomas Hobbes ultimately derived this revolutionary doctrine. This will necessitate an examination first, of the powers actually translated to the king by the statutes of

6. See above, pp. 14–18.
7. Hobbes, *Leviathan*, Chap. 42.

the Reformation Parliament; and second, of the exact nature of the theory of Royal Supremacy advanced by the
Henrician pamphleteers to justify that actuality.

The Reformation Parliament and succeeding parliaments during the reign of Henry VIII threw over altogether the traditional relationship between the *regnum*
and *sacerdotium*. Papal hegemony was repudiated, the
Church *in* England was identified with the English State,
and the king was made the absolute head of the Church,
unrestricted in his ecclesiastical prerogative by either convocation or parliament.

But this revolution by statutory enactment was not accomplished all at once. It was only by degrees that English
lords and commons were persuaded to scrap the medieval
Church entirely, and to sign away any control which they
themselves might have hoped to gain over the new English
Church. Roughly speaking, it may be said that the Henrician anti-ecclesiastical legislation passed through four
well-defined stages. From 1529 to 1531 only the abuses of
the medieval Church, against which reformers had protested for centuries, were attacked. During these years the
principles upon which the medieval fabric had been based
were left untouched, and it was the middle class, even
more than the crown, which stood to profit most by the
statute book. The year 1532 was one of hesitation, during
which it could not have been predicted whether king and
parliament would go to further extremes or turn back. In
1533, however, it became clear that Pope Clement VII had
no intention of granting Henry VIII a legal annulment of
his marriage to Catherine of Aragon. Consequently, by
the Act of Appeals of 1533, parliament proclaimed England an "empire," free from all foreign control, and especially papal control. The fourth and final phase of the
struggle was heralded by the Act for the Submission of the
Clergy in 1534. This act was the signal for a statutory
attack on the Church *in* England. Henceforth, archbishop
and bishop, as well as pope, were subjected to a relentless

parliamentary offensive. The trend of the statute book from 1529 through 1539 was thus evolutionary as well as revolutionary.

The years 1529–1531 constituted the formative phase of the Reformation Parliament. During these years Henry VIII was still hopeful of having his great matter successfully decided at Rome, and accordingly the medieval philosophy of the *regnum* and *sacerdotium* remained intact in the statute book. Acts were passed abolishing abjuration by sanctuary men,[8] and restricting benefit of clergy to those of the order of subdeacon or above.[9] But nothing was said of theory. Something was done to remedy the abuse of pluralities and non-residence,[10] and Henry had such "tender pity, love, and compassion" for the English clergy that the latter were obliged to pay £118,840 to extricate themselves from a charge of *praemunire*.[11] But as yet no attack was leveled against the legislative and judicial powers of the medieval Church. In short, the first three sessions of the Reformation Parliament represented a joint campaign of crown and middle class against clerical abuses, the former perhaps largely as an interested onlooker, the latter perhaps more aggressive because its pocketbook was involved. The statutes restricting fines exacted by the clergy for probates of testaments[12] and fixing mortuary rates,[13] and especially the act which prohibited spiritual persons from farming, buying and selling merchandise, and maintaining breweries,[14] were all to the advantage of a rising middle class. The king had not yet benefited materially by the anti-ecclesiastical campaign except to the extent of £118,840.

8. 22 Hen. VIII, c. 14.   9. 23 Hen. VIII, c. 1.

10. 21 Hen. VIII, c. 13 (pp. 293, 294–295).

11. 22 Hen. VIII, c. 15, and 23 Hen. VIII, c. 19. According to J.R.Tanner (*Tudor Constitutional Documents*, Cambridge, 1922, p. 20), these acts were important because they put the English clergy, which still had dealings with Rome, in constant fear of another charge of *praemunire*, and thus made them more tractable when the king commenced his attack on Rome.

12. 21 Hen. VIII, c. 5.

13. 21 Hen. VIII, c. 6.

14. 21 Hen. VIII, c. 13 (pp. 292–293, 295).

In 1532 parliament passed its first piece of radical legislation, the first Act of Annates.[15] This act forbade the payment of annates to Rome, and provided for the consecration of bishops and archbishops in England, in the event that bulls of confirmation were not forthcoming from Rome. But this bill must be regarded as a lever by which Henry VIII hoped to coerce the pope into rendering a favorable decision in his divorce case, rather than as a statement of theory. For the king was empowered to withhold his assent to the act by letters patent before the following Easter, and Clement VII is still referred to reverently in the text as "our said Holy Father the Pope."

The Act of Appeals of 1533[16] was the first statute of the reign with real theoretical implications. For Archbishop Cranmer to pronounce the king's marriage with Catherine of Aragon void, it was found necessary to cut the very roots of papal jurisdiction in England. Consequently, the preamble of the Act of Appeals, which provided that all persons appealing to Rome should incur the penalties of *praemunire*, asserted boldly that by "divers sundry old authentic histories and chronicles" it appears that the realm of England is an "empire."[17] This realm is governed, so the statute affirmed, by one Supreme Head, the king, unto whom obedience is owed next to God by both spirituality and temporality, and who possesses plenary power within the country, free from the interference of any foreign prince or potentate. But while a revolutionary document in one respect, the Act of Appeals was eminently conservative in another. By proclaiming England an "empire," the papal jurisdiction in England was repudiated, but the English clergy was as yet left untouched. The medieval principle of Gelasian dual-

15. 23 Hen. VIII, c. 20.
16. 24 Hen. VIII, c. 12.
17. The term "empire" had a much different connotation in the early sixteenth century than it has today. The British Empire of the twentieth century means the extensive territories of which the king of England is the titular head. But in 1533 "empire" signified simply "a country of which the sovereign owes no allegiance to any foreign superior," *i.e.*, pope or emperor (*N.E.D.*).

ism was expressly retained in the Act of Appeals by the assertion that the body spiritual, *i.e.*, the English clergy, has power "when any cause of the law divine happen[s] to come in question or of spiritual learning," just as the other part of the body politic has cognizance of temporal affairs. The independence of the English clergy was further admitted in the provision that henceforth all spiritual appeals shall be made to the archbishops, and that appeals involving the king shall be settled in the upper house of convocation.

Beginning with the year 1534 the Reformation Parliament entered into its fourth and really revolutionary phase. The attack on abuses and on the power of the "Bishop of Rome" was pursued relentlessly, and by two acts the authority of the pope was declared to have been a usurpation contrary to the laws of God and the king's prerogative.[18] But of far more importance for the English constitution was the vigorous offensive launched against the privileges and powers of the English Church, which culminated in the transference to Henry VIII of a jurisdiction which no English king had hitherto enjoyed. By a series of statutes from 1534 to 1545 the crown absorbed the entire legislative, judicial, administrative, financial, and even doctrinal prerogatives of the medieval Church—a "supremacy" in the real as well as the theoretical sense of the word, which was not shared with parliament.

In 1534, by the Act for the Submission of the Clergy,[19] the autonomous legislative and judicial powers of the English Church were destroyed at one blow. By this act it was asserted that convocation might be summoned only by the king's writ, and that henceforth no new canons could be promulgated by convocation without the king's license. Moreover, the clergy "beseeched" his Highness to have all clerical statutes thought to be prejudicial to the royal prerogative, submitted to the judgment of thirty-

18. "Act for the punishment of heresy" (25 Hen. VIII, c. 14), and the "Act abolishing the authority of the Bishop of Rome" (28 Hen. VIII, c. 10).
19. 25 Hen. VIII, c. 19.

two persons, sixteen laymen from parliament, and sixteen clerics, all to be appointed by the king. It was then stated, as supplementary to the Act of Appeals, that all appeals from the archiepiscopal courts should be made to the king's court of chancery. The English episcopacy had, for the most part, loyally supported the king in his earlier attack on the papacy. But with this attack on their own autonomy, the bishops began to grow restive.[20]

Having disposed of the legislative and judicial independence of the Church, king and parliament now turned their attention to administration. By the second Act of Annates of 1534,[21] they virtually established control over episcopal nominations, for though theoretically all elections of archbishops and bishops were to be made by the cathedral chapters, they were to be carried out only with the king's license, and after letters missive naming the person to be chosen had been received from the king. The Dispensations Act of the same year[22] provided that in the future all dispensations and licenses should be issued by the Archbishop of Canterbury, but not until the king had given his assent. In case the archbishop refused to grant licenses in conformity with this act, a writ might be issued from chancery enjoining him to do so. The act also provided that the authority to visit monasteries should be vested in the king, and not in the archbishop. The Act of Supremacy[23] gave the king a title befitting his new powers, and in addition the power to reform errors and heresies committed by the spiritual authorities—in other words, the right of ecclesiastical visitation.

Despite the revolutionary character of this legislation, however, the king was not yet a positive influence in the Church. His Supremacy so far amounted to a kind of

20. As early as 1532 convocation had begun to resist royal attacks on its autonomy. See the "Answer of the Ordinaries," written by Bishop Gardiner in 1532 in repudiation of the theory of royal control advanced by the "Petition of the Commons" of the same year (Gee and Hardy, *Documents illustrative of English Church History*, London, 1896, pp. 154–176).

21. 25 Hen. VIII, c. 20.

22. 25 Hen. VIII, c. 21.   23. 26 Hen. VIII, c. 1.

overlordship which could be exercised to keep the clergy in step, but which could not itself initiate anything. It remained for the last sessions of the Reformation Parliament and later parliaments in the reign to give to Henry VIII the power to legislate by proclamation in the ecclesiastical sphere, and to pronounce on matters of doctrine. This was the logical conclusion, the last step of the Henrician Reformation, and one to which Henry was perhaps driven to make his Supremacy something more than mere theory.

This last phase was heralded by the Act of Proclamations of 1539,[24] which asserted that proclamations set forth by the king with the advice of his council, "as well for and concerning divers and sundry articles of Christ's Religion," should henceforth be obeyed as of equal validity to acts of parliament. The statute, 31 Hen. VIII, c. 9, which empowered the king to appoint new bishops to take care of the religious duties left uncared for by the dissolution of the monasteries, also provided that the king should have authority to make rules and ordinances for the new bishoprics. But the acts, 32 Hen. VIII, c. 26, and 37 Hen. VIII, c. 17, were the most drastic of all. The former definitely gave the king, together with the clergy, the right to make doctrinal decrees by letters patent, independent of parliament. And the latter, in justification of the provision that doctors of civil law, though laymen and married, might exercise spiritual jurisdiction, stated that the king had always had the authority, by virtue of his title of Supremacy, "to exercize all manner of jurisdictions commonly called Ecclesiastical jurisdiction."

It is evident that by the end of his reign, Henry VIII had acceded to a position of preëminence within the ecclesiastical sphere of which his predecessors had never dreamed. The Royal Supremacy in 1547 was a far cry from the medieval position which the king had held in rela-

---

24. 31 Hen. VIII, c. 8. It is Pollard's contention (*Evolution of Parliament,* London, 1926, pp. 267–268) that the Act of Proclamations was passed in order to make the Act of Supremacy a practical reality.

tion to the Church in 1529. Still hampered by natural and positive law in the secular realm, as we shall see below, he had become a sovereign indeed with sovereign power in respect to the Church, absolute, above parliamentary or convocational control.

There was just one step which the Henrician parliaments were not prepared to take. They gave to the king absolute ecclesiastical jurisdiction and the power to interpret doctrine. But they stopped short of making him a spiritual person with the right to consecrate bishops, to preach, and to administer the Sacraments. Henry VIII was made Supreme Head, but not High Priest. The new powers given him by parliament constituted, according to canon law definition, a *potestas jurisdictionis*, or more specifically still, a *jurisdictio fori*, but not a *potestas ordinis*.[25] Canon law teaches that there is in the Church a triple power—orders, teaching, and jurisdiction—of which, for all practical purposes, the last two are indistinguishable.[26] The *potestas ordinis* is the power of conferring grace by consecration and by the administration of the Sacraments.[27] The *potestas jurisdictionis*, on the other hand, consists of the jurisdiction of the internal forum (*jurisdictio poli*), which, by the Sacrament of Penance, the granting of dispensations from vows, etc., treats the relations of man with God; and the jurisdiction of the external forum (*jurisdictio fori*) which has to do with external ecclesiastical relations. This latter jurisdiction is itself

25. That Henry VIII was given a *potestas jurisdictionis*, but not a *potestas ordinis*, is also the opinion of Makower (*Constitutional History and Constitution of the Church of England*, pp. 255–256), Pollard (*Cranmer*, London, 1904, pp. 83–84), and A.S.Barnes (*Bishop Barlow and Anglican Orders*, London, 1922, pp. 55–56).

26. According to the *Dictionnaire de Théologie Catholique*, the power of teaching, "considéré d'une facon concrète, en tant qu'inséparablement uni au pouvoir de commander l'obéissance de la foi, ne se distingue pas adéquatement du pouvoir de juridiction, et c'est pourquoi l'usage commun ne reconnaît que ces deux grandes divisions du pouvoir ecclésiastique, à savoir, le pouvoir d'ordre et le pouvoir de juridiction" (article, "Juridiction," p. 1978).

27. See *Dictionnaire de Théologie Catholique*, article "Ordre."

subdivided into legislative, judicial, and coercive, the first of which has for its object the definition of doctrine as well as the settlement of disciplinary questions.[28] It was manifestly the *jurisdictio fori* only which was transferred to the king by the Reformation Parliament. The king was, for example, given the power to nominate archbishops and bishops by letters missive, and to appoint new bishops to succeed to the religious duties left uncared for by the dissolution of the monasteries, but not the power to consecrate.[29]

According to canon law, of course, only a clerk of at least the rank of priest can exercise even the *potestas jurisdictionis*.[30] But parliament ignored canon law and gave to the king the power of jurisdiction, without at the same time making him a priest. The key to the Henrician attitude is to be found in a single phrase of that statute already referred to as dealing with the doctors of civil law (37 Hen. VIII, c. 17). The ordinances of the Bishop of Rome against the exercise of spiritual jurisdiction by laymen are repugnant, the act reads, to your Majesty's title of Supremacy, "your Grace being a layman." Perhaps some of the members of parliament were familiar with Judge Kingsmill's legal decision of 1506. Kingsmill had asserted in court that under no circumstances can an act

28. See *ibid.*, article "Juridiction." Among the powers listed under the *potestas jurisdictionis* are the following (quotation from Bouix's *Tractatus de principiis juris canonici*): "le pouvoir de définir le dogme et d'obliger les fidèles à donner aux définitions un ferme assentiment, etc."

29. The second Act of Annates (25 Hen. VIII, c. 20) provided that on the king's presentment, the consecration of archbishops and bishops should be made with all speed and celerity *by the appropriate ecclesiastical persons*. The title given in the statute book to 31 Hen. VIII, c. 9—"An Acte for the King to make Bisshopps"—is obviously misleading.

30. The *Dictionnaire de Théologie Catholique* quotes from Gregory IX's *Decretals* in this connection: "Quum laicis, quamvis religiosis, disponendi de rebus Ecclesiae nulla sit attributa potestas, quos obsequendi manet necessitas, non auctoritas imperandi." It goes on to say that "le pape Innocent IV, au concile général de Lyon, en 1245, établit que tout clerc appelé à gouverner une Église devait, dans l'année même, recevoir l'ordre de la prêtrise" (article, "Juridiction," p. 1987).

of parliament make the king a "parson," or give spiritual jurisdiction to a layman.[31]

In conclusion, it is well to remember that according to canon law neither the English Parliament, nor any other body of secular men, had any authority whatever to hand over to the king powers which the Catholic hierarchy claimed to have received originally from Christ himself. The *potestas jurisdictionis*, as well as the *potestas ordinis*, could be exercised legally only by priests and bishops who had been duly confirmed and consecrated according to the rules of Holy Church. No king or layman could exercise spiritual jurisdiction by virtue of an act of parliament, for parliament had no authority to meddle with such matters. But there precisely was the significance of the Reformation Parliament. It usurped powers formerly exercised by popes, general councils, and clergy, and transferred them—illegally, of course—to the king. It accused the pope of usurpation, but in point of fact parliament was itself guilty of that sin. Actually, there has never yet been a revolution in the history of the world in which the successful violators of the *status quo* are not guilty of usurpation.

31. Year Books, 21 Hen. VII, Hil. pl. 1, partially printed in Chrimes, *English Constitutional Ideas in the Fifteenth Century*, App., no. 110. Kingsmill, J., says: "Mes, Sir, l'act de Parliament ne peut faire le Roy d'estre person; Car nous per nostre ley ne pouvons faire ascun temporel home d'aver Jurisdiction spirituel; car nul poit ceo faire sinon le supreme teste. . . ."

III

THE KING AND THE CHURCH:
THE HENRICIAN PAMPHLETS

All men agree that the Catholic Church may expound Scripture: and if the clergy can prove that they be the Catholic Church, then it belongeth to them to expound it. But if the emperors, kings, and princes with their people, as well of the clergy as of the laity, make the Catholic Church, and the clergy but a part of that Church: then may the emperor, kings, and princes with their people expound it. But for as much as the universal Catholic people cannot be gathered together to make such exposition, therefore it seemeth that kings and princes, whom the people have chosen and agreed to be their rulers and governors and which have the whole voices of the people, may with their counsel spiritual and temporal make exposition of such Scripture as is doubtful so as they shall think to be the true understanding of it. CHRISTOPHER ST. GERMAN, *An Answer to a Letter*, Chap. 7.

IN order to impress the English people with the fact that usurpation is not usurpation, and that for centuries Christians had been deliberately misled by popes and church doctors about the proper relationship between the *regnum* and *sacerdotium*, the Henrician government had to supplement the statutes by scriptural and historical "proof." The enactment of statutes does not of itself insure obedience to the law, much less does it imply intellectual conviction on the part of the people. In an age of transition the people presumably have to be educated, persuaded by concrete proof that their habitual ways of thinking are erroneous. It is to Henry VIII's and Cromwell's credit that they perceived this necessity almost at once, and that they accordingly devoted almost as much attention to the printing press as to the sessions of parliament. The use of the printing press was rigidly denied to the proponents of the old school, while the administration saw to it that a veritable flood of literature was issued in support of the new creed.[1]

1. For a full discussion of Henry VIII's dictatorship of the press see Appendix A, "Henry VIII's Propagandist Campaign." See also in this connection Pierre

It is for this reason that the Henrician political pamphlets issued between 1529 and 1547 went through an evolution roughly corresponding to that already noted in the statute book. It may be said, for example, that the pamphlets of 1538 and 1539 were far more radical than those written during the nascent years of the Reformation Parliament, just as the Act of Proclamations of 1539 was more thoroughgoing than the earlier statutes aimed at clerical abuses; that the year 1532, which saw the hesitant first Act of Annates passed, was also a year of uncertainty for the pamphleteers, who challenged the pope's dispensatory power, but not his supremacy over the English Church;[2] that the literary attack on the papacy was begun in earnest in 1533,[3] the same year in which the revolutionary Act of Appeals was passed; and that 1534, the year of the famous Act for the Submission of the Clergy, witnessed the beginnings of a concerted intellectual attack on the *potestas jurisdictionis* of the English Church.[4]

This rough correspondence of the Henrician pamphlet

Janelle's *L'Angleterre Catholique à la veille du schisme* (Paris, 1935; hereafter referred to as *L'Angleterre Catholique*). Janelle devotes two chapters to what he calls "l'expression intellectuelle du schisme."

2. Neither the anonymous pamphlet, *A Glasse of the Truthe* (reprinted in *Records of the Reformation*, edited by Nicholas Pocock, Oxford, 1870, II, 385–421), nor Christopher St. German's *A Treatise concernynge the diuision betwene the spiritualtie and temporaltie* (reprinted in *The Apologye of Syr Thomas More, Knyght*, edited by A.I.Taft, E.E.T.Soc., London, 1930, Appendix; hereafter referred to as *Spirituality and Temporality*), both of which were published in 1532, attacked the papal power directly. The former, defending Henry VIII's divorce aspirations, maintained that popes cannot dispense with the law of God, but not that their universal power is usurped.

3. This was the year in which Bishop Fox probably wrote, but did not publish, his *Opus eximium de vera differentia regiae potestatis et ecclesiasticae* (London, 1534; hereafter referred to as *De vera differentia*); and in which Bishop Sampson possibly published his *Oratio, qua docet . . . omnes, potissimum Anglos, regiae dignitati cum primis ut obediant, quia verbum Dei praecipit. . . .* (London; hereafter referred to as *Oratio*). Both of these works vigorously attacked the theoretical claims of the papacy.

4. In 1534 and 1535 appeared Fox's *De vera differentia* and St. German's three most radical treatises: *A treatyse concerning the power of the clergye and the lawes of the realme* (London; hereafter referred to as *Power of the Clergy*); *A treatise concernynge diuers of the constitucyons prouynciall and legantines* (London; hereafter referred to as *Constitutions Provincial and Legatine*); and *An Answere to a Letter* (London; hereafter referred to as *Answer*).

literature to contemporary statutory evolution can be illustrated from the works of a single writer. In another place, I have shown that the apologetic treatises of Christopher St. German, prominent Henrician lawyer, underwent a change between 1530 and 1535 from a moderately conservative to a radical point of view.[5] As the statute book during these years introduced more and more radical innovations, St. German himself became more and more audacious, and in his last pamphlet, *An Answer to a Letter*, ended by ascribing to the king in parliament all the jurisdictional powers formerly wielded by both pope and English clergy.

It will be the purpose of this chapter to determine precisely the extent to which the Henrician pamphlet literature, whether in printed or manuscript form, reflected the spirit of the statute book. Precisely what did the Henrician political writers have to say about the king's position in relation to the English Church that was different from the views held by Fortescue and the fifteenth century? What, in their opinion, was the true nature of the pope's power in England? What were their views as to the proper relationship between the king, as Supreme Head of the English Church, and general councils? Did they regard England as still part of an international whole, or as fully sovereign within its own borders? Did the doctrine of Royal Supremacy mean simply freedom from foreign control, or did it imply as well the absorption by the king of the medieval functions of the English clergy, that is, the clergy's legislative, judicial, and doctrinal powers? Did the pamphleteers regard the Royal Supremacy as the prerogative of the king alone, or of the king in parliament? And finally, did they tend to overreach the statute book and to ascribe to the king a *potestas ordinis* as well as a *potestas jurisdictionis?*

It must be stated parenthetically that it is no easy matter to answer these questions from the literature of the

5. "Christopher St. German. The Political Philosophy of a Tudor Lawyer," *Amer. Hist. Rev.*, XLII, 631–651.

early sixteenth century. To begin with, the terms of a new creed giving expression to new political facts are always of necessity less comprehensible than the phraseology of a theory matured by long use and acceptance. Men cannot make up their minds all at once, and they do not generally perceive the full implications of the revolution being accomplished before their eyes. Thus, it was easier for Hooker and Hobbes to write something intelligible about the doctrine of Royal Supremacy than it was for Bishop Gardiner or Christopher St. German. One should not expect Henry VIII's pamphleteers to be quite sure of what was implied by the word "supremacy," nor should one expect them always to express unanimity of opinion. The statute book is cut and dried, but the theory justifying the statute book is often hopelessly confused.

This confusion is accentuated by the medieval method of exposition employed by sixteenth-century authors. The reader is so overwhelmed by scriptural quotations and historical references that he often cannot see the woods for the trees.[6] He seldom encounters a real critical analysis of the precise meaning of the Royal Supremacy, but is asked rather to believe that the king is in fact the Supreme Head of the English Church because St. Paul said so, or because the pope is the "whore of Babylon." One is therefore continually impressed with *the fact* of the king's supremacy, but not always with its precise theoretical meaning. It might mean a lot or very little, depending on how much success the reader has in penetrating the mazes of scriptural quotations.

Moreover, the conditions under which the pamphlets were written make it even more difficult for the historian to arrive at the truth. One can never be quite sure whether the opinions expressed in the pamphlets are genuine, or whether they are the product of sycophants writing to

6. See, for example, the first two chapters of St. German's *Power of the Clergy* which are entitled, "Authorities to proue that kiges [*sic*] and princes haue theyr auctoritye imediatly of god," and "Certayn partyculer auctorityes concernynge kynges and princes." They are, as their titles imply, simply long lists of scriptural authorities.

please their royal master. This dilemma is directly attributable to the fact that the Henrician political writings were to some extent, at any rate, propagandist. Henry VIII exercised a dictatorship of the press which, judged by results, was just about as effective as any western Europe has ever seen. The opposition, denied the use of the English printing press, was either driven abroad to publish, or else forced to circulate its views in manuscript. And the government was meanwhile encouraging men, indeed forcing influential men, to write in favor of the changes implemented by the Reformation Parliament.[7] Doubtless, many of the pamphlets were sincere, for after all the middle class had no great love for the Church.[8] But others, for example Bishop Gardiner's *De vera obedientia*, cannot be treated with too much caution, for they were written under the threat of the executioner's ax.[9]

With these difficulties in mind an attempt can be made to analyze the doctrine of Royal Supremacy as it was understood in the early sixteenth century.

1. KING AND POPE

FIRST and most obviously, the Royal Supremacy implied the freedom of the English king from any foreign interference whatever in spiritual as well as temporal affairs. This doctrine was unavoidable in view of the contemporary political situation. To procure a divorce from Catherine of Aragon sanctioned in some manner by ecclesiastical law, Henry VIII had realized the necessity of acquiring either the assent of the pope or of the Church in England. By 1533 it had become evident that the assent of the pope

7. See Appendix A, "Henry VIII's Propagandist Campaign."

8. St. German's pamphlets, for example, were probably sincere, for before the ecclesiastical controversy had fairly gotten under way, St. German had already begun his attack on clerical privileges. As a common lawyer, he was jealous of ecclesiastical jurisdiction and needed no governmental pressure to stir him into action.

9. For a brief account of Gardiner's submission to the king after defending ecclesiastical privileges in convocation, and of his obligation to give literary proof of his volte-face, see Janelle, *Obedience in Church and State* (Cambridge, 1930), pp. xiii–xiv.

would not be forthcoming .because Clement VII was bound hand and foot by the emperor, Catherine of Aragon's nephew. Consequently, Henry had determined on the second alternative which involved the repudiation of papal jurisdiction, and the elevation of the archiepiscopal court of Canterbury to the eminence of a final court of ecclesiastical appeal. Without the abolition of papal authority from England, Henry would have laid himself open to a charge of disobedience to Christ's vicar on earth. But with the anti-papal legislation of the Reformation Parliament, he provided himself with a plausible excuse, namely that obedience is not owed to a power whose divine authority is usurped. Thus, what had begun as a purely empirical offensive calculated to obtain the king's immediate objective—annulment of his first marriage—had ended as an attack on the whole traditional conception of papal hegemony. The significance of this transformation is easily apparent from a comparison of the king's own words in 1521 with the phraseology of the Act of Appeals of 1533. "I will not wrong [the pope] so much, as troublesomely, or carefully to dispute his Right, as if it were a Matter doubtful," Henry had written in 1521 in refutation of Luther. "For . . . the Indians themselves (separated from us by such a vast Distance, both of Land and Sea,) do submit to the See of Rome."[10] Only twelve years later the statute

10. *Assertio Septem Sacramentorum,* edited by Rev. Louis O'Donovan (New York, 1908), p. 202. The translation is the editor's, but I would take issue with him on one word. He has translated "pontifex" as "Bishop of Rome," an expression which did not come into use in England until 1533, except among the radical Protestants. A more accurate rendition would be "pope," as I have indicated in the text, or simply "pontiff." The passage quoted is one which Sir Thomas More is reported to have urged the king to delete from his book. Accused at his trial by Cromwell, Cranmer, and others of having incited the king to write the *Assertio* upholding papal authority, More rejoined that at the time of the writing of the book, he had, on the contrary, argued with Henry that the papal authority should be "more sclenderly touched" therein. Whereupon the king had allegedly answered, "Whatsoeuer impediment be to the contrary, we will set forthe that aucthoritye to the vttermost. For we receaued from that Sea our crowne Imperiall" (Roper, *Life of More,* E.E.T.Soc., Oxford, 1935, pp. 67–68). The *Assertio,* incidentally, was the book which won for Henry VIII the title of *Fidei Defensor.*

book was declaring that England was an "empire," governed by one Supreme Head, the king, and a body spiritual called the English Church, which has always been considered self-sufficient "without the intermeddling of any exterior person or persons."[11]

The political pamphlets took up this "empire" theme with avidity and by degrees undermined the whole position of the medieval papacy. In this respect, the pamphlets reflected scrupulously the spirit of the statute book and broke definitely with the views of Fortescue and the fifteenth century.[12] The pamphleteers warmed up to their task slowly, however, and except for the radical reformers, Tyndale and Barnes,[13] at first confined themselves to an attack on papal abuses only.[14] But in 1533 two books were issued by the royal printer, Thomas Berthelet, which denounced the papacy unequivocally and which set out deliberately to "expose" Rome's usurpations.[15] Henceforth, the attack on the "Bishop of Rome" knew no limitations. Bishops Fox and Gardiner,[16] profiting doubtless by the current translations into English of Marsilius of Padua's *Defensor Pacis* and the anonymous *Disputatio inter militem et clericum*, developed what had been im-

11. 24 Hen. VIII, c. 12.
12. See above, pp. 14–18.
13. Tyndale's *Obedience of a Christian Man* (1528) and *Practice of Prelates* (1530), and Barnes' *Supplication to Henry VIII* (1534?), were all attacking the papacy at a time when Henry VIII had not yet made up his mind to break with Rome. For the full titles of these and subsequent books to be mentioned, see Appendix B.
14. For example, St. German's *Doctor and Student*, which was completely written by 1531, denied that the pope might present to benefices voiding at Rome (Dialogue II, Chap. 37), or, of his own authority, specify places of sanctuary within the realm (Dialogue II, Additions, Chap. 4). But in this work St. German avoided attacking the theoretical basis of papal power. As noted above, this was also true of the anonymous pamphlet, *A Glasse of the Truthe*, published in 1532, which questioned the pope's dispensing power and asserted his subordination to a general council, but said nothing of the Royal Supremacy.
15. I refer to the *Articles devisid by the holle consent of the kynges moste honourable counsayle* (London; hereafter referred to as *Articles devised by king's council*), and Sampson's *Oratio*.
16. Fox was elected Bishop of Hereford in 1535. Gardiner had been appointed Bishop of Winchester in 1531.

plicit in the works of 1533[17] and set to work to undermine completely the medieval papal claims to *plenitudo potestatis*. Where Bishop Sampson,[18] in his *Oratio* of 1533, had been content to prick various weak points in the papal armor, Fox and Gardiner erected a new national state in which the king rather than the pope was the Supreme Head. It is astonishing to see how well these two writers performed their task, for by 1536 and 1537, ideas which five years before would have been regarded as radical had now become cant. Stock phrases, original to a certain extent with the earlier writers, were mechanically reiterated over and over again in the sermons, pamphlets, and letters of later years.[19] Indeed, very little originality was displayed in any of the anti-papal tracts published after 1535.[20] Henry VIII's propagandist campaign had done its work thoroughly, and henceforth the attack on the papacy was to be carried on by scurrilous pamphleteers only, who were at pains to expose the crimes, but not the weaknesses in the theoretical position, of the pope.[21]

Granted, however, that the propagandist campaign against the papacy was successful, just what arguments

17. Janelle is of the opinion that Fox's *De vera differentia* was written before Sampson's *Oratio* (*L'Angleterre Catholique*, pp. 271, 281). However that may be, it is nevertheless true that Fox dealt with the subject of the papacy at greater length and with more theoretical completeness than did Sampson.

18. Sampson was made Bishop of Chichester in 1536, and translated to Coventry and Lichfield in 1542.

19. See, for example, Simon Matthew's *Sermon at St. Paul's* (1535), Bishop Longland's *Sermon before the king* (1537), Bishop Tunstal's *Sermon on Palm Sunday* (1539), and Tunstal and Stokesley's *Letter to Reginald Pole, Cardinal* (printed in 1560, but written in 1537). The arguments employed by all these writers are of the talking-machine variety, amazingly alike, and consisting for the most part of phrases which had been hackneyed years before.

20. The only pamphlet after 1535 which displays any signs of originality is the anonymous *Treatise provynge by the kynges lawes, that the byshops of Rome, had neuer ryght to any supremitie within this realme* (London, 1538; hereafter referred to as *Treatise proving by the king's laws*), the first chapter of which advances the amazing thesis that the Bishops of Rome had never, even during the middle ages, commanded any allegiance in England.

21. See, for example, *The Sum of the Actes and decrees made by diuerse bisshops of rome* (1540?), *Here begynneth a boke, called the faule of the Romyshe churche . . .* (1540?), and *A proclamacyon of the hygh emperour Jesu Christi, vnto all his faithfull Christen* (1547). All these tracts are purely sensational.

were adduced by the pamphleteers to persuade Englishmen that the pope had no legitimate power in England, when in point of fact he had been head of the *ecclesia Anglicana* for centuries? This task of persuasion was a staggering order, for countless generations had to be shown to have been wrong, and an age-old tradition flouted. The Henricians were fond of using the argument —particularly pertinent to the king's divorce—that the pope has no authority "extra suam provinciam," that in fact he ought to be entitled "Bishop of Rome" rather than pope, for he has no more power in England than has the Archbishop of Canterbury in Rome.[22] In support of this contention, the pamphleteers boldly asserted, following the example set by Marsilius of Padua and Sampson, that Peter had had no more authority given him by Christ than the other apostles; that the primitive Church had accordingly not recognized Peter's superiority;[23] that the early oecumenical councils had known nothing of Roman hegemony;[24] and that the Church Fathers themselves had spoken against it.[25]

To prove that this was actually the case, some of the more enterprising writers delved into English history and produced precedents for their preconceived opinions. The classical example of this method of attack was the anonymous *Treatise proving by the king's laws that the bishops*

22. On this point, see Sampson's *Oratio*, printed in Strype's *Ecclesiastical Memorials*, (Oxford, 1822), I (2), 167. All subsequent citations from the *Oratio* are taken from Strype's edition (*Eccles. Mem.*, I (2), 162–175).

23. Sampson argued that Paul and the other apostles had never admitted Peter's supremacy (*Oratio*, p. 168). And one writer averred that Christ had exhibited an especial affection for John the Evangelist (see Pocock, *Records of the Reformation*, II, 102).

24. An oft-cited example was the Council of Nicaea where, according to Sampson, the Bishop of Rome had been accorded first place, but only a primacy of honor (*Oratio*, p. 172); and where, according to Fox, there had been only three patriarchs present, the Bishop of Rome, who was fourth in order, being absent (*De vera differentia*, printed in Melchior Goldast's *Monarchiae S. Romani Imperii siue Tractatvvm de Iurisdictione Imperiali*, III, Francofordiae, 1613, p. 28). Henceforth, all citations from Fox's treatise will refer to Goldast's edition.

25. According to Fox, St. Jerome said that a priest and bishop were originally all one, and that the Church had originally been governed by a common council of priests (*De vera differentia*, p. 28).

of *Rome had never right to any supremacy within this realm*, which pulled a rabbit out of the hat in the form of the astounding thesis "that the bishops of Rome had never rightful power or authority of supremacy in any country, nor their writings, certificates, or process were at any time obeyed here by the laws of this realm"! English kings have often in the past rejected papal bulls of excommunication against English subjects, says the author. Moreover, if the said bishop were actually "head of all Christians," he could not be sued for debt by Englishmen. Yet facts prove that he has been liable to prosecution frequently in the king's court like every other man. Actually, the king has always enjoyed full supremacy within this realm and has often put that supremacy into execution.[26]

For those who were partially convinced by the historical argument, but yet loath to repudiate the accumulated wisdom of centuries, the government had an additional trick up its sleeve. If you can show people that what you are saying is nothing new, but that prominent men have expressed those same opinions in the past, you go far toward quieting the people's better judgment. Accordingly, Cromwell saw to it that Marsilius of Padua's radical *Defensor Pacis* and the anonymous *Disputatio inter militem et clericum* were done into English.[27] English medieval

---

26. *Treatise proving by the king's laws*, Chap. 1.
27. Marsilius of Padua was the apologist for the Emperor Ludwig the Bavarian in his controversy with Pope John XXII in the first half of the fourteenth century. The *Defensor Pacis*, for the most part a polemic against the pope's claim to temporal power, was finished in 1324. Although not actually printed until 1522 (Basle edition), it was a well-known work, and Cromwell must very soon have perceived its significance for his purpose. For William Marshall's English translation was ready in manuscript form as early as the spring of 1533 (*Letters and Papers of Henry VIII*, VII, 423), and it was printed by Robert Wyer in 1535. That the government was behind this translation may be inferred from Marshall's letter to Cromwell in 1534 in which he says that he has begun to print the *Defensor Pacis*, counting on Cromwell's promise to lend him £12 for the purpose. The *Disputatio inter militem et clericum* was written at the end of the thirteenth century to support Philip the Fair of France against Boniface VIII. Translated into English, it was entitled *A dialogue betwene a knyght and a clerke concernynge the power spirituall and temporall* (hereafter referred to as *Dialogue between a knight and clerk*). It was published by Berthelet, probably in 1533.

treatises like those by William of Ockham and Wiclif could not be used because they assumed the headship of the pope, or because they were tainted with heresy.[28] But there was no reason why continental tracts would not do almost as well.

Other arguments against papal supremacy were also frequently used. Scriptural texts cited by papal apologists in the middle ages to justify the papal supremacy were reinterpreted.[29] Some writers went out of their way to illustrate the avaricious origin of papal authority,[30] while others sought to refute Sir Thomas More's contention that papal power was based on unwritten tradition.[31] It was also fashionable, of course, to recite papal enormities in the hope that this would prove the pope's moral ineptitude.[32]

But what were the consequences of these arguments for English political theory, and especially for the theory of kingship? More precisely the "empire" theory became a device in the hands of the Henrician pamphleteers for

28. For a discussion of this point, see Janelle, *L'Angleterre Catholique*, pp. 236–237.

29. See, for example, Fox's *De vera differentia*, p. 25. The scriptural passages, Matthew 16:18 ("Thou art Peter, and upon this rock I will build my church"), and Matthew 18:18 ("What things soever ye shall bind on earth shall be bound in heaven"), were invariably re-interpreted to suit the needs of the Henrician Reformation, as indeed they were to justify the continental Reformation as well.

30. The chapter in the *Defensor Pacis* (Dictio II, Cap. 18) proving that the Bishop of Rome's temporal power was purely "historical" may well have served as the model for English sixteenth-century writers on this score.

31. See Thomas Swinnerton's *A mustre of scismatyke bysshoppes of Rome, otherwyse naming themselues popes, moche necessarye to be redde of ąl the kynges true subiectes* (London, 1534), pp. Ej^b–Eij^b. Swinnerton says "that as concernyng the necessite of our saluacyon, it is false that there lacketh any thyng in scripture writen. . . ." True, he continues sarcastically, there are other things necessary to be believed of good reason which do not appear in Scripture, "as to byleue . . . that poules steple cannot ryde .xl. myles vpon a day, no though Lyncolne mynstre were the horse." Swinnerton was a Protestant divine who used the pseudonym "John Roberts" to shield himself against persecution for heresy.

32. Gardiner's tract, "Si sedes illa" (printed in Janelle, *Obedience in Church and State*, pp. 21–67) is one continuous slander against the papacy. The pope, Gardiner writes therein, has been wont to triumph by a wanton slaughter of infants, boys, and women. This tract, not printed until 1930, was written in 1535 as a reply to Paul III's brief to Francis I declaring Henry VIII deprived of his crown.

transferring to the king that *plenitudo potestatis* which
the extreme papalists had claimed for their master in the
late middle ages, and which Fortescue had himself enunciated. This was where Marsilius of Padua's *Defensor
Pacis* and the newly translated *Disputatio inter militem
et clericum* came in handy. It had been the purpose of
Marsilius and the anonymous author of the second work to
repudiate the extreme papal theory, and to restate the
doctrine of Gelasian dualism in the interest of their masters, Ludwig the Bavarian and Philip the Fair. These two
works could now be used by the Henrician pamphleteers
in the interest of their own master, Henry VIII. According to Marsilius, Jesus had sought no earthly dominion
but had, on the contrary, refused to be called King of the
Jews with the words, "Regnum meum non est de hoc
mundo."[33] It is therefore fitting, Marsilius had said, that
the spirituality should confine itself to purely "spiritual"
duties, leaving all worldly affairs and coercive jurisdiction in the hands of the temporal power.[34] Such being the
case, he had concluded, the papal claim to *plenitudo
potestatis*, which would subject the emperor to papal overlordship, is obviously of no validity. It is not only against
the law of God, but subversive of orderly government as
well.[35]

Fox and Gardiner found these conclusions so much to
their liking that, as Janelle has pointed out, they followed
their model almost slavishly.[36] In the introduction to the
De vera differentia, Fox states the extreme papal case and
then proceeds in the body of his work to cut it to pieces.
The papalists, he says, "make him (bishop of Rome) not
a minister of the word and a servant, but the vicar of God.
They give unto him authority of Dominion, that he may
do all things . . . , Judge all men, and that none ought

33. *Defensor Pacis*, edited by C.W.Previté-Orton (Cambridge, 1928), p. 130.
34. For Marsilius' distinction between *temporale* and *spirituale* see *ibid.*, pp.
118–119, 159–160.
35. *Ibid.*, Dictio II, Cap. 23–26.
36. *L'Angleterre Catholique*, p. 275. Janelle shows that Fox got many of his
ideas from Marsilius, and that Gardiner in turn copied Fox. "Nous avons ici un
exemple typique de la chaîne qui va de Marsile à Foxe, de Foxe à Gardiner."

to Judge him, that he hath dominion over Emperors and kings, and in few words that he hath pre-eminence over all men and is moreover above a general council."[37] This doctrine is manifestly fallacious, Fox asserts, for God gave to his bishops authority, but not dominion.[38] The authentic gloss of John 18:36, "Regnum meum non est de hoc mundo," is to the effect that "I am not to rule or reign as with temporal dominion, for that is the office of kings." [39] As the fourth council of Carthage once ruled, a bishop should give himself up to prayer and to preaching the word of God, and leave worldly business entirely to princes.[40] Gardiner, in his *De vera obedientia*, goes one step farther and abandons the principle of Gelasian dualism altogether.[41] The distinction, he says, between the government of a prince, and that of the Church, "that is, that the Prince should govern in temporal matters and the Church in spiritual," is full of darkness. It is absurd to suppose that the king, who by the testimony of the Old Testament controlled and appointed priests, should confine himself entirely to worldly business and overlook spiritual men's sins.[42]

To prove, however, that the king alone had the right to *plenitudo potestatis*, the pamphleteers had obviously to re-define the term "Church" according to their own predilections. For to say, as the medieval Church had said, that the *ecclesia* is "a body of men united together by the profession of the same Christian Faith, and by participa-

37. *De vera differentia*, p. 24. I use here, as well as in subsequent passages, the English of Henry, Lord Stafford, who published an English translation of Fox's treatise in 1548.

38. *Ibid.*, p. 29.

39. *Ibid.*, p. 30.

40. *Ibid.*

41. In point of fact, Marsilius and Fox had also abandoned the principle of Gelasian dualism as originally conceived. They retained the theoretical distinction between "spiritual" and "temporal" jurisdiction, but assigned to the latter powers which Pope Gelasius would never have conceded, *e.g.*, the administration of church property, jurisdiction of the ecclesiastical courts, etc. For a discussion of this point, see below, pp. 67–69.

42. *De vera obedientia*, printed in Janelle, *Obedience in Church and State*, p. 102f. I quote from Bale's English translation when accurate. Henceforth, all citations from the *De vera obedientia* will refer to Janelle's edition.

tion in the same sacraments, *under the governance of law-ful pastors, more especially of the Roman Pontiff, the sole vicar of Christ on earth,*"[43] was to admit the pope's hegemony. Far more to Henrician tastes was the definition once offered by Marsilius of Padua when at loggerheads with Pope John XXII. The Church of primitive times, according to Marsilius, had had nothing to do with the pope and his cardinals, but had consisted simply of the general congregation of all faithful believers, laity as well as clergy *(universitas fidelium credentium)*.[44] Christopher St. German drew the obvious sixteenth-century inference from this definition. "All men agree," he says in one of his strongest passages, "that the Catholic Church may expound scripture: and if the clergy can prove that they be the Catholic Church, then it belongeth to them to expound it. *But if the emperors, kings, and princes with their people, as well of the clergy as of the laity, make the Catholic Church and the clergy but a part of that Church;* then may the emperor, kings, and princes with their people expound it."[45] Bishop Gardiner was no less emphatic on the subject. Since the "realm" and the "Church" are in fact identical, he says, what possible objection can there be to calling the king, who is head of the realm, also head of the Church of England?[46] As a matter of fact, so fashionable had this Marsilian definition become by 1537,[47] that it was incorporated as dogma in the *Bishops' Book* of that year.[48]

43. Cardinal Bellarmine's definition, quoted from the *Catholic Encyclopedia*. Italics mine.

44. *Defensor Pacis*, edited by C.W.Previté-Orton, pp. 116–117.

45. *Answer*, pp. Giiii–Gv. See also St. German, *Power of the Clergy*, pp. Diiii–Diiii*b*. Italics mine.

46. *De vera obedientia*, pp. 92, 94. According to Gardiner, the Church meant "eam demum populi multitudinem, quae Christiana professione unita in unum corpus coaluerit. Hoc enim usus obtinuit, ut ecclesiae appellatio, alioqui communis, excellentioris tamen corporis propria efficeretur."

47. St. German and Gardiner were by no means the only writers who defined "Church" in the Marsilian sense. See, for example, Fox's *De vera differentia*, p. 25; and *A Litel Treatise ageynste the mutterynge of some papistis in corners* (London, 1534), printed in Pocock's *Records of the Reformation*, II, 543.

48. According to the *Bishops' Book*, the Catholic Church is inclusive of all the saints now in heaven and all the faithful who are now living, or who shall live

The pamphleteers further fortified their position by developing concomitantly the theory that kings, and not popes, are God's vicegerents on earth, and that therefore to rebel against kings is a religious sin. But more of this below. Suffice it to say here that the pamphleteers clearly reflected the anti-papal legislation of the Reformation Parliament by enunciating an uncompromising "empire" theory. The realm, they declared, is free from papal interference, and the entire *plenitudo ecclesiasticae potestatis* is thereby transferred to the king. The "empire" theory marked the first step toward making the king truly sovereign in the spiritual realm.

2. KING AND GENERAL COUNCIL

BUT if the Royal Supremacy was understood to mean first of all, freedom from papal control, did it imply as well independence of general councils? Or was the "empire" theory restricted in its meaning, referring to popes alone and not to councils? Here again, the pamphlets are sensitive to the political barometer and accordingly return opportunistic answers. In the early days of the Reformation Parliament they are conservative; by the end of the reign, however, their authors have seen fit to discard the mask and to attribute to the king full spiritual sovereignty in respect to councils as well as the pope. In the beginning, they are content to rest on tradition; in the end they anticipate the phraseology of the Thirty-Nine Articles and the considered statement of the judicious Hooker.

hereafter in this world, "of which number our Saviour Jesus Christ is the only head and governor." But apparently there is a visible organization of this invisible Church, for the *Bishops' Book* goes on to say that within the Church there is no difference in pre-eminence or authority among the particular churches. "And therefore," reads the text, "I do believe that the Church of Rome is not, nor cannot worthily be called the Catholic Church, but only a particular member thereof, and cannot challenge or vindicate of right, and by the word of God, to be head of this universal Church, or to have any superiority over the other churches of Christ which be in England, France, Spain, or in any other realm. . . ." See *Formularies of Faith put forth by authority during the reign of Henry VIII*, edited by Charles Lloyd (Oxford, 1825; hereafter referred to as *Formularies of Faith*), pp. 52–55. For further comment, see J.W.Allen, *History of Political Thought in the Sixteenth Century* (London, 1928), pp. 162–163.

Certainly, during the early life of the Reformation Parliament the Henrician pamphleteers stated without qualification the superiority of general councils in purely spiritual matters to both pope and king. This was because in 1532 and 1533 the pamphleteers were concentrating on the pope and did not wish to weaken their position by appearing too radical all at once. Then, too, before 1536 the king's followers could appeal from pope to council with a feeling of security, for the possibility that a council might be convoked seemed then sufficiently remote. Few Englishmen during these years would therefore have disagreed in theory with Sir Thomas More when he said, just prior to his execution, that England "being but one member and (small) part of the Church, might not make a particular law disagreeable with the general law of Christ's Universal Church, No more than the city of London, being but one poor member in respect of the whole realm, might make a law against an act of parliament to bind the whole realm."[49] Many would have quarreled with More as to whether or not the repudiation of papal authority was specifically contrary to "the general law of Christ's Universal Church." But all would have admitted that a general council, convoked under the proper auspices, was in the final analysis sovereign in spiritual matters, and not the king.

Accordingly, we find the early pamphleteers appealing the king's great matter and the question of papal authority not to a plenary royal jurisdiction, but to the early oecumenical councils, to the great fifteenth-century councils, and to conciliarists like Gerson.[50] In the words of one anonymous writer, "The general council lawfully gath-

49. Roper, *Life of More*, pp. 92–93. See also More's two letters written in the Tower in which he asserts the same principle (*Letters and Papers of Henry VIII*, VII, 289, 575).

50. The author of *A Glasse of the Truthe*, for example, appeals to the Councils of Nicaea, Constantinople, and Chalcedon to prove that the Bishop of Rome has no authority "extra suam provinciam" (Pocock, *Records of the Reformation*, II, 402–404). Gerson is cited by the same author to prove that general councils are above popes (*ibid.*, p. 407). The author of the *Articles devised by consent of king's council* refers to the Council of Basle for a similar purpose (*ibid.*, pp. 526–527).

ered is, and ought to be, superior to all Jurisdictions, either usurped and suffered (as the papal), or justly holden as kings, in all matters concerning the faith and direction of the whole Church of Christ." Princes, the author continues, have two ways of obtaining justice from one another: "in causes concerning the soul being mere spiritual, appellation to the general council; in temporal causes, the sword only."[51] No more summary statement of the spiritual sovereignty of general councils is conceivable.

These early pamphleteers did not, unfortunately, take the trouble to define precisely what a general council "lawfully gathered" was. But very likely this omission was intentional, for the very vagueness of a conclave meeting sometime in the future gave them the opportunity of lauding the Royal Supremacy without positing the latent conflict in spiritual sovereignty between king and general council.

Beginning with 1536, however, the pamphleteers were obliged to be more specific, for in that year Pope Paul III issued a bull summoning a general council to meet the following year at Mantua. The possibility of a general council was now no longer remote, and the Henrician apologists had to muster their forces accordingly. The government took the initiative by causing two pamphlets on the subject of councils to be struck off at once by the royal printer. The first, entitled *A Protestation made for the King of England wherein is declared that no prince is bound to come to the pretended council of Paul bishop of Rome*,[52] was published in 1537, and the second, entitled *An Epistle from Henry VIII to the Emperor*, in the following year. Neither of these tracts, it is true, repudiated

51. British Museum, Cotton MSS., Cleopatra, E. VI, f. 333. This manuscript is a piece of a sermon or exhortation in defense of Henry VIII, written probably in 1533 or 1534.

52. Hereafter referred to as *Protestation*. This pamphlet and the *Epistle from Henry VIII to the Emperor* of the following year were published by Berthelet in both English and Latin, possibly so as to reach a foreign as well as a native public. For full titles, see Appendix B.

conciliar jurisdiction altogether, but they did mark a considerable change of attitude from the stand taken before 1535. The *Protestation* begins conservatively by asserting that the king and his clergy had never refused to attend a general council, and that they had never intended to break the unity of the Christian faith.[53] But its author maintains with equal emphasis that the king will not submit to a council summoned and dominated by the Bishop of Rome, where no man can speak freely, and where errors will only be perpetuated.[54] Actually, the pamphlet states, the authority to summon councils is vested in the emperor, kings, and princes, certainly not in the aforesaid Bishop of Rome.[55] And if a council cannot be called under their

53. *Protestation* (Berthelet edition, 1537), pp. Avi–Avi[b]. The assertion that by repudiating the papacy England had in no sense broken away from the unity of Christian faith, was a common one among sixteenth-century pamphleteers, and indeed it is still maintained by Anglo-Catholics. In Henry VIII's reign, of course, it was important for Englishmen to impress foreigners with the fact that the Act of Supremacy did not imply doctrinal heresy. Bishop Gardiner, for example, went out of his way to state that separation from the Roman See did not mean separation from the universal Church ("Si sedes illa," printed in Janelle, *Obedience in Church and State*, p. 36). In his *De vera obedientia*, he asserted, moreover, that Christ is the head of the Catholic Church "cum neque Anglicana [ecclesia] sola sit, sed etiam Gallicana, Hispana, neque non Romana, quippe nullo loco circumscripta. . . ." (*ibid.*, p. 114). That this habit of thinking is still very much alive is evident from a manifesto recently issued in England by the Anglo-Catholic Advisory Council attacking alleged errors in Anglican doctrine. It begins as follows: "The Church of England in the Book of Common Prayer, the Ordinal and the Thirty-Nine Articles has expressly adhered to the faith and order of the Catholic Church and in matters of controversy has ever appealed to the teaching and practice of the undivided church. It is on this principle that Anglicans give their allegiance to the Church of England. They cannot, therefore, recognize any claim on their loyalty which conflicts with that which they owe to the Church Catholic, *of which the English church is a part.*" Italics mine; quoted from *New York Times*, April 22, 1938. On the other hand, the Henrician theorists had to leave room for the king to exercise his Royal Supremacy. They asserted therefore that although the English Church is part of the Catholic Church and as a result must teach the same essential doctrines as the French and Spanish Churches, nevertheless there is room for diversity in traditions and ceremonies. The assertion in the Thirty-Nine Articles concerning Church traditions (Article 34, "Traditiones atque ceremonias easdem, non omnino necessarium est esse ubique, aut prorsus consimiles") gave the king as Supreme Head plenty of room to provide for the English Church as he listed, and still theoretically to remain within the fold of the Catholic Church.

54. *Protestation, passim.*   55. *Ibid.*, p. Aviii.

auspices, it is better that each prince should convoke a provincial council and care for his own realm personally.[56]

In the formulation of a more radical English opinion in respect to councils, Marsilius of Padua's *Defensor Pacis* was probably of no little importance. It is possible, of course, that the later Henrician pamphleteers may have derived their conciliar ideas from the works of conciliarists other than Marsilius—William of Ockham, for example. No one can deny that the conciliar idea was "in the air" in the first half of the sixteenth century when men were audibly expressing dissatisfaction with the papal monarchy. Yet, what scanty English evidence we possess points to the fact that the *Defensor Pacis* exercised a greater influence on contemporary conciliar thought than did any other book.[57]

As already noted, William Marshall translated the *Defensor Pacis* into English between 1533 and 1535. It is true that the chapters of the *Defensor Pacis* dealing with conciliar theory are carefully deleted from this translation, doubtless because Marsilius had retained the pope as the titular head of his hypothetical council.[58] But the pamphleteers could easily have consulted Marsilius in some unabridged version, either in the printed Basle edition of 1522, or in manuscript. In point of fact, internal evidence from the pamphlets themselves shows that they probably did do so. Marsilius, as stated above, had expanded the definition of the Church to include all faithful Christians, lay as well as clerical. He had then pro-

---

56. *Ibid.*, p. Cv[b].

57. As a matter of fact, the importance of the *Defensor Pacis* as an influence on Henrician political theory as a whole was not slight. Elsewhere, I have pointed out the influence of Marsilius on the political thought of Thomas Starkey and Christopher St. German ("Thomas Starkey and Marsilius of Padua," *Politica*, London School of Economics, II, no. 6, and "Christopher St. German," *Amer.Hist.Rev.*, XLII, 637–638). C.W.Previté-Orton has indicated the Marsilian strain in Cranmer ("Marsilius of Padua," British Academy *Proceedings*, London, 1935), and, as stated above, Janelle has demonstrated the importance of the *Defensor Pacis* for the political ideas of Fox and Gardiner.

58. Chapters 20–22 are left out of Marshall's translation "as not of moche value."

ceeded to make his ideal general council truly representative of the Church so constituted. At his council there
were to be present lay as well as clerical representatives,
duly chosen by the *legislator humanus*, that is, the people,
or the magistrates of the various countries—not simply
cardinals, bishops, and abbots attending *ex officio*, as had
formerly been the case. The enforcement of all conciliar
decrees was then to be left exclusively to that same *legislator humanus*, or to its special representative, the *princi-
pans*.[59]

Now this was almost exactly the theory advanced by
the Henrician pamphleteers after 1536. Indeed, the two
official tracts already discussed reflect that theory to some
extent, for example, in the idea that it is for kings to
summon councils. But other pamphlets reflected the Marsilian theory even more scrupulously. This is true, for
example, of an unpublished tract entitled "A Treatise
concerning General Councils" which was written in 1537
or 1538, possibly by Archbishop Cranmer.[60] This tract
states that the power to summon general councils was
originally vested in kings, not in the Bishop of Rome,[61]
and that from the very beginning laymen had been asso-

59. *Defensor Pacis*, Dictio II, Cap. 21, *passim*.
60. This MS. is at Hatfield House (hereafter to be referred to as Hatfield
MS.). It is calendared in the *Calendar of the Manuscripts of the Most Hon. the
Marquis of Salisbury*, Part I (London, 1883–1933), no. 47, and in the *Letters
and Papers of Henry VIII*, VII, 691(2). The date suggested by the editors of
the latter is 1534, but this is manifestly wrong. For in chapter 6 the author
refers to a council which the Bishop of Rome has called of late to a place where
he has great power—obviously a reference to the Council of Mantua called in
1536. Moreover, in chapter 11 the definition of the Church in the *Bishops' Book*
is referred to. The treatise must therefore have been written during or after
1537.
61. Hatfield MS., Chap. 7. This was also the opinion of the author of another
unpublished treatise, written about the same time and entitled "By whatt authorite and whow generall counsayles may bee callyd" (British Museum, Cotton MSS., Cleopatra E. VI, ff. 331–331ᵇ). The author maintains therein that in
calling general councils the pope usurps the authority of Christian princes "to
whom (as to the Immediatt Rulers under god of ther subiectes specially Summe
of them having an hole entier and supreme monarchie seuerally in ther own
Realmes yt apperteynith to call by ther commen agrement and none otherwise
a generall counsayle. . . ."

ciated with clerics in conciliar business.[62] That this is as it should be, the author remarks, is evident from the true definition of the Church, for "to say that Bishops and priests make the universal Church is a great error, for the universal Church is *the congregation of all faithful people*, and not only of Bishops and priests."[63] As to the execution of conciliar decrees, this, according to the author, is the exclusive prerogative of kings "as heads and governors over the people."[64] Is any more faithful reproduction of Marsilian ideas conceivable?

Even more radical on the subject of councils than this unpublished tract, however, is Thomas Starkey's *Exhortation to Christian Unity*, written probably in 1536 to support the Royal Supremacy. According to Starkey, it is incumbent on good subjects to obey the king's commands *even if contrary to conciliar regulations*, for a general council is a thing "indifferent," not stipulated by divine law. In fact, the decisions of councils are of no authority among the people of any country "till they be confirmed by princely power and common counsel."[65]

This same point was to be made sixty years later by Hooker in the *Ecclesiastical Polity*.[66] Indeed, the whole statement of the Thirty-Nine Articles "de authoritate Consiliorum generalium" is simply a reiteration of the

62. Hatfield MS., Chap. 5. In the beginning, the author says, the power to bind and loose was given by Christ to the apostles alone, but as laymen began to be converted, the apostles associated the seniors of the people with them in their counsels.

63. Ibid., Chap. 7. These words represent very likely an exact translation of the Marsilian phrase *universitas credentium fidelium*.

64. Ibid., Chap. 5.

65. *Exhortation to Christian Unity* (London, 1536?), p. 9. By "common counsell" Starkey probably means parliament.

66. Hooker states that whoever admits the right of Philip of Spain to limit the efficacy of the decrees of the Council of Trent in his own country, "must grant that the canons even of general councils have but the force of wise men's opinions concerning that whereof they treat, till they be publicly assented unto, where they are to take place as laws; and that, in giving such public assent, as maketh a Christian kingdom subject unto those laws, the king's authority is the chiefest" (*Ecclesiastical Polity*, Book VIII, edited by R.A.Houk, New York, 1931, p. 235).

Henrician point of view.[67] Henry VIII's apologists had begun by demanding the determination of spiritual matters in council rather than in papal *curia*. They had ended by labeling general councils as "indifferent." They still allowed that councils might at times be valuable, but they stipulated that the convening of councils and the execution of conciliar decrees must be in the hands of the secular princes. This was practically to make the king free of conciliar as well as papal interference.

3. KING AND PARLIAMENT

BEFORE turning to the problem of the king's position in respect to the English clergy, it will be well to pause and consider for a moment a closely related question. Did the Henrician pamphleteers think of the Royal Supremacy as having to do with the king alone, or with the king in parliament? The statute book, as we have seen, clearly conceived of the Supremacy as being vested entirely in the king's person.[68] But did the pamphlets faithfully reflect the statute book in this particular? During the reigns of Elizabeth and James I, thinking on this subject was hopelessly confused. On the one hand, the queen was as loath to permit the Commons to interfere with religious affairs as she was to have them dictate marriage plans. On one occasion she informed the speaker that if he perceived any idle heads meddling with Church reforms, he should refuse to consider the latter "until they be viewed and considered by those who it is fitter should consider of such things and can better judge of them."[69] On the other hand, the common lawyers and Puritans were be-

67. Article 21 reads as follows: "Generalia concilia, sine iussu, et voluntate principum congregari non possunt, et ubi convenerint, quia ex hominibus constant, qui non omnes spiritu, et verbo Dei reguntur, et errare possunt, et interdum errarunt etiam in his que ad normam pietatis pertinent: ideoque quae ab illis constituuntur, ut ad salutem necessaria, neque robur habent, neque authoritatem, nisi ostendi possint e sacris literis esse desumpta."

68. See above, Chap. II.

69. *Select Statutes and other Constitutional Documents illustrative of the reigns of Elizabeth and James I*, edited by G.W.Prothero (3rd edition, Oxford, 1906), p. 125.

ginning by that time to demand ecclesiastical control by parliament, the lawyers because they were apprehensive lest an unlimited royal prerogative in respect to religion might eventually encroach on the common-law preserve,[70] the Puritans because the monarch consistently refused to hear of religious innovations in the direction of Puritanism. Puritan discontent on the point is epitomized in the *Apology to be presented to his Majesty* formulated by a committee of the Commons in 1604, which states in no uncertain terms that in matters of religion "it will appear, by examination of truth and right that your Majesty should be misinformed if any man should deliver that the Kings of England have any absolute power in themselves, either to alter religion . . . , or make any laws concerning the same, otherwise than as in temporal causes, by consent of parliament."[71] As a matter of fact, this ambiguity regarding the ecclesiastical prerogative was not really cleared up until after the Glorious Revolution when the king ceased legislating outside of parliament on matters of serious import, religious or secular.

During the reign of Henry VIII, speculation on the ecclesiastical prerogative was even more confused than later on in the sixteenth century. This was only natural, for few people were as yet particularly concerned as to whether the Supreme Head's powers were limited by parliament or not. In religious matters, king and parliament were for the moment in alliance. The common enemy was the pope, and men had not as yet had time to consider whether they were Episcopalians or Puritans. Consequently, there was little or no jealousy of the king's ecclesiastical prerogative, and most political writers simply ignored the problem altogether.

However, it is possible to discern, albeit faintly, two schools of thought on the subject in early sixteenth-century England. One group, which was to become the divine-

---

70. On this point, see J.W.Allen, *History of Political Thought in the Sixteenth Century*, pp. 170–171.
71. Prothero, *op. cit.*, pp. 290–291.

right party under James I, left out parliament altogether
in its discussion of the Royal Supremacy. A second group,
which was to constitute the Puritan faction of a later
day, was disposed to speak of the "king in parliament" in
connection with the Supremacy.

To begin with, declarations of faith drawn up during
the reign of Henry VIII were all issued in the name of
the king, or of the king and clergy, without implying the
necessity of parliamentary sanction. This was in line with
the Act of Proclamations which, it will be remembered,
admitted the king's right to issue edicts "as well for and
concerning divers and sundry articles of Christ's Religion." Thus, the *Articles of 1536* were "set out by the
convocation, and published by the king's authority." The
Bishops' Book was addressed to Henry VIII whom the
bishops humbly besought to permit and suffer the book's
publication.[72] The *Homilies of 1547* were promulgated by
Edward VI with the advice of Somerset and the Council.[73]
And although the *King's Book* of 1543 asserted that "the
lords both spiritual and temporal, with the nether house
of our parliament, hath both seen and like very well" the
doctrine set forth therein, it was actually issued in the
name of the king with the advice of the clergy.[74]

This hypothesis that the government of the Church
was the exclusive prerogative of the king was, moreover,
the assumption on which many of the leading pamphleteers wrote their tracts. Bishops Sampson, Fox, and
Gardiner set up the king, not the king in parliament, as
Supreme Head, and there is not a single reference in their
treatises to parliament in a spiritual capacity. It was the
prince alone, not the prince advised by the lords and commons, whom the Henrician bishops lauded as God's vice-

72. See Lloyd, *Formularies of Faith*, pp. 26–27.
73. Promulgated by "the kynges moste excellent maiestie, by the prudent
auise of his moste deere beloued vncle, Edwarde Duke of Somersett, . . . with
the reste of his moste honorable Counsaill." Parliament is not mentioned. See
Certayne Sermons, or Homilies, appoynted by the kynges Maiestie (London, 1547;
hereafter referred to as *Homilies of 1547*), p. Aij.
74. Lloyd, *Formularies of Faith*, pp. 215–216.

gerent on earth. The words of Edward Hall, chronicler and member of parliament, reflect this same attitude toward the ecclesiastical prerogative. Speaking before the parliament of 1540, Hall asserted that inasmuch as we laymen are unlearned in the Scriptures and ancient doctors, it is our duty as subjects to observe such things touching religion as our prince, especially with the concurrence of the clergy, shall set forth to be believed.[75] It is surely of no little significance that a member of parliament descanting on the Act of Six Articles should thus have ignored parliamentary jurisdiction in spiritual matters.

A second group of political writers, however, construed the Royal Supremacy less in line with the statute book. Of this group, Christopher St. German was the outstanding example. As a common lawyer, St. German had at first been jealous of the ecclesiastical courts. But once the submission of the clergy had been achieved, he seems to have become apprehensive of the mighty powers transferred to the king. In his rôle as champion of the sovereignty of parliament in spiritual as well as temporal matters, he was the forerunner of those men of the law who in James I's reign attacked the Court of High Commission and challenged the kings' ecclesiastical prerogative. It was St. German's definition of the Church which provided him with the proper lever for driving home his point. If the Church represents all the people of the realm, lay as well as clerical, why then, St. German asks, "should not the parliament [notice that St. German does not say the king alone] which representeth the whole Catholic Church of England expound scripture rather than the convocation which representeth only the state of the clergy?"[76] By identifying the Church with the

75. Foxe, *Acts and Monuments*, edited by G. Townsend and S. Cattley (London, 1837–1841), V, 504–505.

76. *Answer*, pp. Gvi–Gvi[b]. This was exactly Hooker's position at the end of the century. According to Hooker, "to define of our own church's regiment, the parliament of England hath competent authority. Touching the supremacy of power which our kings have in this case of making laws, it resteth principally

State, St. German was in fact saying that just as the king shares his rule of the State with parliament, so the Royal Supremacy must be interpreted to mean the rule of the Church by the king in parliament.[77]

That this was his contention is clearly evident from other passages in his works. The *king in parliament*, St. German says in the *Doctor and Student*, has charge over both the bodies and the souls of his subjects, and may therefore decide who is the rightful pope in case of schism.[78] In the *Power of the Clergy*, St. German constantly refers spiritual matters to the king in parliament for redress. It is, for example, within the power of parliament to change Church holidays, he says, if their number be too large for the good of the commonwealth.[79] And it depends on the "king and his parliament" to see that ecclesiastical excommunications are not abused.[80]

Another lawyer who assumed that the Royal Supremacy referred to the king in parliament was the author of the *Treatise proving by the king's laws*.[81] "The king, and his parliament," says the author in one place, might give the clergy larger powers or appoint them less.[82] If a schism should arise in the Universal Church upon articles concerning Christ's religion, and princes had not time to call a general council, "in such cases kings of this realm might . . . call their parliaments, and set an order therein for their subjects . . . , for kings are heads upon earth over the people, and have power by their

in the strength of a negative voice. . . ." (*Ecclesiastical Polity*, Book VIII, edited by R.A.Houk, p. 244). Like St. German, Hooker felt that the identity of Church and State gave the king in parliament, rather than the king alone, the right to determine ecclesiastical affairs.

77. In the passage quoted above, St. German was, of course, attacking the clergy, not the king. Nevertheless, it is evident that the lawyer understood the Royal Supremacy to refer to the king in parliament, and not to the king *solus*.

78. *Doctor and Student*, Dialogue II, Additions, Chap. 8.

79. *Power of the Clergy*, p. Ei^b.

80. *Ibid.*, Chap. 12.

81. That the author of this treatise was in all probability a lawyer is inferred from his copious use of legal phraseology.

82. *Treatise proving by the king's laws*, p. Cii.

supremacy and prerogative royal, *with their parliaments* to redress all such defaults and enormities."[83]

Bishop Gardiner propounded a similar doctrine after the death of his master, Henry VIII. In his *De vera obedientia* of 1535 he had advanced the thesis of the absolute spiritual sovereignty of the king. But in 1547 he refused flatly to obey the royal injunctions ordering the use in churches of a new *Book of Homilies* and Erasmus' *Paraphrase upon the New Testament* (both of which taught Protestant tenets with which Gardiner was not in sympathy), *on the ground that both these books were contrary to act of parliament.* The *Book of Homilies*, Gardiner said, "teacheth the clear contrary to the doctrine established by the act of Parliament," *i.e.*, the *King's Book*, and ought not therefore to be obeyed.[84] This was to assume that parliament had the right in the first place to determine matters of doctrine, and that the king might not therefore issue spiritual injunctions without parliamentary sanction. It is true that Gardiner's real reason for refusing to obey the injunctions was his doctrinal conservatism. Yet it is important that he should have sought to justify his conservatism by taking refuge in the theory of parliamentary sovereignty in spiritual matters.

More striking still in this connection is a letter written by an unknown to Cromwell, probably in 1533 or 1534.[85] The writer wonders whether his Lordship thinks it convenient that certain matters be proved in convocation, that, for example, "the King's Majesty in his Parliament" hath authority to determine what causes shall be determinable in spiritual courts, and "that the King's Majesty hath as well the care of the souls of his subjects

83. *Ibid.*, p. Di. Italics mine.
84. See *Letters of Stephen Gardiner*, edited by J.A.Muller (New York, 1933), p. 382.
85. The editors of *Letters and Papers of Henry VIII* include this letter under the year 1536 (XI, 84), but this is hardly likely since the matters proposed for deliberation therein had already been determined by that time. Strype's suggestion (*Eccles. Mem.*, I (1), 209) that its date is 1534 seems more likely.

as their bodies; and may, by the law of God, *by his Parliament*, make laws touching and concerning as well the one as the other."[86]

Thus, it is obvious that the Henrician political writers were not all of one mind in deciding whether the Royal Supremacy applied to the king alone, or to the king in parliament. Indeed, one of them, Bishop Gardiner, could in 1535 ignore parliament altogether in his declaration of the Royal Supremacy, and in 1547 stake his life on the theory of parliamentary sovereignty. In regard to this question, it is evident that the pamphlets did not always reflect the spirit of the statute book.

4. KING AND ENGLISH CLERGY

WITH this ambiguity in mind, we may turn to the third great problem of ecclesiastical sovereignty, namely the relation of the king to the English clergy. So far, we have determined that in the minds of the Henrician political writers the Royal Supremacy implied first, the king's absolute freedom from papal control, and second, his practical independence of general councils. For all practical purposes, this left king and clergy supreme in England in respect to ecclesiastical dominion, for there was small likelihood of a general council being called jointly by such loving brothers as the Emperor, His Most Christian Majesty, and the Defender of the Faith. Henry VIII and the English clergy therefore found themselves confronting each other as the sole combatants for the prize of spiritual sovereignty in England. The contest was not even, and, as we have seen, was decided entirely in the king's favor by the Reformation Parliament. By statutory legislation, the whole legislative, judicial, and doctrinal machinery of the medieval clergy was translated—illegally, if you like—to the crown, which by that act acceded to powers never before enjoyed by an English monarch.[87] The Church was identified with the State, and

86. Strype, *Eccles. Mem.*, I (1), 209. Italics mine.
87. See above, Chap. II.

the clergy henceforth performed their functions not *jure divino*, as before, but by sufferance of the king. But what had the pamphleteers to say of this combat? After all, many of them were bishops, and, as such, naturally jealous of their spiritual prerogatives. As a matter of fact, the episcopacy, assisted to a certain extent by old-line conservatives like Sir Thomas More, put up something of a fight for the *status quo*. Just before his death, Archbishop Warham drafted a speech in which he said in no uncertain terms that it is against God's law to suppose that an archbishop's power in any sense depends on a prince's temporal power.[88] Bishop Fisher wrote a treatise defending the privileges of the clergy.[89] And of the laymen, Sir Thomas More, though for the most part avoiding the issue of Church and State in his controversial tracts, did likewise by consistently maintaining the divine authority of Church tradition.[90]

It was Bishop Gardiner, however, who proved to be the most inveterate opponent of the king's proposed changes. As royal secretary, Gardiner had gone along with the king on his divorce project, and he had no particular objections to repudiating the papal authority. But as

88. *Letters and Papers of Henry VIII*, V, 1247. This speech, designed to be spoken in the House of Lords, was never actually delivered.

89. P.R.O., St.P. 6: 11, 15; *cf. Letters and Papers*, VIII, 887(6). Fisher's treatise consists for the most part of examples from the Old Testament of kings who had reverenced and honored the clergy as God's representatives on earth. In fact, Fisher writes, the clergy "represent christes own person and . they shuld be obeyd and herd evyn as men wold obey and here Christ hymselfe" (f. 447). Bishop Tunstal was another who for some time caused Henry embarrassment. Several times he protested against the title of *Supremum Caput*, and suggested that it should read "in temporalibus, post Christum" to avoid offense (*Letters and Papers*, V, 819).

90. More's point was that by the words, "I am with you all the days to the end of the world" (Matthew 28:20), Christ had promised to be ever present in his Church. This meant that all the deliberations of the Church would be divinely inspired, and superior in authority even to the Scriptures. Indeed, More says, the Scriptures themselves were selected by the Church which existed before the Scriptures were ever written down. See More's *Dialogue concerning Tyndale*, edited by W.E.Campbell (London, 1927), *passim*, but especially Book I, pp. 73–74, 124. Had More applied this principle of the infallibility of Church tradition, he would have been led logically to recognize the divine right of the clergy to the entire *potestas jurisdictionis*.

Bishop of Winchester, he flew to the rescue of his class, and stood forth as the champion of an independent convocation. When in 1532 the so-called "Petition of the Commons" demanded that henceforth canons passed in convocation should require royal assent,[91] Gardiner framed a vigorous reply. The "Answer of the Ordinaries," which was apparently largely inspired by Gardiner,[92] rejoined that it was against divine law to submit canons to the judgment of the secular sovereign.[93] About the same time a similar treatise was written in manuscript entitled "That the bishops have immediate authority of Christ to make such laws as they shall think expedient for the weal of men's souls." [94] In this the author maintained naïvely that since the priests of Egypt, Ethiopia, and Palestine had been venerated in times gone by, so now their privileges and liberties ought equally to be respected by secular sovereigns.

By 1535, however, the opposition had petered out, and henceforth few voices were raised conspicuously against the Submission of the Clergy. A combination of luck and governmental pressure saw to that. Archbishop Warham tactfully died in 1532. Fisher and More were executed for their pains. And Gardiner turned king's evidence with the publication of that most extreme of all anti-ecclesiastical tracts, the *De vera obedientia*. Henceforth, the doctrine of the absolute sovereignty of the State in ecclesiastical affairs reigned supreme, and the pamphlets

91. See Gee and Hardy, *Documents Illustrative of English Church History,* p. 146.

92. On this point, see Janelle, *L'Angleterre Catholique,* pp. 152–153.

93. This pertinent rejoinder reads as follows: "And as concerning the requiring of your highness's royal assent to the authorizing of such laws, as have been by our predecessors, or shall be made by us, in such points and articles as we have by good authority to rule and order by provisions and laws; we, knowing your highness's wisdom, virtue, and learning, nothing doubt but that the same perceiveth how the granting thereunto dependeth not upon our will and liberty, and that we, your most humble subjects, may not submit the execution of our charges and duty, certainly prescribed by God, to your highness's assent; although, of very deed, the same is most worthy. . . ." (Gee and Hardy, *Documents Illustrative of English Church History,* p. 157).

94. P.R.O., St.P. 6: 1, 8; *cf. Letters and Papers,* V, 1020.

proceeded arm in arm with the statute book—if not in detail, at least in general approach.

Like the statute book, the anti-clerical pamphlets began conservatively, and gradually came to expound a more and more radical philosophy. Back in 1515 when the Hunne case was arousing anti-clerical feeling in London, Dr. Henry Standish, among others, had outspokenly attacked the privilege of benefit of clergy.[95] And during the first years of the Reformation Parliament, Simon Fish and the radical Protestants fairly outdid one another in writing anti-clerical diatribes.[96] It was not, however, until 1532 that a really serious and respectable literary offensive was set in motion against the clergy. No doubt Fish and Tyndale were serious enough, but they were hardly respectable. They were, unfortunately, tainted with heresy, and as a result, their abusive language was not calculated to influence public opinion to nearly the same extent as the broadsides of pillars of society like bishops and lawyers. Respectability was then, as now, a primary requisite for the success of a public appeal, and the radical Protestants had not yet achieved respectability in England.

The soul of the respectable anti-clerical campaign was Christopher St. German, who, during the years 1530–1535, directed no less than seven treatises against the medieval prerogatives of the clergy.[97] As a common lawyer, St. German was jealous of the jurisdiction of the

95. Benefit of clergy had been a lively issue in 1515. The Abbot of Winchcombe, in a sermon at St. Paul's Cross, had defended the old order and denounced the law, 4 Hen. VIII, c. 2, which restricted benefit of clergy to the higher orders, as being "enconter le lei de dieu." The king had thereupon chosen several doctors and canonists to argue the matter at Blackfriars. The defendant had proclaimed that the conventing of clerks before temporal judges "est peccatum in se." Whereupon Dr. Standish, as king's counsel, had replied that "cest decrée d'exemption des Clerkes ne fuit jammes resceive cy en Engleterre." See Keilwey's *Reports* (London, 1688), pp. 181–182.

96. For example, Fish's *Supplication for the Beggars*, Tyndale's *Practice of Prelates*, and Barnes' "Men's constitutions not grounded in Scripture bind not the conscience."

97. I include Dialogue II and the Additions to the *Doctor and Student*, both of which were written separately from Dialogue I, and which contain a good deal of anti-clerical material.

spiritual courts, and as a bourgeois, he typified that fierce hatred of clerks for which London merchants had long been renowned. It was therefore only natural that the clergy should have been more especially anathema to St. German than the pope himself. For six years the law-yer pursued the attack relentlessly, and both in perspi-cacity and in perseverance he may be said to have been the leader of the anti-clerical campaign.

Indeed, so important was St. German in this connec-tion, that the evolution of anti-clerical opinion between 1530 and 1540 was largely synonymous with the evolu-tion of the lawyer's own point of view. His earlier treatises —Dialogue II of the *Doctor and Student* (1530), the Additions to the *Doctor and Student* (1531), the *Spiritu-ality and Temporality* (1532), and *Salem and Bizance* (1533)—were, to be sure, sometimes anticipatory of the statute book,[98] but they were confined to an attack on the legislative and judicial functions of the clergy. It was not until his later works, particularly the *Answer* (1535), that he took the final step and transferred the entire *potestas jurisdictionis* of the clergy, including the right to define doctrine, to the secular power.[99]

This radical evolution of St. German's thought. was precisely the development which the Henrician political writings as a whole experienced. The "Petition of the Commons" of 1532, which, as various authorities have pointed out, resembles St. German's *Spirituality and Temporality*,[100] attacked convocation's legislative pre-rogative and the abuses of the ecclesiastical courts, but forbore from asking that the power to interpret Scripture be assigned to the temporality. Nor did the *Disputatio*

98. St. German's idea, advanced as early as 1532, that the legislative and judicial powers of the clergy ought to be subject to secular supervision was, for example, given concrete form in the Act for the Submission of the Clergy (1534).

99. For a more detailed account of the development of St. German's political thought in a radical direction, see my article, "Christopher St. German," *Amer.Hist.Rev.*, XLII, 631–651.

100. See A.I.Taft, *Apologye of Syr Thomas More, Knyght*, p. xxxvii, note 4, and Janelle, *L'Angleterre Catholique*, p. 150.

inter militem et clericum, published in English probably in 1533, make any such claims. It was not until the publication of Fox's *De vera differentia* and Gardiner's *De vera obedientia* during the next two years that precedents began to be cited for the absorption by the king of the entire *potestas jurisdictionis* of the medieval clergy. The political writers devoted the next decade to elaborating this point, which was given official expression in the introduction to the *Bishops' Book* of 1537.

The outstanding argument by which the pamphleteers undermined the position of the clergy was the same which they had used against the papacy—a re-definition of Gelasian dualism. As originally stated by Pope Gelasius I and restated by Fortescue and others in the fifteenth century, this doctrine, as we have seen, stated that each of the two powers, the spiritual and temporal, derives its authority directly from God, and each is therefore independent within its own peculiar sphere. As applied practically, this theory meant that the spirituality has authority to legislate concerning the spiritual life of the people, to render decisions in its own courts, and to define doctrine —in other words, to exercise the whole *potestas jurisdictionis* of the medieval Church.

Now the Henrician pamphleteers basically altered this scheme. The fundamental hypothesis, the idea that the spirituality and temporality are independent within their own spheres, they retained, but its specific application they profoundly modified. They maintained that the term "spiritual" does not comprise powers of jurisdiction, but only of orders. The distinction between "spiritual" and "temporal" thus came to mean the distinction between the *potestas ordinis*, and the *potestas jurisdictionis* plus the temporal jurisdiction of the secular government. The clergy were left with a realm of their own, but with a realm empty of content except for the power to confer grace through the Sacraments.

This re-definition followed by the Henrician writers was essentially the same as that propounded by Marsilius of Padua in the *Defensor Pacis*. Marsilius had distinguished sharply between the terms *temporale* and *spirituale*. *Temporale*, he had said, refers to all corporal things calculated to supply the needs and desires of man for this present life. *Spirituale*, on the other hand, has to do with the law of God, and all things applicable to the life to come. Practically speaking, Marsilius had continued, this means that the learning and teaching of the divine precepts, the administration of the Sacraments, and other like things, are the only prerogatives of the clergy. To extend this word *spirituale* to include the mundane actions of priests, their temporal goods, moveable and unmoveable, tithes, and coercive jurisdiction, is to upset the order originally instituted by God himself.[101]

Christopher St. German, followed by Bishop Fox, reflected this point of view in all his controversial works. "Mere spiritual" things, he said, that is, the administration of the Sacraments, etc., are derived by the spirituality directly from God, and are therefore not to be tampered with by the laity. But other powers now exercised by the clergy are not theirs by divine right, but originate through a medium, "that is to say, by the mean of princes."[102] The altercations between clergy and laity in this realm, he affirmed, are due entirely to the fact that the clergy have encroached on the peculiarly secular sphere. To put an end to this division, it would be necessary for all men, spiritual and temporal, "to be ordered and ruled by one law in all things temporal."[103]

Bishop Fox advanced a similar thesis. He admitted that the clergy have received a special mandate from God to exercise a *potestas ordinis*, but hastened to add that laws, punishments, judgments, and restraints are reserved for the secular power.[104] Stated in other words, God has given

---

101. *Defensor Pacis*, pp. 118–120.

102. *A Dialogue betwixte two englyshemen, whereof one was called Salem, and the other Bizance* (London, 1533; hereafter referred to as *Salem and Bizance*), p. lxxx^b.

103. This is the main contention of St. German's *Spirituality and Temporality*.   104. *De vera differentia*, p. 30.

his bishops authority, but not dominion.[105] Fox proceeded to distinguish sharply between *cleros* and *laos*. A clerk, he said, has nothing to do with corporal business, but should live in poverty, holding all things in common with other clerks.[106] A layman, on the other hand, has the right to possess temporal things and judge between man and man.[107] It is evident that although St. German and Fox saved the appearances by retaining the principle of Gelasian dualism, they both re-defined the latter in such a way as to deprive the clergy of everything but a *potestas ordinis*.

Bishop Gardiner and the author of the anonymous *Treatise proving by the king's laws* were of a similar mind except that they stated the issue in a somewhat different way. They, too, took away from the clergy everything but the *potestas ordinis*, but in so doing, they abolished Gelasian dualism altogether. Some people will wonder, Gardiner said, that he has abandoned the old distinction which would differentiate between the government of a prince and that of the Church; according to which the prince, like the moon which is called the lesser light, should have charge of the affairs of the night, and the Church, like the sun, should reserve to itself the government of the day. Actually, said Gardiner, this distinction is full of darkness, for it is absurd to suppose that the king, whom God has enjoined to feed the people, should neglect spiritual matters and spiritual men's sins.[108] The anonymous writer of 1538 likewise denounced the distinction between spiritual and temporal men. Such a distinction, he asserted, is palpably false, for a layman by good living may be spiritual, and a bishop by evil living may be temporal. Similarly, he said, the distinction between spiritual and temporal, which would have all cases

---

105. *Ibid.*, p. 29.
106. *Ibid.*, pp. 31–33. This idea, that the clergy should observe absolute poverty, had been previously espoused by Marsilius and the Spiritual Franciscans in the fourteenth century. See, for example, *Defensor Pacis*, Dictio II, Cap. 12.
107. *De vera differentia*, pp. 31–33.
108. *De vera obedientia*, pp. 102–104.

involving sin tried in the spiritual courts, is built on a false premise, for all offenses against the laws of the realm are sin, and yet have always been tried in the king's courts.[109]

But what, it may be asked, were the practical implications of this new type of thinking? What, specifically, were the powers which, in the process of re-defining Gelasian dualism, the pamphleteers transferred from the clergy to the king, or the king in parliament, as the case may be? The answer is, as has been indicated above, the whole *potestas jurisdictionis* of the medieval clergy—the powers of legislation, jurisdiction, and interpretation of doctrine. The pamphleteers, like the statute book, endowed the crown, or the crown in parliament, with a sovereignty in spiritual matters complete except for the nebulous superiority of a general council.

In the first place, the pamphleteers proclaimed the sole authority of the king, or the king in parliament, to legislate on spiritual as well as temporal matters. Arguments differed, but the thesis that convocation functioned only by delegation from the secular power was generally agreed upon. For six years St. German unceasingly inculcated the doctrine that to parliament belongs the exclusive right to legislate on all matters having to do with property, goods, and money, and that, indeed, convocation has no right to legislate at all except by the king's consent.[110] Pushing his re-definition of Gelasian dualism to its logical conclusion, the lawyer maintained that parliament might pass laws concerning mortuaries,[111] tithes,[112] the

109. *Treatise proving by the king's laws*, pp. Bii^b–Biii^b.
110. St. German said, for example, that he saw no authority for benefit of clergy except laws of the clergy's own making "which be therin of no strength for them in this realme excepte certayn lybertyes that they haue in that behalf by the kyng and his progenytours and by the lawes and customes of the Realme" (*Constitutions Provincial and Legatine*, pp. Bv–Bv^b).
111. *Doctor and Student*, Dialogue II, Additions, Chap. 1. Parliament had already passed an act fixing mortuary rates in 1529 (21 Hen. VIII, c. 6).
112. *Power of the Clergy*, p. Bi. "Though tythes be called spyrituall," St. German says, "yet they be in dede temporall: as all goodes be in whose hands soeuer they come. And so the parliament hath full power to ordre them so that the lawe of god be nat broken by their ordre."

disposition of Church goods,[113] and the exaction of money by visitors of religious foundations.[114] All these measures he justified on the ground that they are temporal and concern the body. Summing up his theory in one succinct paragraph, he said that "it is holden by them that be learned in the law of this realm, that the parliament hath an absolute power as to the possession of all temporal things within this realm, in whose hands so ever they be, spiritual or temporal, to take them from one man and give them to another without any cause or consideration."[115] St. German, in other words, despoiled the clergy of their traditional right to legislate without the king's consent, and thus gave effect in literary form to the principles of the "Petition of the Commons" and the famous Act for the Submission of the Clergy.[116]

Bishop Fox maintained a similar doctrine in the *De vera differentia*. Canon laws, he said, "have not their strength and virtue by the authority of bishops that be the makers thereof, but by the people receiving them willingly."[117] Citing numerous examples from the Old Testament and English history, he sought to prove that in the past kings had always legislated concerning things

113. *Constitutions Provincial and Legatine*, Chap. 21. The constitution, St. German says, which forbids a layman to order and dispose Church goods, is not enjoined by the law of God, for it appertains to laymen, and not to clerks, to look after such things.

114. *Doctor and Student*, Dialogue II, Additions, Chap. 13. "For the money that they [the visitors] receive," says St. German, "though it be given by occasion of a spiritual thing is temporal, and is under the power of parliament, as all temporal lands and goods are." St. German could well remember the days when Wolsey, in his capacity as *legatus a latere*, had reaped a handsome income from his ecclesiastical visitations.

115. *Spirituality and Temporality*, p. 228 (all page citations from this treatise refer to A.I.Taft's edition in *The Apologye of Syr Thomas More, Knyght*, Appendix). This statement comes in connection with a discussion on mortuaries.

116. The "Petition of the Commons" complained to the king that the clergy in convocation had "heretofore made and caused to be made, and also daily do make, many divers fashions of laws, constitutions, and ordinances, without your knowledge or most royal assent, and without the assent and consent of any of your lay subjects" (Gee and Hardy, *Documents Illustrative of English Church History*, p. 146; a passage from the "Answer of the Ordinaries" to the "Petition" has been quoted above, p. 64, n. 93).

117. *De vera differentia*, p. 31.

which the clergy now regard as "spiritual." With rather
more emphasis on ecclesiastical regulations, and less on
the pecuniary aspect of Church law than St.

German,
Fox summoned the ghosts of Kings Cnut, Ethelred, Ed-
gar, and Edmund to illustrate how once upon a time
English kings had issued enactments of a "spiritual"
nature, independently of convocation. Laws concerning
the sums to be paid at burial, the payment of tenths, the
length of Sunday, the prohibition of business and hunting
on Sunday, and the number of times the Sacrament of the
altar should be administered, were among the accomplish-
ments of these early English heroes.[118] Fox, like St. German, re-defined Gelasian dualism in such a way as to repudiate the independent right of the clergy to legislate.

Fox's historical thesis, that the clergy have no right to
legislate independently because in fact they have not done
so in the past, was one which appealed to the author of the
Treatise proving by the king's laws as well. We have already seen how this writer argued against papal primacy
on the ground that in the past papal primacy had never
been recognized in England.[119] He now turned this same
argument against the English clergy. Since parliament,
he asserted, has often heretofore passed laws regulating
preaching, usury, and perjury—all offenses involving sin,
which the clergy claim as their exclusive prerogative—
parliament has the right to do so today if it chooses.[120]
Moreover, the mere fact that convocation is called by the
king's writs, and that parliament has at times legislated
concerning convocation itself, indicates clearly enough
that the king in parliament is of more authority than
convocation.[121] With both Fox and this anonymous writer,
the argument of custom and precedent counted almost as
heavily as that of divine law.

118. *Ibid.*, pp. 39–40.
119. See above, pp. 43–44.
120. *Treatise proving by the king's laws*, p. Cviii[b]. The author also argues
(*ibid.*, p. Bii) that bishops may not enact laws to bind kings and their subjects
because they too are the king's subjects and ministers to the people.
121. *Ibid.*, pp. Ciiii[b]–Cv.

In denying convocation its ancient rights, the rest of the pamphleteers simply followed the arguments enunciated by St. German, Fox, and the anonymous writer. Repetition, rather than ingenuity, was the order of the day. In only one other tract that I have consulted can there be detected a note of originality. An author in manuscript turned the tables on the conservatives by maintaining that the clergy's assertion of their right to make laws, either spiritual or temporal, or to bind kings and princes, is actually "heresy," rather than *vice versa*, and that the apostles had exercised a legislative power only until enough laymen had been converted to Christianity to take over the burden.[122] Most of the pamphlets, however, were simply variations on the same dominant themes.

In the second place, the pamphleteers asserted that the clergy have no judicial rights independent of the secular power. In addition to rejecting the notion that cases involving property and money might be tried in clerical courts,[123] St. German denied the latter cognizance of other causes like adultery, fornication, matrimony, and the proving of wills.[124] The lawyer was especially vehement against the clerical claim that a spiritual judge might act as overseer of the secular courts.[125] To put it in

122. P.R.O., St.P. 6: 1, 24, ff. 213, 217–218; cf. Letters and Papers, XI, 85. This tract is entitled "Of dyuers heresies which haue not ben taken for heresies in tyme paste," and is over thirty folio pages long. It is calendared in the *Letters and Papers* under the year 1536. The unique passage in question reads as follows: "Also to saie that the bisshop of Rome and the Clargie maye make lawes to bynde kynges and prynces and ther subiectes and obstynatly defende it is heresie for it is ayenst this texte of scripture Psalmo. 2. Where it is saied O kynges vnderstande ye, be ye lerned that iudge the worlde and sithe the kynges be iudges of the worlde noone maye make lawes to bynde them, for if they myght then shulde not kynges be iudges but vnder them that make the lawes."

123. St. German said, for example, that all cases of annuities belonged in temporal courts (*Doctor and Student*, Dialogue II, Additions, Chap. 9), and that a man indicted in a spiritual court for debt, trespass, or any other thing belonging rightfully to the king's courts might have a *praemunire facias* against the party suing him (*ibid.*, Dialogue II, Chap. 33).

124. *Answer*, Chap. 1.

125. *Salem and Bizance*, p. lxxviii. One of the false "pretences" of the clergy, St. German says, is the claim of the spiritual judge to compel the secular judge to do justice, "orels supplie his roume and here the cause."

Fox's strong language, "neither the Scriptures of the Evangelists nor of the Apostles do give them [that is, priests] Judicial power nor court to make examination or determination of punishment."[126] Fox's argument was, indeed, strongly Marsilian, for he attacked the clergy's right to jurisdiction on the ground that God gave coercive power exclusively to the secular government. The author of the *Treatise proving by the king's laws* employed an argument similar to that used in his invective against convocation. The king's courts, he said, have always been higher in authority than the courts christian.[127] The clergy receive their jurisdiction not from God, but from custom and the sufferance of princes. What jurisdiction the clergy do possess began, according to the author, "to the only intent, to ease the king's higher courts, that they should not be letted in greater and weightier matters, by such light causes, as most of them be, whereof the clergy doth hold plea."[128]

To translate the entire *potestas jurisdictionis* of the medieval clergy to the king, or the king in parliament, the pamphleteers had still, however, to assign to the latter the power of interpreting Scripture. This the pamphleteers were all prepared to do, with the reservations already noted concerning general councils. The official statement in the *Bishops' Book* of 1537, which, according to its introduction, was submitted to His Majesty "to be recognized, overseen, and corrected,"[129] was actually the reflection of a point of view already standardized by the pamphleteers of the preceding three or four years. St. German's statement is again the most significant. Everybody admits, he said in a passage already quoted in another connection, that the Catholic Church may expound

126. *De vera differentia*, p. 37.
127. *Treatise proving by the king's laws*, pp. Bvii–Bvii[b]. In illustration of this point, the author says that when the clergy have held plea of anything appertaining to the king's courts, the latter have always sent to the clergy a writ of prohibition.
128. *Ibid.*, p. Dii[b].
129. Lloyd, *Formularies of Faith*, pp. 26–27.

Scripture, and if the clergy can prove they constitute the Catholic Church, then it is their duty to expound it. If, on the other hand, the laity as well as the clergy make the Catholic Church, "why should not the parliament then which representeth the whole Catholic Church of England expound Scripture rather than the convocation which representeth only the clergy?"[130] Fox and Gardiner cited Justinian to prove that princes had made laws concerning doctrine in the past.[131] And the author of a manuscript already referred to was of St. German's mind, that parliament ought to declare the meaning of the various articles of faith, and none other.[132]

The effect of this manner of thinking was to create an opinion like that of Edward Hall toward the end of the reign. Anticipating Hobbes, the chronicler announced that to obey the king in the exposition of Scripture was sufficient discharge for his loving subjects before the face

130. *Answer*, pp. Giiii[b]–Gv. It is worthy of notice that St. German had not held this extreme view in his earlier treatises. In his *Spirituality and Temporality*, for instance, he had thought (p. 223) "that the temporall men maye not iudge, what is heresie and what not."

131. See Fox, *De vera differentia*, p. 39, and Gardiner, *De vera obedientia*, pp. 116–118. Gardiner's statement in this connection is extremely significant. "Itaque," he wrote, "quis unquam improbauit Iustiniani factum, qui leges aedidit de summa trinitate, et de fide catholica, de episcopis, de clericis, de haereticis, et caeteris id genus." Janelle notes (*ibid.*, p. 118, note 1) that Gardiner is here simply copying from the Justinian Code.

132. P.R.O., St.P. 6: 1, 24, ff. 238–239. In answer to the question, who should interpret doubtful Scriptural passages, the author says: "But no doctour ne other maye take vppon hym to iudge such doubtes of scripture . . . but onely they that haue auctorite therto of god, that is to saie the generall councell gathered and ordred by the auctorite of kynges, and prynces or els by euery kyng or prynce in his dominyon after such maner as lawes be made there and that in this Realme is by the kyng and his parliament, and that maye the kyng and all other kynges and prynces do for acquyetyng of ther people till a generall Councell maye come." The author of the *Treatise proving by the king's laws* reproduced this idea exactly. "Yf any Scisme shoulde fortune to aryse in the uniuersall churche," he says (Di), "upon articles concerning Christis religion, which had nede to be spedely redressed, and princes by occasion of other matters canne not haue tyme to agree, to haue a generall Councille: in such cases kynges of this realme myght, and yet may, call their parliamentes, and set an ordre therin for their subiectes, untyll a generall council maye be conueniently be had, which ordre so set by parlyament, shall bynde the hole realme in the meane tyme, as well the clergy, as other. . . ."

of God.[133] Henry VIII himself, in a speech delivered before the parliament of 1545, assumed a position very like this. If members of the laity, he said, suspect a preacher of teaching perverse doctrine, let them declare it to the council or to the king, to whom the authority to order such causes is committed by God. "Be not judges yourself, of your own fantastical opinions, and vain expositions, for in such high causes you may lightly err."[134] It is evident that by the end of the reign men had come to think in terms of the infallibility of the king, or of the king in parliament, rather than of the medieval Church. The pendulum had swung completely over, and the *potestas jurisdictionis* of the *sacerdotium* had been entirely transferred, albeit illegally, to the *regnum*.

This conception of the infallibility of the king, or the king in parliament, was not only highly significant for English constitutional history, but also indispensable to the Henrician pamphleteers as an argument against the clergy. It was all very well to re-define Gelasian dualism, but there still remained some doubt as to just what cases could be called "mere spiritual," and which temporal. It was very useful, in the event of altercation, to point to the king, or the king in parliament, as an infallible oracle to decide the issue. In all his controversial treatises, St. German took refuge in this pious principle. "It cannot be thought," he said, "that a statute that is made by authority of the whole realm, as well of the king and of the lords spiritual and temporal, as of all the commons, will recite a thing against the truth."[135] This was to make

133. Foxe, *Acts and Monuments*, V, 504–505. This view implied, of course, that if the king denied any doctrine necessary for salvation, and his subjects followed him in that denial, God would hold the king alone responsible. Said Hobbes later in the *Leviathan* (Chap. 42), "This we may say, that whatsoever a subject . . . is compelled to in obedience to his Soveraign, and doth it not in order to his own mind, but in order to the laws of his country, that action is not his, but his Soveraign's; nor is it he that in this case denyeth Christ before men, but his Governour, and the law of his countrey."

134. Edward Hall, *Chronicle* (London, 1809), pp. 864–866.

135. *Doctor and Student*, p. 279. This doctrine of parliamentary infallibility was probably St. German's main contribution to the development of parlia-

the king in parliament an absolute sovereign in spiritual affairs, and to establish beyond a shadow of doubt that the *potestas jurisdictionis* of the medieval Church—legislative, judicial, and doctrinal—was the prerogative of the State.

By the end of the reign, therefore, the doctrine later to be classicized in the pages of Hooker[136] and Hobbes was thoroughly familiar to Englishmen. Hobbes' statement, already quoted, that "all Pastors, except the Supreme, execute their charges . . . *Jure Civili.* But the King . . . executeth his Office of Supreme Pastor . . . *Jure Divino,*"[137] might have been uttered by any Henrician pamphleteer after 1534. And, curiously enough, it was the bishops who partially signed their own death warrant. For although St. German may be said to have been the most prominent priest-baiter, Bishops Fox and Gardiner abetted no little the destruction of their own order.

5. *POTESTAS JURISDICTIONIS* OR *POTESTAS ORDINIS?*

IT is important to notice again, however, that for all their radicalism, the majority of the Henrician pamphleteers did not abandon the principle of Gelasian dualism altogether. Although, as we have seen, they re-defined the

mentary sovereignty. In his *Salem and Bizance* he remarked sarcastically (pp. lxxiii–iv) that "if Master More can shew any lawes, that haue ben made by parliament, concernyng the spiritualtie, that the parliament had none auctoritie to make . . . it wyl be wel done that he shewe them." In another place, he maintained that the parliamentary statutes requiring priests to answer for their crimes in secular courts were according to divine law, "for it is nat to presume that so many noble princes and their counseyle, ne the lordes, and the nobles of the realme, ne yet the Comons gathered in the sayde parlyamente wolde fro tyme to tyme renne in so great offence of conscyence as is the brekynge of the lawe of god" (*Power of the Clergy*, Chap. 6). Moreover, the whole *Treatise proving by the king's laws* was written on the assumption of parliamentary infallibility. The clergy must be wrong, so the argument goes, because anti-clerical statutes have been passed in parliament.

136. That the clergy have no power *jure divino* to call and dissolve ecclesiastical assemblies, to make laws for the Church, or to exercise jurisdiction, but that they derive such power from the secular sovereign, Hooker was later to enunciate clearly in the *Ecclesiastical Polity*, Book III (particularly, Chaps. 5, 6, 8).

137. See above, p. 25.

words "spiritual" and "temporal" in Marsilian terms, and although they deprived the spirituality of its *potestas jurisdictionis*, they nevertheless reserved to the latter a narrow sphere within which it was to be supreme, unmolested by secular encroachments. This sphere was the *potestas ordinis*, the power of conferring grace through consecration and the Sacraments, which the pamphleteers, like the legislators, could never bring themselves to include under the Royal Supremacy. They denied, in contradistinction to medieval Gelasianism, that the clergy had been given powers of coercive jurisdiction by God, but they refrained from repudiating the medieval scheme altogether. They rather re-defined it in their own words and then gave it their blessing. The king, or the king in parliament, they said in effect, is supreme administrator of the Church, but he is not a priest *ex officio*. He must not interfere with the *potestas ordinis* which the clergy wield *jure divino*. In this respect, the pamphlets for the most part scrupulously reflected the statute book.

In the first place, if the pamphleteers had wished to attribute to the king the power of orders, they would doubtless have seen the advantage of amplifying the unctional character of the coronation. But nowhere in their writings is there mention of a *persona mixta* who partakes of the nature of a clerk as well as a layman.[138] On the contrary, the Henrician writers usually went out of their way to repudiate the notion that the king might interfere with things "mere spiritual," that is, the administration of the Sacraments.[139] "Such ministration the king may not take upon him, nor he intendeth it not," said St. German.[140] In fact, the lawyer asserted, if parliament and

138. See L.G.W.Legg, *English Coronation Records* (London, 1901), pp. xvi–xvii. Legg observes that the coronation unction did not confer on the king power to perform functions appertaining to priests. But if the sixteenth-century writers had desired to extend to the king a *potestas ordinis*, they could obviously have used the coronation ceremony to some advantage.

139. To St. German the expression "mere spiritual things" was, I think, always synonymous in his mind with the *potestas ordinis*.

140. *Answer*, p. Aiiii. See also *Power of the Clergy*, Chap. 17, where St. German says that the king "hath none auctorite to minister any of the sacramentes, ne

convocation had granted to the king, along with the title
of Supreme Head, authority over things "mere spiritual,"
"it is no doubt but that the grant had been void; for they
have no authority to change the law of God."[141] Bishops
Tunstal and Gardiner, and the author of the *Treatise
proving by the king's laws*, were unquestionably of a
similar mind, though applying themselves to the problem less directly.[142]

More illuminating on this point than even the pamphlets, however, are the answers given by the bishops and
theologians to certain questions put them by the king in
preparation for the *King's Book* of 1543.[143] Some of the
rejoinders, indeed, seem to ascribe to the king a *potestas
ordinis*, but for the most part they repudiate the notion
vigorously. The opinions of Dr. Redman, of the Archbishop of York, and of Dr. Edgeworth are particularly
noteworthy.[144] In answer to the question whether the

to do any other thing spyrituall whereof oure lorde gaue power only to his
apostles and discyples."

141. *Answer*, p. Biii.

142. By inference, all these men were of St. German's mind. In the *Letter
written by Tunstall and Stokesley to Reginald Pole, Cardinal* (London, 1560),
Tunstall explains to Pole that it is no argument against the Royal Supremacy
to say that the king cannot exercise the chief office of the Church in preaching
and the administration of the Sacraments. "It is not requisite to euery body
naturall," he says (p. Ciiii), "that the heade shall exercyse ether al maner of
offices of the body, or the chiefe office of the same." Gardiner refers to the matter
indirectly where he says that the Bishop of Rome has no more power than other
bishops, "uidelicet ut commissam in sua diocesi plebem diuini uerbi, et sacramentorum ministratione alant, et pascant" (*De vera obedientia*, p. 128). The
author of the *Treatise proving by the king's laws* also observes (p. Bii) that
"the clergie of this realme, as bysshops and priestis, haue power by the lawe of
god, and by the wordis of the gospelle, to consecrate, to make priestis, to assoyle,
and to preache the word of god. . . ." There is a similar passage in the Hatfield
MS. Priests "onely" may consecrate, the author says (Chap. 2), "and none but
theye. And they may also babtise by the lawe of god: and soo maye every laye
man but none may vse the Ceremonyes therof but prestes."

143. Printed in Burnet, *History of the Reformation of the Church of England*,
edited by Nicholas Pocock (Oxford, 1865), IV, 443–496. For comment, see
R.W.Dixon, *History of the Church of England* (Oxford, 1891–1902), II, 302f.

144. All these men were staunch supporters of the Royal Supremacy, and
were not therefore leading an opposition. Dr. John Redman was one of Henry
VIII's chaplains. Edward Lee, Archbishop of York, was one of those who from
the very beginning had backed up the king in both his divorce and the Royal

apostles, not having a Christian king among them, made bishops by that necessity, or by authority given them by God, Redman asserted that the "making" of a bishop or priest may be taken two ways. If it is to be understood as "ordaining" or "consecrating," he said, then it pertains to the apostles and their successors only; if taken, however, to mean simply "appointing" or "naming" to the office, then it pertains to princes as Supreme Heads of the Church.[145] Redman further rejected the idea that appointment alone is necessary to a bishopric without consecration,[146] and he remarked that in case all the bishops of a region were dead, it were better to send for bishops dwelling near by than to allow the king to supply this function.[147] The Archbishop of York, though less emphatic, was equally certain that the Royal Supremacy did not imply a *potestas ordinis*. Appointment to a bishopric, he said, is not sufficient without consecration,[148] and even if a prince, accompanied by only secular men, should conquer infidel regions, he could not lawfully make priests there, "forsomuch as no man may use this or any other authority which cometh from the Holy Ghost, unless he have, other commission grounded in scripture, or else authority by tradition, and ancient use of Christ's church universally received over all." [149] Dr. Edgeworth's opinion is also worthy of attention. Under no conditions, he observed, ought a prince to administer Sacraments other than Baptism, unless he receive a special commission from God, as Moses once did.[150] Nor did these opinions represent a minority, for on all the really important questions

Supremacy. Dr. Roger Edgeworth was also a typical Tudor churchman who swam with the tide. He adhered to the religious innovations introduced by Henry and Edward VI, and still could become a good Catholic under Mary.

145. Burnet, *History of the Reformation of the Church of England*, IV, 469–470, 476.

146. *Ibid.*, p. 479.

147. *Ibid.*, p. 486.

148. *Ibid.*, p. 478.

149. *Ibid.*, pp. 481–482.

150. *Ibid.*, p. 484.

the majority of the answers returned were either equivocal, or else in line with those of Redman and York.

Archbishop Cranmer, it must be admitted, represents a very important exception. He answered equivocally when asked whether any other than a bishop may "make" a priest,[151] and for the most part he does seem to have thought that the king might assume on occasion a kind of *potestas ordinis*. He is certain that a priest or bishop need not be consecrated if he has been duly elected and appointed.[152] And under extraordinary circumstances, as for example if a prince had nothing but temporal men with him in an infidel country, or if all the priests of a region were dead, he had no doubt that the king might constitute priests. "There be histories," he said, "that witnesseth, that some Christian princes, and other laymen un-consecrate have done the same."[153]

The majority of the divines agreed with Cranmer that under the peculiar conditions described above, "necessitas non habet legem," and that the king, for lack of spiritual persons, might teach and even administer the Sacraments. But it must be repeated that in answer to the really vital question, they agreed in principle with Redman and York, that the power of orders is the exclusive prerogative of the clergy.

In point of fact, few men were prepared to go as far as Cranmer in the early sixteenth century. Cromwell is reported to have summoned various bishops before the council for the purpose of asking them whether the king could

151. *Ibid.*, p. 475. Cranmer successfully dodges this question. He reads the word "make" as "elect," and therefore comes to the obvious conclusion that often in the past princes have "made" bishops.

152. *Ibid.*, pp. 468, 478. Just what Cranmer implies by this assertion however, is not clear. For he says (*ibid.*, p. 468) that "there is no more promise of God that grace is given in the committing of the ecclesiastical office, than it is in the committing of the civil office." This would seem to indicate that even if royal appointment be sufficient to make a bishop, without the necessity of consecration, even so this would not constitute a *potestas ordinis*, for by the act of appointment the king would not be conferring grace on the appointee.

153. *Ibid.*, p. 481.

not make and unmake bishops at pleasure.[154] But it is not certain that he did not mean by "faire et deffaire" simply "elect and depose." Moreover, Bishop Fox's interesting examples of the king's spiritual capacity in *De vera differentia* are presented without theoretical comment, and it may be that the Bishop of Hereford was merely permitting his enthusiasm to run away with him for the nonce. According to Matthew Paris, Fox says, the king gave the archbishopric of Canterbury to the Bishop of London "and did consecrate him by a ring and crosier" (*annulus et baculum*). He also presented William Gifford with the see of Winchester, "and by and by put him in possession of all things pertaining to the bishopric and did consecrate him as well."[155]

Whatever the attitude of men like Cranmer and Fox, however, it is clear that the king himself consistently denied that he was aiming at a *potestas ordinis*. It may be true, as one Catholic historian maintains, that at one time in his career Henry VIII, contemplating an alliance with the Lutherans, tried to get the English divines to admit that the source of episcopal power lay in lawful appointment by the civil power, and not in consecration. But as Barnes himself admits, this demand was calculated to increase the king's jurisdictional control over the episcopacy, not to regale the Royal Supremacy with the power of conferring grace.[156] That Henry had no such designs is apparent from other sources. In 1532 he is reported to have said that the bishops are the doctors of men's souls, but ought not to meddle with their bodies, conceding to the episcopacy thereby the *potestas ordi-*

154. *Letters and Papers of Henry VIII*, VIII, 121 (Chapuys to Charles V, Jan. 28, 1535).
155. *De vera differentia*, p. 40. This interesting passage reads as follows: "Rex (vt scribit idem Matthaeus) dedit Episcopatum Vinthoniensem Gulielmo Gifford, & continuo de possessionibus cunctis ad Episcopatum pertinentibus, tam fratrisans quam patrisans, illum inuestiuit; non obstante statuto Vrbani Rom. Pontificis, sub Ecclesiasticis censuris prohibentis; *ne aliquis Clericorum de manu Principis aut aliorum Laicorum Ecclesiasticas dignitates recipiat.*" Italics mine.
156. A.S.Barnes, *Bishop Barlow and Anglican Orders*, pp. 26–27.

nis.[157] In 1533 he wrote to the clerics of the province of York reproving them for quibbling over the Supremacy on the ground that it involved the *potestas ordinis*. Actually, he replied, *"no man will deny* the ministration of spiritual things to have been by Christ committed to priests, to preach and minister the sacraments, them to be as physicians to men's souls."[158] And more important than even this admission was the fact that the *Bishops' Book*, which was published with the king's permission in 1537, set forth this idea boldly. "We may not think," it read, "that it doth appertain unto the office of kings and princes to preach and teach, to administer the sacraments, to absolve, to excommunicate, and such other things belonging to the office and administration of bishops and priests."[159] This was the official view of the government, and as such it is typical of the contemporaneous outlook.

In conclusion, it may be said that the English political writers of the early sixteenth century threw overboard the whole medieval philosophy of the *sacerdotium* and *regnum*. Conservative in some of their ideas of kingship, they blazed a new trail in the ecclesiastical sphere, and proclaimed the king head of the English Church, supreme in England above pope and clergy alike. Unwittingly, they propounded a doctrine of sovereignty[160]—the doctrine that the king, or the king in parliament, will brook no rival jurisdiction within the confines of the State. On the whole, the Henrician writers were, in this respect, simply following the trend of events. They were justifying theoretically the revolutionary legislation of the Reformation Parliament.

In certain respects, it is true, the pamphleteers were not prepared to push the new doctrine to its logical conclu-

157. *Letters and Papers*, V, 1013 (Chapuys to Charles V, May 13, 1532).

158. Wilkins, *Concilia Magnae Britanniae et Hiberniae* (London, 1737), III, 762. Italics mine.

159. Lloyd, *Formularies of Faith*, p. 121.

160. Not, however, a doctrine of unlimited sovereignty. This will appear more clearly below.

sion. They exalted the prerogative of the State at the expense of pope and clergy, but they made the reservation that a general council, lawfully convoked, was still the supreme ecclesiastical sovereign of western Christendom. Moreover, men like St. German and Gardiner were not quite clear as to whether the powers of the medieval Church had been transferred to the king or to the king in parliament. This was an issue over which battles were to be fought in the seventeenth century. And finally, the political writers, almost to a man, disclaimed any intention of conferring on the king the *potestas ordinis*. The *potestas jurisdictionis* they were willing to concede him, but not that power which would have given him control of the sacramental, as well as the administrative, system of the Church.

Despite these reservations, however, it is evident that by 1547 parliament and the political theorists had made the king by all odds the most important force in the English Church. With the enunciation of the "empire" theory, the principle of English nationalism won the day over internationalism, and the national sovereign was enabled to shake off papal and, to a large extent, conciliar control. With the redefinition of Gelasian dualism, the king was justified in wresting the internal control of the English Church from the clergy. It was this doctrine of the Royal Supremacy which, more than any other, differentiated the sixteenth-century theory of kingship from that of the fifteenth.

IV

THE CULT OF AUTHORITY

Indeed, God, according to his exceeding great and unspeakable goodness toward mankind, . . . substituted men, who, being put in authority as his vicegerents, should require obedience which we must do unto them with no less fruit for God's sake than we should do it (what honor soever it were) immediately unto God himself. And in that place he hath set princes whom, as representatives of his Image unto men, he would have to be reputed in the supreme and most high place, and to excel among all other human creatures. . . . By me (sayeth God) Kings reign, in so much that, after Paul's saying, whosoever resisteth power resisteth the ordinance of God. BISHOP GARDINER, *De vera obedientia.*

THE Henrician pamphleteers departed from fifteenth-century political theory in another important respect. They enunciated a doctrine of absolute non-resistance to the king—a novel doctrine in the early sixteenth century, one which had enjoyed little vogue during the middle ages. To medieval publicists, the legality of rebellion against the king in certain instances—*e.g.*, in the event of the king's violation of the feudal contract, or of his repudiation of certain dictates of Holy Church —had been unquestionable. In the middle ages, Law and the Church had been supreme, not the king. The fifteenth-century publicists had largely adhered to this tradition, although, to some extent, it is true, they had begun to stress the heinousness of rebellion.[1] The Henrician political writers, however, broke with the medieval tradition altogether. They taught that non-resistance is essential for the security of the state. Indeed, they set up a veritable cult of authority in which the king was lauded as God's vicegerent on earth. Rebellion they denounced as a religious sin, as a sin against God himself. The Henrician cult of authority was not so extreme, perhaps, as the Roman imperial cult, and it may have lacked the precise

1. See above, pp. 13–14.

ceremonial of Louis XIV's "levers" and "couchers." But
it succeeded admirably in its main purpose—the exaltation of the king as a semi-divine figure against whom rebellion constituted a grievous sin.

Thus, during the early English Reformation encomiums in praise of kingship, and a doctrine of authority
sufficiently vague—rather than precise analyses of the
actual powers wielded by a king—became the order of
the day. One writer "dares not cast [his eyes] but side-
wise upon the flaming beams of [the king's] bright sun,
which [he] in no wise can steadfastly behold."[2] Another
likens Henry VIII to the "Son of Man."[3] Still another
lauds him for possessing the same virtues as Solomon,
Sampson, and Absalom, and as being comparable to the
sun, no less.[4] Absolute non-resistance to the king's man-
dates was enjoined by practically all the respectable
writers of the day, and by many non-respectable people,
such as the radical Protestants, as well. The king, it was
the general consensus, "representeth as it were the image
of God upon earth," and must be obeyed "yea, though he
were an infidel." Scripture recognizes no limitations whatever to this obedience, which God has enjoined without so
much as "one syllable of exception."[5] To sum up, "the
king is, in this world, without law, and may at his lust
do right or wrong, and shall give accounts but to God
only."[6]

2. British Museum, Reg. MSS. 7, C XVI, f. 181. This manuscript is a letter
written by an unknown person to the king, in which, after a lengthy panegyric
on Henry VIII's virtues, the writer requests that he be given the appointment
to a Hebrew lectureship. As a test of his skill, he submits a translation from the
Hebrew of the gospels of James and Jude.

3. British Museum, Lansdowne MSS. 97, Plut. LXXV, E 13, ff. 148–153.

4. These were the flattering metaphors used by Sir Richard Rich, speaker of
the commons, in his orations at the beginning and end of the June-July parliamentary session of 1536 (Lords' Journals, I, 86, 101).

5. See Gardiner, De vera obedientia, pp. 96, 98. For a good, short discussion
of the doctrine of non-resistance in sixteenth-century England, see Allen, History of Political Thought in the Sixteenth Century, Part II, Chap. 2.

6. Tyndale, Obedience of a Christian Man, printed in Doctrinal Treatises by
W. Tyndale, edited by Rev. H. Walter (Parker Soc., Cambridge, 1848), p. 178.
Henceforth, all citations from Tyndale's Obedience of a Christian Man will refer
to the Parker Society edition.

The necessity for such a doctrine during the early English Reformation is fairly obvious. In the first place, England had only just a short time before emerged from the anarchy of the Wars of the Roses, the disorders of which were, at least in part, attributable to a lack of respect for the reigning sovereign. Moreover, the current example of Germany, disfigured and torn by the Peasants' Rebellion and by religious strife, left an indelible impression on the average Englishman's mind.[7] Was it not natural that in their dread of anarchy, Englishmen, radical Protestant and Anglican alike, should have stressed the divine retribution involved in disobedience to the king? It was for this same reason, among others, that Bodin was later in the century to emphasize the sovereignty of the French king, and that Le Bret and Bossuet were to preach divine-right monarchy at the court of Louis XIV. Frenchmen in the late sixteenth and seventeenth centuries no more desired a repetition of the Huguenot wars or the Fronde than Henrician Englishmen wanted a second Tewkesbury or Bosworth.

The exaltation of the king was necessary, in the second place, to offset the threat of foreign invasion as well as internal anarchy. It is seldom appreciated that during the early Reformation "the Enterprise of England" was as live an issue as during the reign of Elizabeth.[8] Henry VIII—at least in the minds of contemporaries—was in no less danger from Charles V and Paul III, than was his daughter at a later date from Philip of Spain and Greg-

7. I am inclined to think that the current example of Germany was of more importance in this connection than the Wars of the Roses. For by 1530 Englishmen had already experienced forty-five years of fairly stable government. By that time, doubtless, the political chaos of the fifteenth century had been largely forgotten.

8. It is interesting to note that the phrase "Enterprise of England," so common during Elizabeth's reign, was used as far back as 1533. In that year, Chapuys, the imperial ambassador to England, wrote Charles V that civil war in England was imminent, and that under these circumstances "it can hardly displease you to make an enterprise against this kingdom" (*Letters and Papers of Henry VIII*, VI, 324). In 1538 such an "enterprise" was actually broached when Cardinal Pole was dispatched by the pope to consult with Charles V and Francis I regarding a league of Christian princes against Henry VIII.

ory XIII. The king's divorce from Catherine of Aragon
and his consequent break with the Catholic Church had
inevitably incurred the displeasure of both emperor and
pope. In September, 1533, Clement VII had issued a bull
of excommunication against Henry, declaring the king to
be deprived of his kingdom, and his subjects to be absolved
of their oath of obedience to their lawful monarch. And
in 1535 Paul III had written indignant briefs to Ferdinand, King of the Romans, and to Francis I, His Most
Christian Majesty, requesting those sovereigns to avenge
the execution of Cardinal Fisher, and to "enforce justice
against the said Henry."[9] The fact that neither Charles V
nor Francis I could find the necessary time to execute the
papal bull, and that the bull was actually suspended for
three years after 1535, does not gainsay the fact that
after 1533 England was constantly apprehensive of "the
Enterprise." Henry was forever looking to his fortifica-
tions, and well he might, for the imperial ambassador to
England, Eustace Chapuys, was currently plotting with
English nobles to overthrow the king, and urging his master to invade England.[10]

To counterbalance the theory of rebellion implied in
the papal bull of excommunication and the projected
"Enterprise," the Henrician pamphleteers quite naturally
stressed the sacrosanctity of the king and emphasized
the doctrine of non-resistance.[11] The Henrician cult of
authority, in other words, typified English nationalism
as personified by the king, as against the internationalism
of the papacy and the Catholic Church.

9. The pope's brief to Francis I is printed in Janelle, *Obedience in Church and State*, pp. 11–19.

10. For a résumé of Chapuys' numerous intrigues against Henry VIII, see Pickthorn, *Early Tudor Government, Henry VIII* (Cambridge, 1534), especially pp. 204–205, 211–212. That Lords Darcy and Hussey were, moreover, actually in communication with Chapuys regarding an imperial invasion of England is evident from another of the ambassador's letters (*Letters and Papers*, VII, 1206).

11. Lord Burghley did precisely the same thing in 1583 when he wrote his *Execution of Justice in England* to refute the theory enunciated in Pius V's bull of excommunication against Elizabeth. He went out of his way to stress the inherent sinfulness of rebellion against the queen.

In the third place, the idea of non-resistance fulfilled an important function in ensuring the practical effectiveness of the Royal Supremacy. Though not essentially a political thinker, Martin Luther had understood that to give the secular sovereign control of the Church within his own territory, and yet to admit the validity of rebellion in certain cases, was to create a dangerous ambiguity. To the Henrician political writers this point was no less apparent. In order to safeguard the Royal Supremacy, it had to be proved that *under no circumstances*, "yea, even though the king were an infidel," had subjects the right to rebel against their prince. Otherwise, any man differing with the king's religious views might raise the standard of revolt and rejoin, as indeed both English Catholics and Marian exiles did at a later date, that God is to be obeyed rather than man, and that the Royal Supremacy is valid only so long as the Supreme Head adheres to "right belief." In order to guard against such a contingency, the pamphleteers had to promise the rebels a warm reception in Hell even if they so much as raised a finger against the Lord's anointed. To save the Royal Supremacy, a cult of royal authority had of necessity to be set up, and the king's person suffused with a glow of divinity. To an English Catholic or a radical Protestant ready to don armor for the true faith, what more effective rejoinder than the words of the poet:

> "Not all the water in the rough rude sea
> Can wash the balm off from an anointed king.
> The breath of worldly men cannot depose
> The deputy elected by the Lord."

It may be added that up to 1538 the English Puritans preached the doctrine of non-resistance for other reasons of their own. Tyndale and Barnes hoped for much from Henry VIII. The king was opposed to the papacy. Might he not also be persuaded in time to purify the English Church further still, to purge it of all its popish trappings, in other words, to make it into the kind of Church

of which Tyndale and Barnes approved? Better play safe
and preach non-resistance to a king who is the one real
hope of English Puritanism. Besides, Tyndale and
Barnes, like Calvin, felt themselves bound to refute the
contention of their enemies—that Lutheranism and
Zwinglianism are identical with Anabaptism, that the
English Puritans, like the Anabaptists, preach communism and revolt against the constituted authorities. Obviously, the best way to rebut this charge was to insist on
their loyalty to the king, and to preach the doctrine of
absolute non-resistance.[12]

It is evident, then, why the doctrine of non-resistance
should have enjoyed so much popularity in Tudor England. The New Monarchy—implying the absorption of
all rival jurisdictions, secular or ecclesiastical, into the
hands of the royal government—needed just such a doctrinal justification to make its work permanent. So long
as there was danger of England lapsing back into a state
of feudal disorder or being destroyed altogether by continental invaders, or of the Royal Supremacy being repudiated, Englishmen believed that the king was God's
vicegerent on earth, and that disobedience to the king was
a mortal sin. Once those dangers were removed, presumably after 1588, they could afford to be sceptical. Before
1588 the cult of authority was fashionable in England.
After that date it became to a certain extent an object
of ridicule, and was at any rate cultivated by only a
minority. That disobedience to Henry VIII and Elizabeth was a religious sin, the majority of sixteenth-century
Englishmen were willing to believe. But that Charles I
might not be resisted for fear of hell-fire was hard to
impress on Stuart Englishmen. The doctrine of non-resistance, expanded into the theory of divine right, lived
on, to be sure, into the seventeenth and even the eighteenth
century. But its vitality had been spent during Eliza-

12. See M.M.Knappen, *Tudor Puritanism* (Chicago, 1939), Chaps. 1, 2,
passim.

beth's reign when the central government had definitely triumphed over feudal and papal sovereignty, and when the foreign invader had been forced to beat a humiliating retreat. In 1688 its day was over, and Archbishop Sancroft's and Charles Leslie's were voices crying in the wilderness.

The doctrine of non-resistance, like most political ideas, was, in other words, opportunistic. It flourished during the sixteenth century when there was a definite need in England for strong monarchy. It declined in popularity during the ensuing centuries when strong monarchy became more of a liability than an asset. During the sixteenth century, especially after 1533, the usefulness of the doctrine of non-resistance was understood by every political group in favor of the *status quo*. Indeed, it may be stated without exaggeration that "non-resistance" was the slogan of the ruling parties throughout the Tudor era, that it was preached by Anglicans, Puritans, and Catholics alike, depending on which group happened to be in power. Under Henry VIII non-resistance was preached principally by the Henrician party, led by Bishops Gardiner and Fox, and also by the radical reformers—men like Tyndale and Barnes, who realized that their only hope of triumph or even toleration lay in the king's good will. Cardinal Pole, the leader of the Catholic opposition after the death of Fisher and More, meanwhile proclaimed the right to rebel from the continent. During the reign of Edward VI the radical reformers, now possessing real political power, were more vehement than ever in pronouncing the virtues of non-resistance. With Mary's accession the balance shifted. The reformers, driven into exile, turned a complete volte-face and pronounced the righteousness of resistance, even tyrannicide, against a popish queen. On the other hand, the Catholics, now taking their turn at the political helm, stopped playing with fire, and espoused the highly respectable doctrine of non-resistance. Under Elizabeth, the Catholics again became sowers of sedition, and it was the Anglican clergy, depending on the Royal Supremacy for maintenance, who became the pillars of the state.

It must be stated at this point, however, that the doctrine of non-resistance preached by the ruling groups in the Tudor state was by no means identical with the theory of the divine right of kings advanced by James I, Dr. Cowell, Archbishop Sancroft, and others, in the seventeenth century. According to Figgis, the divine right of kings includes four fundamental propositions, (1) that monarchy is a divinely ordained institution, (2) indefeasible hereditary right, (3) that sovereignty is invested entirely in the king who is incapable of legal limitation, and (4) non-resistance.[13] As Allen notes, the Henrician political writers did not concern themselves with inquiring into the origins of monarchy, and certainly they did not propound any idea of indefeasible hereditary right.[14] The truth of the matter is that the Henricians were not apprehensive of a Charles Stuart who might destroy their fundamental rights, but of a Paul III or a Charles V who might conceivably lead a crusade against their schismatic king. They therefore scrupulously avoided raising debatable points like sovereignty, and concentrated entirely on non-resistance. Almost everyone could agree that rebellion against the king would endanger the state. A discussion of the principle of succession or of the location of sovereignty would, on the other hand, breed furious argument. And Henry VIII was wiser than James I in perceiving that it is better to let sleeping dogs lie.

However, non-resistance, if not divine-right monarchy, was held to be essential for the security of the Tudor state. England was in danger of rebellion and invasion. Who could predict whether the majority of Englishmen, to

13. *Divine Right of Kings* (2nd ed., Cambridge, 1914), pp. 5–6.
14. *History of Political Thought in the Sixteenth Century*, Part II, Chap. 2. The argument of indefeasible hereditary right might have proved embarrassing during Henry VIII's reign, for the king's father had been a *de facto*, not a *de jure*, king.

whom the Royal Supremacy had come as a shock, would continue to abide by the royal control in matters religious? Any day now the emperor might find the opportunity to execute the papal bull of excommunication against the king, rallying all pious Englishmen to his standard with the plea that God is to be obeyed rather than man. Small wonder that patriotic publicists should have produced a special body of literature between 1530 and 1550, emphasizing the sacrosanctity of the king and the heinousness of rebellion under any conditions, even where a subject disagreed with his sovereign's religious creed or with the very principle of the Royal Supremacy. "Obedience" was the magic catch-word by which the pamphleteers proposed to save England for the English, and to preserve the newly acquired powers of the New Monarchy. During these two decades almost every English political writer enunciated the doctrine of non-resistance at the same time that he was attacking the papal, and proclaiming the royal, supremacy. This was true, for example, of both the radical reformer, William Tyndale, and of the moderate bishop, Stephen Gardiner.

But in addition to works like Tyndale's *Obedience of a Christian Man* and Gardiner's *De vera obedientia,* there was a large number of tracts dedicated exclusively to the non-resistance theme. In 1536, for example, the year of the Pilgrimage of Grace, there appeared in print Sir John Cheke's *Lamentation in which is showed what ruin and destruction cometh of seditious rebellion,*[15] and the anonymous *Remedy for sedition, wherein are contained many things, concerning the true and loyal obedience, that commons owe unto their prince and sovereign lord the king.*[16] In 1539, the year after a truce had been concluded between Charles V and Francis I, and when it seemed that at last the papal bull against Henry VIII might be executed, Sir Richard Morison published his *Exhortation*

15. Hereafter referred to as *Lamentation.*
16. Hereafter referred to as *Remedy for sedition.*

to stir all Englishmen to the defence of their country[17]
and his *Invective against the great and detestable vice,
treason,*[18] the second in no less than three editions. Cheke
wrote another pamphlet in 1549 entitled *The hurt of sedition how grievous it is to a commonwealth,*[19] and Archbishop Cranmer and Thomas Lever, among others, delivered sermons on the subject for the edification of the
faithful. During Mary's reign the Catholic Bishop of
Chichester, John Christopherson, published a long and
ponderous tome entitled *An exhortation to all men to take
heed and beware of rebellion.*[20] These are only a few examples of that special *genre* of Tudor literature devoted
exclusively to the cult of authority and the doctrine of
non-resistance. Their number alone is ample testimony to
the popularity enjoyed by the non-resistance theme during the early English Reformation.

To prove the sacrosanctity of the king and the heinousness of rebellion, the Henrician pamphleteers had recourse to all kinds of arguments. Indeed, the thoroughness
with which they sought to drive home their point and to
argue down the opposition reveals just how much they
thought was actually at stake. In their opinion, the prizes
were nothing less than the salvation of souls and the security of the state. They appealed to divine and natural law
to show that obedience is owed to the king, and to no one
else, in this world. They summoned the authority of the
Old and New Testaments to prove that even tyrants must
not be resisted. They drew upon historical examples to
demonstrate that never before had rebellion been crowned
with success, except where God had directly countenanced
it himself. They exalted the eminently Christian virtues of
patience and humility to lull the intractable into a mood
of acceptance. They kept alive the medieval functional

17. Hereafter referred to as *Exhortation to stir all Englishmen.* "The merry
Morison," as Sir Richard Morison was called, served under Wolsey, and in 1535
received an official appointment from Cromwell.
18. Hereafter referred to as *Invective against treason.*
19. Hereafter referred to as *Hurt of sedition.*
20. Hereafter referred to as *Exhortation to all men.*

ideal of society to show that the order established by God must not be tampered with. They conjured up all sorts of imaginary horrors to impress their readers with the chaos into which society would be plunged in the event of rebellion against the Lord's anointed. No argument, it seems, was overlooked in exalting the king as God's vicegerent on earth, and as being therefore ultimately beyond human control.[21]

The appeal to divine law was the most telling argument used by the advocates of non-resistance. In the sixteenth century men were still peculiarly sensitive to biblical quotations. If the pamphleteers could prove from the Scriptures that God had unquestionably commanded absolute obedience to the king, the field was theirs without a fight. It is significant that the *Homilies of 1547*, the official mouthpiece of the government on many aspects of the early English Reformation, should have used this argument to no inconsiderable extent. The passage on non-resistance therein fairly bristles with scriptural quotations. Proverbs 8 is cited to prove that kings were instituted directly by God, and that therefore their laws are the ordinances not of man, but of God himself. The example of David, who, despite the wrongs done him by King Saul, nevertheless refused to touch the Lord's anointed, is referred to as proof that under no conditions must kings be resisted. The authority of Romans 13, 1 Peter 2, and John 19 is summoned to prove a similar teaching from the New Testament.[22]

21. "To be in this world without law" did not, however, mean the same thing to Henricians as it later did to James I and Dr. Cowell. As we shall see below, few Henricians believed that the king was not subject to law, divine and positive, and that for all normal purposes he was not required to rule in conjunction with parliament. "To be in this world without law" signified to a Henrician that in case the king chose to rule as a tyrant, his subjects might not resist him forcibly. *Ultimately* he was therefore beyond human control.

22. *Homilies of 1547*, pp. Rij–Sij. These particular Old and New Testament references were used over and over again in the Henrician pamphlets. For the story of David and Saul, see, for example, Tyndale, *Obedience of a Christian Man*, p. 176; and "A document of the year 1531 on the subject of the Pope's supremacy," printed in Pocock's *Records of the Reformation*, II, 100. An excellent account of Christ's alleged attitude toward non-resistance is to be found in a

The non-resistance pamphlets of the preceding fifteen years constitute for the most part variations on this same central theme, appeal to divine law. Their authors were particularly anxious to point out that according to the Scriptures no one can doubt to whom obedience is specifically due. This they rightfully understood to be the essential point. Obedience is a great virtue, Bishop Sampson wrote, but it is a grave sin to render obedience where it is not due. The Scriptures are clear that it is the king, and no other, whom God would have us obey. Whoever resists the king under any circumstances, either by word or deed, merits damnation. "O! magnum praeceptum, et ab omnibus observandissimum!"[23] Other writers, for example Bishop Gardiner and Richard Taverner,[24] stressed the king's divine origin in order to demonstrate further that obedience is owed to the king above all others. By asserting that kings "represent unto us the person even of God Himself," and that God "adorneth them with the honorable title of his own name, calling them Gods,"[25] they effectively rebutted the contention that kings derive their power from the pope. One pamphleteer, writing in manuscript, devoted his efforts to explaining away all possible exceptions to this scriptural rule. Some men will object, he wrote, that the children of Israel frequently fought against their kings with God's consent. This, however, was due to God's especial commandment and can in no

manuscript at the P.R.O. (St.P., 1: 99, 219), written probably about 1534. The stories of the tribute money, Christ's meek subjection to Herod and Pilate, though both were infidels, and the payment of taxes to the emperor by Joseph and Mary, are all reproduced here.

23. *Oratio*, pp. 164–165. Starkey added that in case of conflict between general councils and kings, men are bound by divine law always to obey the latter (*Exhortation to Christian Unity*, p. 9).

24. Taverner was a religious reformer who for some years was employed in Cromwell's service. He was appointed a clerk of the privy seal and, under Cromwell's direction, devoted himself to producing and publishing works to encourage the Reformation.

25. *The garden of wysdom wherin ye maye gather moste pleasaunt stowres, that is to say, proper wytty and quycke sayenges of princes, philosophers, and dyuers other sortes of men* (London, 1539; hereafter referred to as *Garden of wisdom*), II, Bvi. See also Gardiner, *De vera obedientia*, p. 88.

wise be taken as a general rule. Others say that if a religious father, by revelation from heaven, or an angel, should preach rebellion, men can follow these without prejudice to their souls. Clearly, however, the time wherein God was wont to speak to men by direct revelation is past, and the final truth is now contained in the Scriptures.[26] The author was frankly sceptical of venerable patriarchs and angels.

The extreme reformers took care to turn this scriptural argument of non-resistance against their arch-enemies, the papists and anabaptists. Like Calvin in the preface to his *Institutes of the Christian Religion,*[27] they were at some pains to assure their king that it was the "whore of Babylon," and the "cursed Anabaptists," and not themselves, who had violated the law of God in this respect. Their statements, intended to convey the impression that Protestantism was in no sense a danger to the state, contained the germs of the later idea that obedience to Rome and treason are identical. In Robert Barnes' strong language, the pope is guilty of treason for claiming, contrary to Scripture, that he may depose kings and absolve subjects from their obedience to their lawful lords.[28] Morison accused the papists of having broken the fundamental bond of society which God had ordained to hold society together, namely the obedience of subjects to their sovereign.[29] Taverner condemned the Anabaptists to hell, averring that they too go about plucking men from their

26. P.R.O., St.P. 1: 99, 214 f; *cf. Letters and Papers,* IX, 1064. This manuscript is thirteen folios long, and is devoted entirely to an exposition of the doctrine of non-resistance. It is in a much mutilated condition, as though it had suffered from rough handling and wetness. The writing is very faint in spots, and occasionally whole parts of pages are missing. But it represents the most complete expression of the doctrine of non-resistance that I have yet encountered in sixteenth-century literature.

27. Calvin, in his dedicatory epistle to Francis I in the *Institutes,* protested that it was not "our religion" which preached sedition against the constituted authorities. On the contrary, it was the Catholics who advocated rebellion.

28. *Supplication to Henry VIII,* printed in *The whole workes of W. Tyndall, Iohn Frith, and Doct. Barnes* (London, 1573), pp. 185–186.

29. *Exhortation to stir all Englishmen,* pp. Bi^b–Bii.

allegiance to their prince, contrary to the teaching of St. Paul.[30]

The pamphleteers frequently appealed to the law of nature, as well as the law of God, to demonstrate the doctrine of non-resistance—a type of argument which was to become popular among the royalists toward the end of the seventeenth century.[31] Usually, of course, the two higher laws were spoken of in the same breath, as, for example, in the *Bishops' Book* and Starkey's *Exhortation to Christian Unity.*[32] Occasionally, however, an author would appeal to the law of nature separately, as though it added force to the scriptural argument. Bishop Christopherson, for example, cited the case of the bees who ever obey their ruler implicitly. "Doth not nature herein teach all subjects to tender and love their prince, as the poor bees do their king?"[33]

The pamphleteers added that, according to divine and natural law, vengeance should be entirely remitted to God. Christ himself taught this lesson, Tyndale asserted, and Peter was accordingly rebuked when he drew his sword. God utterly forbids men to avenge themselves, for no man is an indifferent judge in his own cause, and at any rate vengeance does not make for peace but only serves to stir up additional strife.[34] Bishop Gardiner reiterated this view by denying that the pope had any right whatever to avenge Cardinal Fisher's execution, seeing that God has expressly reserved vengeance to himself.[35] But God, it

30. *Garden of wisdom*, II, Eiij[b].

31. I refer particularly to Filmer and Nalson who, just prior to the Glorious Revolution, preferred to argue divine right and non-resistance in terms of natural law and the natural constitution of society, and to push divine law into the background. This preference for natural law was, no doubt, a symptom of the growth of rationalism.

32. To the great majority of sixteenth-century political writers these two laws were largely synonymous. Starkey's statement that men are bound to obey the princely authority "by the lawes of god and nature" (*Exhortation to Christian Unity*, p. 8[b]) is typical. For a further discussion of this point, see below, p. 128*n*.

33. *Exhortation to all men*, p. Ovii.

34. *Obedience of a Christian Man*, pp. 165–166, 174.

35. "Si sedes illa," printed in Janelle, *Obedience in Church and State*, p. 60.

seems, does not always wait until people are dead to exercise his prerogative of vengeance. He sometimes uses tyrants and persecutors as his instruments here on earth. These act as his scourge and rod to chastise sinful people, and they are removed by God only when the sinners offer themselves up to the divine will.[36] That "Nero-like" tyrant, the Great Turk himself, was, according to Thomas Becon, God's scourge to punish the Europeans for their abominable living.[37] Some men will ask, said Thomas Lever in one of his sermons, how it is that evil rulers can be of God when God is the author of good only. There can be no doubt about the answer. "It is God, 'Qui facit hypocrita regnare propter peccata populi.' . . . It is not therefore repining, rebelling, or resisting God's ordinances, that will amend evil rulers."[38] In the light of this doctrine, papists would not be justified in resisting a Henry VIII or an Edward VI even though these kings were heretics and tyrants.

The advocates of non-resistance appealed to history, as well as to the Scriptures, to drive home their point. They cited examples from Old Testament, Roman, English, and contemporary history to prove that rebellion against lawfully constituted authority had always failed in the past. One section of Archbishop Cranmer's notes for a homily against rebellion bears the significant heading, "how God hath plagued sedition in time past." Under it the Archbishop enumerated six examples from the Old Testament

36. See, for example, John Johnson's *An confortable exhortation: of oure mooste holy Christen faith, and her frutes Written (vnto the Christen bretherne in Scotlande) after the poore worde of God* (Parishe, 1535), pp. Ev[b]–Evi. Johnson's argument, even to the choice of words, is almost identical with a similar discourse in Tyndale's *Obedience of a Christian Man*, p. 140.

37. *The Policy of War wherein is declared how the enemies of the Christian Public Weal may be overcome and subdued*, printed in *The Early Works of Thomas Becon*, edited by Rev. John Ayre (Parker Soc., Cambridge, 1843), pp. 240–250. This book, which maintains that only by the strict obedience of subjects to their sovereigns can enemies like the Great Turk be overcome, was first published in London in 1542.

38. *English Reprints. Thomas Lever. Sermons. 1550*, edited by Ed. Arber (London, 1871), pp. 33–34.

in which rebels had been cast down by divine wrath.[39] In his sermon on rebellion in 1549 he dwelt at greater length on this theme, citing for particular edification the fate of the children of Israel who used themselves seditiously against Moses.[40] Sir Richard Morison, a true son of the Renaissance,[41] preferred to demonstrate the futility of rebellion by references to Roman history. "I trust by things past, you shall perceive it very unlikely," he wrote, "that any traitor hereafter may or can hurt His Highness [Henry VIII]."[42] God has plucked wit and prudence away from malicious traitors even when they contemplated the death of tyrants like Nero.[43] Men like Perennis and Plautianus were soon enough frustrated in their attempt to set themselves up as emperors.[44] Bishop Christopherson drew up a catalogue of rebels who had come to evil ends resisting the legitimate Roman emperors.[45] And Thomas Paynell, erstwhile monk and chaplain to Henry VIII, translated a work into English entitled the *Conspiracy of Lucius Catiline* the purpose of which, he said, was to show that if God would not suffer rebels to succeed among Gentiles, much less will he suffer them to prevail against a Christian prince, "his very image on earth."[46]

Citations from English and contemporary German history were even more popular. The wretched end of the Taborites in Bohemia, the utter failure of the Peasants' Rebellion in Germany, and the capitulation of Münster

39. *Miscellaneous Writings and Letters of Thomas Cranmer*, edited by Rev. J.E.Cox (Parker Soc., Cambridge, 1846), p. 188.

40. *Ibid.*, p. 199.

41. Morison lived for some time in Venice and Padua, and was a proficient scholar of Greek and Latin.

42. *Invective against treason*, p. a vi.

43. *Ibid.*, pp. av–avi.

44. *Ibid.*, p. aiii. Perennis virtually ruled the Roman Empire under Commodus, but was finally put to death by the army in 186 or 187. Plautianus was executed in 203 for attempting to destroy the Emperor Severus and his son-in-law Caracalla.

45. *Exhortation to all men*, pp. Evii–Fj.

46. *The Conspiracie of Lucius Catiline translated into englishe by Thomas Paynell* (London, 1541), p. Aii[b].

by the Anabaptists served as excellent examples to discourage would-be English rebels.[47] Jack Straw, Jack Cade, John Oldcastle, and Richard III were cited as examples of unsuccessful rebels in English history,[48] and the finger of God was seen currently in the failure of the Pilgrims of Grace, Cardinal Pole, Northumberland, and Sir Thomas Wyatt. Morison devoted most of his *Invective against treason* to showing how the machinations of the "archtraitor" Reginald Pole and his brother Henry, Edward Neville, and Henry Courtenay, were revealed to the trusting king by God himself.[49] Bishop Christopherson, a Catholic, naturally cited the dismal failure of Northumberland and Wyatt to cheat Mary out of her heritage.[50]

The early sixteenth-century exponents of non-resistance also fully appreciated the value of emphasizing the Christian virtues of patience and humility. Meek acceptance had always, of course, been regarded as one of the cardinal Christian virtues, even when crusades and papal bulls of excommunication had belied it in practice. But during the English Reformation humility received a special emphasis, and the king's subjects were urged to be more and more patient. Not only were long passages in many of the political treatises devoted to this theme, but entire books were written on the subject, of which Sir Thomas More's *Dialogue of Comfort against Tribulation*,[51] and William Hughe's *The Troubled Man's Medicine*[52] may serve as examples. The existence of this literature is testimony to the fact that the Reformation politi-

47. For references to the failure of rebellion in Bohemia and Germany, see Christopherson, *Exhortation to all men*, p. Cciij; also *Miscellaneous Writings and Letters of Thomas Cranmer*, pp. 188, 199–200. Cranmer says in one place (*ibid.*, p. 200) that over 100,000 rebels were killed in Germany within three months, and in another place (*ibid.*, p. 188) that 200,000 were killed in one month.

48. See, for example, Christopherson, *Exhortation to all men*, pp. Cciij, Ccv^b; also *Miscellaneous Writings and Letters of Thomas Cranmer*, p. 188.

49. *Invective against treason*, pp. Avii^b–Bi.

50. *Exhortation to all men*, pp. Oii–Oiii.

51. More wrote this work, along with several treatises on the Passion, during his imprisonment in the Tower. It was first published by Richard Tottel in 1553.

52. *The troubled mans medicine verye profitable to be redde of al men wherein they may learne pacyently to suffer all kyndes of aduersitie* (London, 1546).

cal writers sensed a real need for emphasizing habits of
thought diametrically opposed to resistance and rebellion.
Patience they lauded as a two-fold virtue. Through
exercising patience it is clear that the individual benefits
both society and himself. Does not history prove that the
individual benefits society far more as a martyr than as a
conqueror by the use of the sword? Is not the participa-
tion of the individual in Christ's suffering a primary
requisite to entrance into the kingdom of heaven? Both
the erstwhile Bishop of Chichester, John Scory, writing
from exile during Mary's reign, and his Catholic successor, Bishop Christopherson, expatiated on the glories of
martyrdom as opposed to rebellion. Scory, of course,
lauded the Protestant martyrs, Hooper and Rogers, who
through their patient sufferings had won a greater victory for Christ than ever the sword could have done,[53]
while Christopherson eulogized the medieval saints.[54]

Scory's opinion is of especial value. For though he
could well afford to play the philosopher from his safe
retreat at Emden in Germany, yet as an exile he had
everything to gain by arousing English Protestants to
revolt against the Catholic queen. Somewhat smugly, it
must be admitted, he urged those who were repining in
English prisons to rejoice, "for even as you be now made
like unto the image of the son of God in suffering, and be
partakers with him in dying; even so shall you most certainly be partakers of his life, and reign with him hereafter in his celestial kingdom."[55] This was only another
way of saying that "tribulation for righteousness is not a
blessing only, but also a gift that God giveth unto none
save his special friends."[56] Since eternal salvation is the

---

53. *An Epistle wrytten by John Scory* . . . *unto all the faythfull that be in
pryson in Englande* . . . *wherin he dothe as well by the promises of mercy as also
by then samples of diuerse holy martyrès, comfort, encorrage and strenghten them
paciently for Christes sake to suffer the manifolde cruell and moste tyrannous persecutions of the Antichristian tormentours,* etc. (Southwark, 1555), pp. A 3–A 4.
Rogers and Hooper were both martyrs of the Marian persecution in 1555.

54. *Exhortation to all men,* pp. Giij^b–Gvii^b.

55. Scory, *Epistle,* p. A 4^b.

56. Tyndale, *Obedience of a Christian Man,* p. 138.

end of life, it is not, then, advantageous to resist the unjust commands of the tyrant. In Tyndale's unequivocal expression, there is no other way into the kingdom of life save through persecution and death itself, after the example of Christ.[57] It appears that prosperity is really a curse which God gives only to his enemies.[58] For if a person did not sometimes fall into mishap, whence God alone could deliver him, he would never know the meaning of faith. Likewise, if rulers were always kind, a subject would have no way of telling whether his obedience was sincere or not.[59] Or, as Sir Thomas More put it, if it were not for tribulation, our patience would never be tested, and consequently we would never have to call on God for help.[60] Arguments of this order were obviously of no little importance in teaching the people the absurdity as well as the sin of rebellion.

To further emphasize the heinousness of rebellion some of the exponents of non-resistance restated the medieval doctrine of the functional ideal of society.[61] Medieval political theorists had conceived of earthly society as a whole to which every group, every individual, is subordinated. They had seen society as a great hierarchy of ascending orders in which each man—peasant, nobleman, clergyman, and king—has his God-appointed function. The welfare of this society, like the health of the human body, depends on the faithful fulfilment of every function, however humble. Some of the Henricians ingeniously twisted this doctrine around to prove specifically that under no circumstances must a subject revolt against his prince. To strike at the king or his magistrates, to upset the caste system of society created by God himself, was, in their opinion, to question God's wisdom, and therefore to

57. *Ibid.*, p. 140.
58. *Ibid.*, p. 138.
59. *Ibid.*, p. 193.
60. *Dialogue of Comfort against Tribulation*, I, Chap. 4.
61. For a brief discussion of the functional ideal of society in early sixteenth-century political literature, see Allen, *History of Political Thought in the Sixteenth Century*, Part II, Chap. 3, "The Very and True Commonweal."

invite God's vengeance. Edmund Dudley used the functional ideal of society in this fashion in his *Tree of Commonwealth*. He warned the "commoners" against the pursuivant of rebellion who will tell them false tales. He will tell them, for example, that they are made of the same mold as noblemen—that they are as much the descendants of Adam as noblemen, that Christ bought them with his blood no less than the aristocracy, and that their souls are equally precious in God's eyes. Disregard this devilish argument, Dudley admonished the commoners. Abstain from coveting the prosperity of the "chivalry," and do not disdain the great power of the king. For "let us all consider that God hath set a due order by grace between himself and angels, and between angel and angel, and by reason between Angel and man, and between man and man, and man and beast, and by nature only between beast and beast, which order from the highest point to the lowest, God willeth us fervently to keep, without any enterprise to the contrary."[62]

The *Homilies of 1547* used this argument even more pointedly. In a passage entitled "An Exhortation, concerning good order and obedience, to rulers and magistrates," this official organ of the government asserted that Almighty God had created all things in heaven and earth in a most perfect order. In heaven there are archangels and angels; likewise on earth "every degree of people, in their vocation, calling, and office, hath appointed to them, their duty and order. Some are in high degree, some in low, some kings and princes, some inferiors and subjects, priests, and laymen, masters and servants, . . . rich and poor, etc." Remove this divine order, and "there reigneth all abuse, carnal liberty, enormity, sin, and babylonical confusion. *Take away kings, princes, rulers, magistrates, judges, and such states of God's order, no man*

---

62. *Tree of Commonwealth*, pp. 50–53. See also in this connection *English Reprints. Thomas Lever. Sermons. 1550*, pp. 106–107. According to Lever, "every man by doing of his duty must dispose unto other that commodity and benefit, which is committed of God unto them to be disposed unto other, by the faithful and diligent doing of their duties."

shall ride or go by the highway unrobbed, no man shall sleep in his own house or bed unkilled, no man shall keep his wife, children, and possessions in quietness, all things shall be common, and there must needs follow all mischief and utter destruction, both of souls, bodies, goods, and commonwealths."[63]

Most of the Henrician political writers agreed with the *Homilies of 1547,* that if the functional order were upset, society could only expect dire consequences. No doubt in any age the delineation of all kinds of imaginary horrors is a most effective argument to use against those who would change the *status quo.* In this respect the sixteenth century was not different from other centuries. Sir Thomas Elyot predicted chaos if a "common" rather than a "public" weal were instituted. It is only in a society of higher and lower degrees, he said, *i.e.,* a "public" weal, and not in a society where all things are held in common, *i.e.,* a "common" weal, that there can be order. According to Elyot, God himself instituted a "public" and not a "common" weal, for he set degrees and estates in all his glorious works—hierarchies in the Church, the four elements in the human body, the higher and lower degrees among plants and animals. It is evident that "without order may be nothing stable or permanent; and it may not be called order, except it do contain in it degrees, high and base, according to the merit or estimation of the thing that is ordered."[64] Morison, in one of his unpublished treatises denouncing the Pilgrimage of Grace, painted vividly the topsy-turvy state into which society would be plunged if the functional ideal were abandoned. Making use of the analogy of the human body, he depicted the absurdity of a commonwealth in which all men desired riches. What kind of a body would it be, he asked, in which the feet would wear a cap like the head, the shoulders and elbows refuse to perform their proper functions,

63. *Homilies of 1547,* pp. Rj–Rj^b. Italics mine.
64. *The Boke named the Gouernour* (hereafter referred to as *The Governour*), edited by H.H.S.Croft (London, 1880), I, 1–8.

and the hands demand that the mouth should feed them?[65]

The threat of anarchy as the only alternative to non-resistance was not confined, however, to those passages only which dealt with the functional ideal of society. As stated above, the Wars of the Roses, the example of civil strife in Germany, and the fear of foreign invasion all combined to make English political writers unusually apprehensive of a state without a strong head. Tudor political literature is replete with passages warning Englishmen of the nightmare of anarchy. These passages invariably emphasized three points; first, the benefits accruing to society from even a tyrant; second, the frightful chaos into which England would fall if the rule of law were abated; and third, the danger of foreign invasion. Tyndale, emphasizing the first point, was of the opinion that the king protects his subjects from a thousand inconveniences, and though he were the greatest tyrant in the world, he still would be a great benefit to society. "It is better to pay the tenth than to lose all,"[66] he warned. Bishop Christopherson was of a similar mind. The rich, he said, have even less cause to rebel than the poor, for, no matter how avaricious the prince, he is the safeguard of all their riches, which otherwise would be a prey to everybody.[67]

There were many different ways of stating the second point. Morison described obedience as the knot of all commonweals, the breaking of which would open the floodgates to destruction.[68] He mused on the miserable state in which men had found themselves at the beginning of the world, when laws had not yet been made, and when the richest were the strongest.[69] In one fanciful passage he

65. P.R.O., St.P. 6: 13, 4, ff. 51–53. This tract, which is written in Morison's own hand, is calendared in the *Letters and Papers*, XI, 1409. It appears to be a more finished draft of St.P., 6: 13, 3.

66. *Obedience of a Christian Man*, pp. 179–180.

67. *Exhortation to all men*, pp. Dij–Diij.

68. *Exhortation to stir all Englishmen*, p. Bii.

69. P.R.O., St.P. 6: 13, 4, f. 53.

described the terrible consequences of sedition. Where might sits above right, he said, laws lose their voices, justice hides her face, and honesty is driven from the field.[70] Other writers, for example, Sir John Cheke, Archbishop Cranmer, and Bishop Christopherson, drove home the point that not only does rebellion throw the commonwealth into a state of anarchy in which the common law is disregarded,[71] but it also thwarts the rebels' own purpose. Cannot the poor people see, asked Cranmer in one of his sermons, that sedition does not remedy their poverty but, on the contrary, increases it? Cannot they perceive that by rebellion they have hindered the harvest for next year, and thus destroyed their own livings?[72] Thomas Lever described rebellion as a "canker" so dangerous to the commonwealth that if an individual, or even a whole shire, be poisoned with it, it should be ruthlessly cut away to save the whole.[73]

The fear of a continental crusade led by the emperor to give effect to the papal bull of excommunication against Henry VIII, aided by conspirators at home, led the protagonists of non-resistance to stress the threat of foreign invasion as well. Sir John Cheke was particularly apprehensive of the imperial danger. Rebellions, he said, by destroying crops and bringing on disease, greatly diminish the strength of realms and leave them a prey to their enemies.[74] In histories "you shall evermore for the most part find that never great realm or commonwealth hath been destroyed without sedition at home." The Romans, for example, became lords of Greece because of the latter's internal dissensions.[75] Writing in 1549, Archbishop Cranmer was more fearful of the Scottish and

70. *Ibid.*, f. 49.

71. See Cheke, *Hurt of sedition*, pp. Eiiii–Fi; also Christopherson, *Exhortation to all men*, pp. Ddij–Ddij[b].

72. "A Sermon concerning the time of rebellion," printed in the *Miscellaneous Writings and Letters of Thomas Cranmer*, p. 194.

73. *English Reprints. Thomas Lever. Sermons. 1550*, p. 76.

74. *Hurt of sedition*, p. Diiii.

75. *Lamentation*, p. B.

French peril.[76] "What greater pleasure," he questioned, "can we do to the Scots and Frenchmen, than to be at variance within ourselves, and so make our realm a prey for them? What joy is this to the bishop of Rome, to hear that the blood of Englishmen (for the which he hath so long thirsted) is now like to be shed by their own brethren and countrymen! But let us be joined together like members of one body, and then we shall have less need to fear our foreign enemy."[77]

But the protagonists of non-resistance were apprehensive of anarchy from still another source—the commonalty. They dreaded popular government by "the fourth sort of men which do not rule,"[78] as much as they dreaded foreign invasion. Rebellion against the king, they asserted, will unleash the force of democracy as well as open up the country to the Spaniard or Frenchman. The country will be ruined from within as well as from without.

Indeed, Tudor political writers evinced a profound distrust of all forms of popular government. This distrust is undoubtedly what lies behind a good deal of their non-resistance talk. The functional ideal of society taught them, to begin with, that only certain people are endowed by nature to rule, and that only these should be entrusted with the reins of government. But they went farther and expressed a contempt for the capacity of the common man which was altogether alien to the medieval idea. The sixteenth-century contention is well summed up in a passage from one of Morison's unpublished treatises. A way must be found, he wrote, "that those may rule that best can, those be ruled, that most it becometh so to be. This agreement is expedient . . . in a commonwealth, both those that be of the worser sort, to content themselves that

76. Taking advantage of Ket's rebellion, the French declared war on England August 8, 1549. The government was fearful of a joint French-Scottish invasion because of the influence of the Guises on Mary of Scotland.

77. *Miscellaneous Writings and Letters of Thomas Cranmer*, p. 193.

78. This is the phrase which Sir Thomas Smith uses to describe the proletariat in his *De Republica Anglorum* (Book I, Chap. 24).

the wiser govern them, and those that nature hath indued
with rare qualities, and fortune set in higher degree, to
suppose this done by the higher providence of God, as a
mean to engender concord, love, and amity between the
higher and the lower, the small and the great."[79] Sir
Thomas Elyot was of the opinion that inferior persons
ought to consider that, although in substance of soul and
body they are equal to their superiors, they have not been
endowed by God with proportional reason.[80] Therefore,
according to an anonymous writer, those whom nature has
endowed with singular virtues should rule and those of
less ability be ruled. "They should rule, which were the
wiser, they obey, that were the stronger."[81]

Other writers went farther than this. Some expressed a
disbelief in the ability of the common man to fill any other
role in society than that of drudge. To most Tudor Englishmen the common man was inconstant, utterly ignorant,
and therefore incapable of ruling. Consequently, his bet-
ters must be warned that in the event of rebellion, the
government might fall into the hands of blockheads, and
society be utterly undone. In the eyes of the political
writers, the only alternative to such chaos was absolute
non-resistance. One of William Thomas' discourses prepared for Edward VI's edification is indicative of this
state of mind.[82] It is impossible, Thomas states dog-
matically therein, that any commonwealth can long pros-
per where the power is in the commonalty. "For like as it
becometh neither the man to be governed of the woman,
nor the master of the servant, even so in all other regi-

79. P.R.O., St.P. 6: 13, 4, f. 50.
80. *The Governour*, II, 209 (all citations are from Croft's edition).
81. *Remedy for sedition*, p. Aiii.
82. As clerk of the privy council, Thomas appears to have acted as a kind of
political instructor to the young Edward VI. He drew up a list of eighty-five
questions on political subjects for the king's contemplation, printed in Strype's
Eccles. Mem., II(1), 156–161; and a series of six political discourses to follow,
also printed in the *Eccles. Mem.*, II(2), 365–389. Ironically enough, when Mary
came to the throne, Thomas participated in Wyatt's rebellion and was executed
at Tyburn.

ments it is not convenient the inferior should have power to direct the superior."[83] The party of the commons is by all odds more dangerous than that of the nobility—for three reasons. First, the multitude is more inconstant, for many men cannot agree on anything. Second, if the people obtain power they become frenzied and destroy both the nobility and themselves.[84] And lastly, "The multitude utterly knoweth nothing, And though some examples of good success may be alleged for the popular estates; yet, if they be well sought, it shall appear they never proceeded of wisdom, but of necessity."[85]

Other writers expressed a similar fear of popular government. Sir John Cheke wrote contemptuously that it was beyond the ken of cobblers to discuss what statutes and laws are most mete for a commonwealth.[86] Bishop Christopherson remarked that poor men sometimes forget that God created both rich and poor. In point of fact, there are degrees in every commonwealth "which be necessary for the good state thereof; and some be higher, and some be lower, as it pleaseth God to appoint them, and the one cannot lack the other." The poor need men of higher estate to defend them from enemies, even as men of honor must have the poor to toil for them.[87] Another anonymous writer epitomized the feeling of the age when he asserted

83. Strype, *Eccles. Mem.*, II(2), 375.
84. Thomas cites Froissart and the Jacquerie of 1358 in this connection (*ibid.*, p. 374). And farther on in the same discourse he challenges Machiavelli whom he quotes as saying that in some cases the commotions of the people are necessary to mitigate the excesses of great men's ambitions (*ibid.*, pp. 375–376).
85. *Ibid.*, II(2), 374–375.
86. *Lamentation*, p. Aiiii. Erasmus' *Institutio principis Christiani* is also full of contemptuous remarks about the political abilities of the common man. "The great mass of people," Erasmus says, "are swayed by false opinions and are no different from those in Plato's cave, who took the empty shadows as the real things. It is the part of a good prince to admire none of the things that the common people consider of great consequence, but to judge all things on their own merits as 'good' or 'bad.' . . . The one thing which he should consider base, vile, and unbecoming to him is to share the opinions of the common people who never are interested in anything worth while" (*The Education of a Christian Prince*, trans. with an introduction by Lester K.Born, Columbia Univ. Press, 1936, pp. 148, 150).
87. *Exhortation to all men*, pp. Cv–Cv[b].

that the multitude "in all places is ignorant, vicious, and beastlike, given to vanities and sensual pleasures." Unless this multitude is stayed by authority, the commonweal will inevitably be given up to violence and destruction.[88] With the threat of popular government as well as foreign invasion in the offing, Tudor political writers were more than ever inclined to preach non-resistance to the king as an absolute essential to the safety of the state.

In contrast to the overwhelming opinion in favor of non-resistance, few were the voices during the reigns of Henry VIII and Edward VI bold enough, or perhaps convinced enough, to proclaim the right to rebel. During the first twenty years of the English Reformation the emphasis in political literature was almost entirely on the sacrosanctity of the king and the necessity of absolute obedience for the benefit of both state and individual. Considering the circumstances—the threat of anarchy and invasion, the strict censorship of the press by the government,[89] and the fact that the opposition was badly organized at first—this was only natural. Besides, both Catholics and radical Protestants had hopes that the Henrician religious changes might be merely transitory, and that revolt might not therefore be necessary. As late as 1565 Pius IV spoke in consistory in favor of a policy of peaceful reconciliation with Queen Elizabeth, on the ground that the queen might yet be won back to the Cath-

88. P.R.O., St.P. 1: 99, 223. It is interesting to note that Christopher Goodman, one of the Protestant exiles in Geneva during Mary's reign, had a somewhat different conception of the average man, no doubt because he was an exile and wanted to return to his country, at the head of a revolt if necessary. The "people," he wrote in 1558, are not slaves or bondmen, but free subjects who ought not to suffer all their power and liberty to be taken away from them, and to become brute beasts "thinking all things lawful without exception which their rulers do." On the contrary, the multitude is entrusted with a portion of the sword of justice, and in the event of defection on the part of the magistrates is enjoined by God to execute divine judgment against the tyrant (*How Svperior powers oght to be obeyd of their subiects: and Wherin they may lawfully by Gods Worde be disobeyed and resisted*, edition Facsimile Text Soc., 1931, pp. 148–149, 180–181; hereafter referred to as *How superior powers ought to be obeyed of their subjects*).

89. See Appendix A, "Henry VIII's Propagandist Campaign."

olic fold. And the radical Protestants had good reason to expect—especially was this the case between 1547 and 1553—that their views might be accepted as the basis for the state religion. It is not surprising, therefore, that up to 1550 the cult of authority should have reigned supreme in England, and that neither the ultra-conservatives nor the ultra-radicals should have raised a vehement protest.

It was only during the second half of the century that English political writers came to question the doctrine of non-resistance seriously. Mary Tudor's accession to the throne aroused the radical Protestants to action, just as twenty years later the Massacre of St. Bartholomew's was to force the French Huguenots to take up the pen in defense of their cause. The Marian exiles—William Whittingham, William Kethe, John Knox, John Ponet, and Christopher Goodman[90]—all united in proclaiming the validity of rebellion against a woman who, in their opinion, was deliberately controverting the word of God; just as a little later the monarchomachs, Francis Hotman and the anonymous author of the *Vindiciae contra tyrannos*, were to enunciate a similar doctrine on behalf of the French Huguenots. Likewise, the accession of Elizabeth and the surge of the Counter-Reformation persuaded English Catholics, especially after 1570, to justify theoretically the doctrine of resistance implied in the papal bull of excommunication against the queen.[91] Force of circum-

90. Ponet and Goodman were the most important political pamphleteers among this group. Ponet published at Strassburg in 1556 his *Shorte Treatise of politike pouuer, and of the true Obedience which subiectes owe to kynges and other ciuile Gouernours, with an Exhortacion to all true naturell English men* (hereafter referred to as *Short treatise of politic power*). Goodman's *How superior powers ought to be obeyed of their subjects* was published in 1558. Whittingham wrote a brief introduction to Goodman's book, and Kethe contributed a poem at the end, entitled "William Kethe to the Reader." Knox's *First blast of the trumpet against the monstruous regiment of women* was also published in 1558. The burden of all these pieces was that rebellion against an idolatrous prince is legitimate.

91. In 1570 the papal bull of excommunication against Elizabeth, withheld for twelve years because the pope could find no one willing to execute it, was tacked to the door of the Bishop of London's palace. This act aroused a number of English Catholic exiles to take up the pen in defense of the doctrine of resistance against a heretical sovereign. Chief among these was Dr. Nicholas Sanders who in 1571 published his *De Visibili Monarchia Ecclesiae* in support of the papal thesis.

stance dictated that after 1550 certain groups would not hold the cult of royal authority in the same respect as heretofore.

The germs of the doctrine of resistance enunciated by the Marian exiles and the English Catholics are, of course, to be found in Henrician and Edwardian political literature. Political ideas are like economic theories; they do not spring up overnight. They represent, rather, a combination between an intellectual heritage and current political circumstance. Thus, neither Protestant Ponet nor Catholic Sanders, the heralds of rebellion against Mary and Elizabeth, were particularly original. They merely emphasized and elaborated ideas which had been implicit in the writings of the previous generation.

For example, many of the early Reformation pamphleteers had qualified the doctrine of non-resistance by the statement that the king must be obeyed implicitly *except* when his commands run contrary to divine and natural law. In the latter case, they had stipulated that the king must be disobeyed, but not resisted. The Henrician doctrine was thus more accurately one of non-resistance rather than obedience. In treatise after treatise the chief supporters of the king—the Henrician clergy and the radical Protestants—had preached obedience to the king's commands on this one condition—"in so far as they do not stand against God's precepts."[92] Even the *Homilies of 1547*, the official mouthpiece of the government, had stated that kings and magistrates are not to be obeyed "if they would command us to do anything contrary to God's commandments."[93] The extreme Protestants had gone a step farther and asserted, doubtless to justify their own uncertain position at the time, that in the event of tyranny

92. See, for example, Gardiner's "Contemptum humanae legis," printed in Janelle, *Obedience in Church and State*, p. 176. See also Sampson's *Oratio*, p. 164. Sampson says that the prince is to be obeyed in everything "modo nihil mandet contra Deum." As an example of the radical Protestant view, there is Barnes' statement that the powers that be must be suffered "always provided that [they] repugn not against the Gospel nor destroy our faith" (*The whole workes of W. Tyndall, Iohn Frith, and Doct. Barnes*, p. 292).

93. *Homilies of 1547*, p. Sj^b.

the subject might try to escape,[94] or even to resist passively.[95] Obviously, it needed only a reversal of political fortune for the Protestants to stretch this theory to justify armed resistance. God is to be obeyed rather than man, wrote Goodman in 1558,[96] and he who commands anything contrary to divine law is the real rebel, not he who resists the king.[97] True obedience consists not of passivity, but of active resistance to unlawful authority.[98]

94. Barnes, for example, realized that his fellow religionists must be given a loophole in case they were at any time jailed for their religious beliefs. If a tyrant incarcerates you for religion, Barnes asserted, you have the right to escape, "and thy conscience is free so doyng, and thou dooste not sinne, nor offende the lawe of God" (The whole workes of W. Tyndall, Iohn Frith, and Doct. Barnes, p. 293).

95. According to Henry Brinkelow, one of the radical reformers, subjects are bound to obey the king and all his laws under normal circumstances. However, "yf they dissent from or be contrary to anye one iote of the Scripture, we must, with Ihon and Peter, say, Actu. iiii, 'Iudge you whether it be better for vs to obeye God or man.'" Subjects must still not rebel, but they must resist the king passively, confessing the truth and not fearing the death of the body (A Supplication of the Poore Commons, edited by J.M.Cowper, E.E.T.Soc., London, 1871, p. 83).

96. Goodman based his entire treatise, How superior powers ought to be obeyed of their subjects, on Acts 4:19. "Whether it be right in the sight of God to hearken unto you more than unto God, judge ye." Ponet made the very interesting addition that obedience is owed not only to God but to the commonwealth as well, before it is owed to the king. "The country and commonwealth is a degree above the king. Next unto God men ought to love their country, and the whole commonwealth before any member of it; as kings and princes (be they never so great) are but members" (Short treatise of politic power, p. Dvii).

97. See Goodman, How superior powers ought to be obeyed of their subjects, pp. 42–44. In this connection, Kethe, in his poem printed at the end of Goodman's treatise, drew a distinction between "rebellion" and "resistance," reminiscent of Thomas Aquinas' differentiation between "sedition" and "resistance." Said Kethe:

> "Rebellion is ill, to resist is not so,
> When right through resisting, is done to that foe,
> Who seeketh, but by ruin, against right to reign,
> Not passing what perish, so the spoil the gain."

98. It is amusing to see how the Protestant exiles utilized the same method, and in many cases precisely the same scriptural and historical texts, as the Henricians, to prove the opposite thesis. Apparently it is true that almost anything can be proved from history. Just as Cranmer and Morison had cited cases from Old Testament and English history to discredit rebellion, so Ponet and Goodman used the Scriptures and historical tradition to prove the opposite. Goodman cited the examples of Peter and John who preached openly in the Temple against the express orders of the authorities; of the Christians revolting against Julian the Apostate; of the deposition of the English kings, Edward II

The Henrician Protestants had believed, too, that God is to be obeyed rather than man, but, hoping for better things to come in peaceable wise, they had not drawn the obvious conclusion.

And so it was with the theory which would differentiate between the office and the person of the king. Occasionally, one of the earlier pamphleteers had made it clear that, while non-resistance is a divine ordinance, there is nothing divine about the king personally. According to Sir John Cheke, for example, the magistrate is called God in the Scriptures "because he hath the execution of God's office."[99] And Bishop Hooper wrote that the king's "office and place" is God's appointment, without saying anything about his person.[100] The evident inference from this distinction would have been that the king is only to be obeyed so long as he does not abuse his divine office. But here again, it remained for the Marian exiles to develop the latent possibilities of this theory. Said Ponet in 1556: the Bible refers to rulers as gods, not because they are "naturally" gods, nor because they have been transubstantiated into gods, but merely because they are God's representatives here on earth. Interpreting the sentence in Romans 13—to the effect that every soul is subject to the powers that be, for there is no power but of God —Ponet asserted that the word "power" does not there refer to the king, mayor, or sheriff. Actually, he said, it is to be interpreted as "the ministry and authority, that all officers of justice do execute . . . : the politic power

and Richard II; of the removal of medieval kings from office by popes who were themselves called to account by general councils. Goodman proceeded to show further that the biblical texts cited by his opponents could in no sense be construed as sanctioning obedience to tyrants. Granted, he said, that St. Paul wrote Romans 13 to show the Romans that Christianity was not a religion of anarchy, but, on the contrary, a religion respectful of the powers that be. But by this statement the apostle had not intended to preach obedience to tyrants. See Goodman's *How superior powers ought to be obeyed of their subjects*, pp. 64, 108–110; and Ponet's *Short treatise of politic power*, pp. Dv^b, Giii–Gv.

99. *Hurt of sedition*, p. Aiiii.

100. "Annotations on Romans xiii," printed in *Later Writings of Bishop Hooper*, edited by Rev. Charles Nevinson (Parker Soc., Cambridge, 1852), p. 104.

or authority being the ordinance and good gift of God
one thing, and the person that executeth the same (be
he king or kaiser) another thing."[101]

The theory of resistance to the king underwent similar
treatment. This theory was by no means entirely unknown
during Henry VIII's reign, but here again it was not until
the second half of the century that it gained anything like
a foothold in England. In the reign of Henry VII, Sir
Thomas More, smarting under his treatment at the hands
of the king,[102] had written a short Latin poem entitled
"Populus consentiens regnum dat et aufert,"[103] and in
the *Utopia* he had prescribed that the prince's office was
to continue for a lifetime "unless he be deposed or put
down for suspicion of tyranny."[104] In his *Dialogue between Pole and Lupset*, Thomas Starkey had, moreover,
scouted the idea that tyrants are God's instruments.
Through his interlocutor, Starkey had concluded boldly
that "this is in man's power, to elect and choose him that is
both wise and just, and make him a prince, and him that
is a tyrant so to depose."[105] Coming from Henry VIII's
chaplain and one of the protagonists of the Royal Supremacy, this opinion is important. During Mary's reign
Ponet took his stand on precisely the same principle, that

101. *Short treatise of politic power*, pp. Av^b, Cv–Cv^b. A similar opinion is to
be found in William Baldwin's dedicatory epistle to the *Mirror for Magistrates*.
God, the ordainer of offices, he says, does not allow tyrants long to escape punishment. "For it is Gods owne office, yea his chiefe office, whych they beare and
abuse" (*Mirror for Magistrates*, edited by Lily B. Campbell, Cambridge, 1938,
p. 65). For a further discussion of the distinction between the person of the king
and his office, see below, Chap. VI, *passim*.

102. According to Roper, More spoke against Henry VII's pecuniary demands in the parliament of 1504, and for this reason incurred the royal disfavor.

103. See More's *Epigrammata* (Basel, 1520), p. 53. This poem is only six lines
in length and reads as follows:

> "Quicunque multis vir viris unus praeest,
> Hoc debet his quibus praeest.
> Praeesse debet neutiquam diutius
> Hi quam volent quibus praeest.
> Quid impotentes principes superbiunt?
> Quod imperant precario?"

104. *Utopia*, p. 136.
105. *Dialogue between Pole and Lupset*, p. 167.

is, that the people to whom kings owe their authority have
the right to take away what they have given, particularly
in the event of tyranny.[106] The theory of the popular
origin of royal authority was soon to have a much greater
vogue in the constitutional struggles of the seventeenth
century.

Nor had the Henrician Catholics been entirely quiet on
the subject of rebellion. Sir Francis Bigod, who had led
an unsuccessful uprising at Beverley in 1537, had written
a book denouncing the Royal Supremacy.[107] And men
like Lord Darcy[108] and Cardinal Pole had connived frequently at "the Enterprise of England." In fact, Pole
had written a book entitled De ecclesiasticae unitatis defensione, in which he had condemned both the king's
divorce and the Royal Supremacy. In the third section of
this book Pole had asserted the constitutional right of insurrection. In conferring the crown at coronation, the
people reserve the right, Pole had stated therein, to depose
the king if he encroaches on their rights. Henry Tudor
has proved himself a traitor to both God and man, and
accordingly Englishmen may now legitimately take up
arms against him and ally themselves with a foreign
power. Pole had exhorted Charles V to turn his attention
to these Turks who are worse than Turks. He had assured
the emperor of help from the English who are the same
that in time past, without any external help, took vengeance on their kings for the evil administration of the
commonwealth. These are also the same Englishmen who

106. *Short treatise of politic power*, pp. Gvᵇ–Gvi. Ponet cites as authority the
ancient office of high constable of England. The high constable, he says, once
had the authority to summon the king before parliament and other courts of
judgment, and, on just occasion, to commit him to ward.

107. See *Letters and Papers of Henry VIII*, XII (1), 201 (pp. 93, 103), 1087
(p. 499). In this book Bigod described what authority pope, bishop, and king
rightfully possessed. He stated that the head of the Church of England might
be a spiritual man like the Archbishop of Canterbury, but not the king.

108. On Chapuys' evidence, Darcy proposed that, if parliament introduced
Lutheranism into England, he should raise the people, and the emperor should
send troops to England. Darcy said that he could not hold himself a good Christian if he consented to the religious changes in England which were outrageous
against God and reason. See *Letters and Papers of Henry VIII*, VII, 1206.

called their kings to account for wasteful spending of money, and who compelled kings to resign their scepters. In fact, they are only waiting for your help, O Caesar, to revenge the injuries inflicted by their present king.[109]

This theory of Pole's was later taken up by the leaders of the English Counter-Reformation, and, in fact, it became the corner-stone of Jesuit political philosophy during the reign of Elizabeth. Dr. Sanders, Dr. Allen, Parsons, and other English Catholics, later asserted the right of subjects to repudiate their oath of allegiance to their royal master, and to execute the papal bull of excommunication against a heretical sovereign.

In conclusion, let it be noted again that it was not until the second half of the sixteenth century that a real theory of rebellion appeared in England. In the first half of the century the political pamphleteers, it is true, sometimes qualified the doctrine of non-resistance by implying that in some cases the sovereign is not to be obeyed, and that the person and office of the king are not synonymous. Also, an occasional political writer like Pole or Starkey expressed the view that subjects have the right to resist the king for heresy or tyranny. But it is important to remember that these implications of early Tudor political theory were not really developed until the reigns of Mary and Elizabeth. And as for the early Tudor monarchomachs, it is significant that Lord Darcy never wrote anything; that Sir Francis Bigod was a man of no importance; that More's attitude throughout the period of his

---

109. *Reginaldi Poli, Cardinalis Britanni, ad Henricum Octauum Britanniae Regem, pro ecclesiasticae unitatis defensione* (Rome, 1539), p. cxii[b]. The passage in question reads as follows: "Mihi crede, integrae adhuc legiones in Anglia latent eorum, qui non conseruauit genua ante Baal. Quos omnes, si uenias, Deus ipse qui conseuauit, ad te adducet. Sunt autem iidem Angli Caesar, qui multo leuiore, de causa ipsi sine auxilio externo, poenas male administratae reipublicae a regibus suis sumpserunt; Qui reges suos ob profusius in reipublicae damnum effusas pecunias, ad rationes reddendas citatos, cum eas approbare non potuissent, corona se & sceptro abdicare coegerunt. Hos porro spiritus cum adhuc retineant, nihil eos a tanta iniuria regis uindicanda retardat, neque iam diu retardauit praeter spem & expectationem tui; . . ."

trial was one of meek acceptance;[110] that Starkey's revolutionary treatise lay in manuscript until 1871; and that Pole's book was published at Rome against his wishes.[111] In other words, the partisans of rebellion during the early Reformation were not very robust, and in any event they produced no body of apologetic literature comparable to that struck off by the partisans of non-resistance.

It is evident, therefore, that during the reigns of Henry VIII and Edward VI political writers were in more complete agreement as to the sacrosanctity of the king and the perniciousness of rebellion than at almost any other time in English history. The Stuart theorists of divine-right monarchy were perhaps more ebullient than the Henrician advocates of non-resistance about the divinity which hedges a king. But they did not command the same universal allegiance. During the early English Reformation, the cult of authority was popular because the king had come to personify English nationalism as against papal internationalism, and because he represented the people's surety against internal anarchy. It was this cult of authority which, in addition to the doctrine of Royal Supremacy, chiefly differentiated the Tudor theory of kingship from that of the fifteenth century.

110. Never at any time during the period of his disgrace and imprisonment did More preach rebellion against the king. His attitude toward rebellion is best summed up by the title of his book, *Dialogue of Comfort against Tribulation*.

111. On this point, see Paul Van Dyke, *Renascence Portraits* (New York, 1905), pp. 383–385.

V

THE KING AND THE LAW

[The law of nature or reason] is written in the heart of every man, teaching him what is to be done, and what is to be fled; and because it is written in the heart, therefore it may not be put away, ne it is never changeable by no diversity of place, ne time: and therefore against this law, prescription, statute nor custom may not prevail: and if any be brought in against it, they be not prescriptions, statutes nor customs, but things void and against justice. And all other laws, as well the laws of God as to the acts of men, as other, be grounded thereupon. St. German, *Doctor and Student*, Dialogue I, Chap. 2.

A T first glance, it would seem that the political writers of the early English Reformation differed from their fifteenth-century predecessors in yet another respect. Some historians contend that the Tudor theorists not only made the king supreme in the spiritual realm, but that they ascribed to the monarch an almost limitless power in the secular realm as well.[1] A superficial reading of books like Tyndale's *Obedience of a Christian*

1. Such is Figgis' undoubted inference when he says (*Divine Right of Kings*, p. 92) that some theory of uncontrolled secular authority had to be elaborated by Tudor political writers to counteract the papal claims to *plenitudo potestatis*. "For the purposes of theoretical consistency and practical efficiency alike," he asserts, "a doctrine of sovereignty vested by Divine Right in the king was the indispensable handmaid of a national Reformation." Another historian of political thought, Raymond Gettell, writes that during the Tudor era, "the dominant political theory was that of divine right monarchy and the passive obedience of subjects" (*History of Political Thought*, New York and London, 1924, p. 196). Even Maitland intimates that the political concepts of the *Corpus Juris Civilis* were creeping into England when he says that the danger of a reception of Roman law in England during the second quarter of the sixteenth century was seriously threatening "the continuity of English legal history" (*English Law and the Renaissance*, Cambridge, 1901, p. 17).

More recent historians have thought otherwise, however. Allen, for example, states emphatically that there was no such thing as a theory of divine right in early sixteenth-century England (*History of Political Thought in the Sixteenth Century*, pp. 121–123). And Sabine says that in Tudor England "because the king's power was not seriously threatened in the sixteenth century, the theory of royal absolutism, or complete sovereignty vested in the king, did not develop. . . ." (*History of Political Theory*, p. 373). Neither of these two last writers has attempted to expand this theme in any detail.

Man and Gardiner's *De vera obedientia* would seem to suggest this. What other interpretation can be placed on Tyndale's statement that "the king is, in this world, without law; and may at his lust do right or wrong, and shall give accounts but to God only"; or to Gardiner's assertion that the king "representeth as it were the image of God upon earth," and that he must be obeyed "yea, though he were an infidel," and without "one syllable of exception"? How else is one to understand the frequent contemporary allusions to Henry VIII's sun-like nature whose flaming beams the lowly subject can in no wise steadfastly behold? Did not Wolsey and Cromwell express a hearty contempt for the political capacity of parliament, and correspondingly magnify the king's position in the state?[2] Can a more unequivocal expression of absolutism be found than the Act of Proclamations of 1539 by which royal proclamations were supposedly made of equal validity with acts of parliament? On the face of it, the evidence does seem to indicate that the fifteenth-century and early Tudor theorists differed profoundly in their conception of the relation of the king to the law. The Henricians, it would seem, advanced a theory of monarchy which Fortescue would never have accepted, and which Hobbes was later to sponsor—that the king is absolute within the secular as well as the religious realm, that he is an unlimited sovereign, unhampered in his prerogative either by law or by parliamentary assembly.[3]

Now it is true that in the world of practical politics, something very like royal sovereignty was becoming an accomplished fact in the England of the early sixteenth century. Indeed, the creation of the strong state, with the king as the near-absolute ruler of that state, was, as we have already had occasion to note, the outstanding political achievement of Europe as a whole during the Renaissance and Reformation. In France, the king had

2. See below, pp. 151–152, 168–170.
3. For definitions of absolute monarchy and unlimited sovereignty, as I understand the terms in this chapter, see above, Chap. I, notes 5, 6.

by 1500 contrived not only to restrict the power of the
Church within France, but to make himself incomparably
the most important secular personage within the state as
well. By the Ordinance of 1439, he had got control of the
public purse, and had consequently become largely independent of the Estates General. With the proceeds of the
taille, he had created a standing army the control of which
he reserved entirely for himself. And under Louis XI the
royal domain had expanded so considerably at the expense
of the great feudatories that it had come to include almost
the whole of France. In Spain, Ferdinand and Isabella,
not scrupling to use the Inquisition as a political device
for crushing their opponents, had by 1500 made the
crown paramount over nobility, *cortes*, and even chartered
towns. In Scandinavia, in the petty principalities of Italy
and Germany, even in far-distant Russia, it was no less
true that the ruler was currently consolidating his temporal as well as his spiritual power.

England, despite her insularity in other respects, was
no exception to this rule. On the contrary, under the first
two Tudors the power of the English crown was so appre-
ciably increased that in the following century the middle
class, just coming of age politically, had to go to war with
the king to establish for itself a permanent place in the
political system. The crown in both council and parliament so magnified its competence during the early Tudor
era that by the death of Henry VIII it had absorbed
almost completely the separate sovereignties of Church,
feudal nobility, and vested corporations. The king in
council, which was the same thing as saying the king
solus since the council in Tudor times had no power independent of the king, came to wield in reality the jurisdiction which during the middle ages it had claimed theoretically. The nobility was kept in check by the summary
justice of the Star Chamber. The prerogative courts of
chancery and requests encroached frequently on the preserve of the common-law courts, either to enforce equity
in the interest of the victims of the enclosure movement, or

to ease the rigidity of the common-law requirements. The councils of the North and Wales, their authority delegated by the king in council, dispensed justice with an iron hand in the north and west country. The council, sitting in its administrative capacity, constantly made its influence felt in the localities by issuing orders to its local representatives, the justices of the peace.

Nor was the increase in power of the king in parliament much less obvious than that of the king in council. During the sixteenth century, the king in parliament, as Pollard puts it, "was emancipated from the control of fundamental law,"[4] and certainly it is true that parliament legislated about things which in the previous century would have been regarded as beyond its competence. We have already seen how parliament effected a revolution by making the king Supreme Head of the English Church. By the statute of 1504, which provided that all acts and ordinances promulgated by corporations must be approved by the chancellor, treasurer, and judges,[5] it accomplished the subordination of corporations as well. And it recorded the swan song of liberties and franchises in the act of 1536 which, among other things, transferred the judicial supremacy of the palatinate of Durham from bishop to king.[6] Clearly, the king in both council and parliament was increasing his powers tremendously during the early Tudor era, and the king *solus* was obtaining an authority which, if not precisely absolute, was immeasurably greater than that of his predecessors.

On the continent there emerged a theory reflecting this practical achievement of royal absolutism and sovereignty. The French civil lawyers went even beyond the theory of the *Corpus Juris Civilis* in attributing to Louis XII and Francis I an almost unlimited power of legislation and jurisdiction. The Roman *princeps*, absolute

4. *Evolution of Parliament*, p. 226.
5. 19 Hen. VII, c. 7.
6. 27 Hen. VIII, c. 14. For a brief discussion of the part of this act dealing with Durham, see G.T.Lapsley, *The County Palatine of Durham* (New York, 1900), pp. 196–198.

within the state and *legibus solutus* but deriving his *imperium* ultimately from the people, was transformed by lawyers like Ferrault and de Grassaille into a monarch equally sovereign within the state but ruling as God's vicegerent rather than as a popular delegate.[7] Later in the century Jean Bodin published his classical disquisition on royal sovereignty, arguing that only when the king possesses "an unlimited right to make, interpret, and execute law"[8] can anarchy be averted. True, Bodin surrounded his sovereign with serious restrictions, indeed so serious as almost to destroy his conception of sovereignty altogether. Nevertheless, the fact remains that in Bodin's *Republic* the idea of absolute monarchy assumed far greater proportions than did its limitations, and Bodin may truly be said to have been reflecting to as great a degree as the French civilians the growth of the strong state throughout Europe.

In Italy, no less than in France, a theory of absolute monarchy made its appearance during the Renaissance. The conception of the prince ruling with sovereign powers as God's representative rather than as the people's delegate, was developed in Italy some years before it reached the hands of the French jurists.[9] And Machiavelli, in the *Prince* at least, was a staunch advocate of the absolute ruler. By natural inclination a republican, Machiavelli regarded human nature as hopelessly corrupt, and held that society's only salvation lay in the use of despotic power. The prince, he argued, must be allowed an unlimited prerogative. To maintain the state, the prince must be omnipotent, above the law, and even outside the common morality.

Of all the countries of Europe, England alone, it seems, failed to propound a theory of absolute monarchy in justification of the new political reality. If it be argued

7. See Allen, *History of Political Thought in the Sixteenth Century*, pp. 280–285.
8. Bodin's definition of sovereignty as translated by Sabine (*History of Political Theory*, p. 407).
9. See Allen, *History of Political Thought in the Sixteenth Century*, pp. 281–282.

that political ideas reflect scrupulously the political and
economic milieu in which they are cast, here at least is an
important exception. At a time when the royal prerogative was increasing in majesty, and when statute law was
absorbing all other forms of sovereignty within the state,
English political writers had little to say about the king
and the law which had not already been said in the preceding century. As we have already seen, they were prepared to elaborate a theory of Royal Supremacy and to
garb the king with the trappings of divinity—two innovations which the political facts of the fifteenth century
had not forced Fortescue to make. But in sharp contrast
to their continental contemporaries, the Tudor theorists
produced no theory of the sovereignty of the king, either
solus or in council or parliament.

What therefore might seem at first glance to be a theory
of absolute monarchy, is actually nothing of the sort. The
high-flown phraseology of a Tyndale or a Gardiner was
decidedly not the normal medium of legal expression in
the early sixteenth century, nor, when used, was it as
startling as it sounds. By reading the works of these writers *in toto*, one is able to see an entirely different picture.
Either the writer, whose literary enthusiasm for royalty
knew no bounds, desired some favor of the king, as in the
case of the supplicant who compared Henry VIII to
Hercules;[10] or the retention of his worldly goods and position depended on complying with the king's wishes, as in
the case of Gardiner; or else, more important still, he
spoke of the king in glowing terms to set up a counterbalance to the pope, or to provide a safeguard against internal anarchy. It is significant, I think, that the king is
eulogized in extravagant terms only when the writer is
attacking the papacy, or at a time when England was in
especial danger of foreign invasion or internal rebellion.
When the political writers, with no ax to grind, turned
their attention to the relation of the king to the law, they

10. See above, p. 86, n. 2.

abandoned encomiums and sought inspiration from the middle ages rather than from the New Monarchy. In other words, Tyndale's statement that "the king is, in this world, without law" is not what it appears to be on the surface, and must not be read without reference to its context.

There are, of course, several good reasons why no theory of unlimited royal sovereignty was advanced during the early English Reformation. It has already been noted in another connection that during the reign of Henry VIII Englishmen were not apprehensive of a Charles Stuart who might destroy their fundamental rights, but of a Paul III or a Charles V who might conceivably lead a crusade against their schismatic king. In other words, the great political issue of the day was not the king *vs.* parliament, but the king in alliance with parliament *vs.* the Church championed by the papacy. Common lawyers and rackrenting landlords might occasionally insist that the king had exceeded his prerogative, and the House of Commons might at times resist the king's financial demands. But, fundamentally, crown and parliament saw eye to eye. Therefore, there was no need on the one hand for the king to make extravagant claims of sovereignty, since he usually had his own way anyhow; nor, on the other hand, for parliament to protest that the king had broken a medieval constitution. Sheer indifference to the subject of the king's relation to the law dictated that neither a theory of divine-right monarchy nor parliamentary sovereignty should have been propounded by Henrician Englishmen. The materials for a study of the king's legal position are therefore scarce in the early sixteenth century. Many writers had vague ideas about the king and the law, but few developed full-fledged theories.

In the second place, as will be noted more fully below, Henry VIII's desire to shift the responsibility for the Reformation to parliament's shoulders precluded any effort on his part to nourish a theory of unlimited royal sovereignty. If he had taken his stand, as James I was later to do, on the proposition that the kingdom was his by conquest, and that parliament derived its right to assist in the legislative process from his prerogative,[11] he would have been forced to admit logically that the revolutionary Royal Supremacy was his handiwork alone. How much more comfortable to inform his continental critics that the extirpation of papal authority from England had been accomplished in parliament "without which he determined no great matter."

In point of fact, no theory of absolute monarchy, and, for that matter, no theory of unlimited sovereignty of any sort, was elaborated in England until the day when royal despotism was beginning to lose its grip. Not until the time of James I, Dr. Cowell, Henry Parker, John Prynne, and Thomas Hobbes did a thoroughgoing theory of sovereignty make its appearance. Such a theory was then advanced because the alliance between crown and parliament had broken down, and both the royalists and parliamentarians were accordingly driven to formulate their views more logically and more precisely.

During the early English Reformation, however, the political writers were content to let sleeping dogs lie. Fortescue, not the *Corpus Juris Civilis*, was their touchstone, and they normally conceived of the king in good fifteenth-century fashion. The king, they maintained, is subject to natural and divine law; he is a legislator in really important matters only in so far as he collaborates with parliament; with the reservation of his medieval prerogatives, he is under the positive law which he himself has a hand in promulgating. Here was decidedly no theory of absolute monarchy such as that propounded currently by the French lawyers and Italian publicists.

---

11. This was James' contention in his *True Law of Free Monarchies*. According to Allen, however, there was little connection between James' theoretical talk and the positive claims which brought him into collision with the House of Commons. Allen says James based his positive claims, not on a theory of divine-right monarchy, but on Tudor precedent and the assumption that *in extraordinary circumstances* the king may act on his own initiative without reference to parliament (*English Political Thought, 1603–1660*, London, 1938, I, Chaps. 1, 2).

1. THE KING AND NATURAL LAW[12]

THE first proof of the fact that the Tudor political writers did not propound a theory of absolute monarchy is the prevalence in the sixteenth century of the natural-law tradition. For it is evident that no society believing firmly in the omnipotence of natural and divine law will advance a full-fledged theory of royal absolutism. As noted above, belief in an immutable *Jus* issuing from either the reason or will of God, a "fundamental" law, precludes automatically the idea that the king's will is law, and therefore irresponsible.[13] However majestically the monarch be exalted above positive law and human interference, *so long as he is held to be subject to an eternal code with specific implications*, he cannot be said to be absolute. The fundamental incompatibility of natural law and absolutism is indicated by the fact that the greatest exponents of absolute monarchy have either excluded natural law altogether from their discussions, or else have described it in such a manner as to deprive it of its sting; whereas the advocates of limited or mixed monarchy have always found it convenient to stress particularly the idea of an eternal code. Thus, Machiavelli, one of the greatest exponents of absolute monarchy, judged rulers solely by their success

12. The terms, natural and divine law, were used, for all practical purposes, as interchangeable terms. There was, to be sure, a theoretical distinction between the two laws. According to St. German (*Doctor and Student*, Dialogue I, Chaps. 1, 2), the law of reason is the law eternal made manifest to human beings "by the light of natural reason"; moreover, it has to do with the activity of man in this present life. The law of God, on the other hand, is the law eternal revealed "by heavenly revelation," and has to do with "the obtaining of the felicity eternal" (*Doctor and Student*, Dialogue I, Chaps. 1, 3). Philosophically speaking, however, St. German regarded the laws of nature and God as merely two different aspects of the same law eternal. And for all practical purposes, the terms may be regarded as almost synonymous. Henry VIII's instructions to Paget, ambassador to the princes of Germany in 1534, are illustrative of the sixteenth-century attitude on this point. Paget is directed to explain that His Highness' marriage to the princess dowager, Catherine of Aragon, was "against the law of God's nature" (*Letters and Papers of Henry VIII*, VII, 148). Ponet also spoke of God's laws "by which name also the lawes of nature be comprehended" (*Short treatise of politic power*, p. Biij[b]).

13. See above, p. 6.

in the political arena, excluding laws of morality almost entirely from his discussion. James I likewise had little to say about natural law in his *True Law of Free Monarchies.*[14] In the *Leviathan,* Hobbes described natural law in such a way as to make it innocuous in its application to the king.[15] On the other hand, Sir Edward Coke, Locke, and the French political philosophers of the eighteenth century—all proponents of limited monarchy—went out of their way to stress the fact that fundamental law, with all its specific implications, is supreme within the state.

Now it is plain that the political writers of the early English Reformation derived much of their legal inspiration from Fortescue and the natural-law tradition. Pollard's statement that "Wolsey was the very embodiment of the idea . . . that unchangeable laws could be interpreted, suspended, dispensed with, and defied by statutes and decrees devised by mortal wit and imposed by human will"[16] is without doubt a most accurate description of the way in which a Tudor statesman like Wolsey was wont to act. It does not, however, indicate how men thought in the sixteenth century. During the Tudor era, the idea of natural and divine law was still very much of a living principle, appealed to by men of all creeds and parties. The number of references made to it in the first half of the century was legion, and the rangeful variety of cases in which its authority was summoned is sufficient proof of the fact that all men, including the king, were still held

14. James does say that by the law of nature the king "becomes a naturall Father to all his Lieges," and that he is accordingly required to care for his subjects as a father cares for his children. But he does not dwell overlong on the subject, and certainly he mentions no specific obligations on the part of the king. See *The Political Works of James I,* edited by C.H.McIlwain, Harvard Univ. Press, 1918, pp. 55–56.

15. Hobbes' natural law was something entirely different from medieval natural law. To Hobbes, natural law signified a general precept forbidding man to do that which is destructive of his life (*Leviathan,* Chap. 14). The rule of self-preservation is surely a far cry from a law of nature enjoining kings to rule justly on pain of the divine displeasure.

16. *Wolsey* (London, 1929), p. 361.

to be subject to a fundamental law beyond human control. In point of fact, natural law may be regarded as the dominant idiom in terms of which the men of the early English Reformation cast their political ideas. Every age has a medium of expression which it uses to make its peculiar concepts intelligible to the public. Eighteenth-century Frenchmen, for example, were fond of describing their predilections in terms of natural reason, and twentieth-century Americans, regardless of party affinities, decide their political views at the bar of the American Constitution. In the early sixteenth century, English political writers were similarly defining their political ideas, whether important or inconsequential, in the language of natural law. Lawyers, churchmen, royal sycophants, refugees, all drank from its fountain and were as native to its phraseology as had been their medieval predecessors. Its theoretical aspects were, for example, discussed at some length in the legal treatises of St. German and Perkins.[17] It was still the habit of speakers at the opening of parliament to descant on its virtues.[18] Sir Thomas More, it will be remembered, devoted the entire second book of his *Utopia* to a description of a society operating under the law of nature. Some men even appealed to it as authority for their views on matters of a distinctly technical nature.[19]

The ubiquity of the natural-law concept during the early English Reformation is even more clearly illustrated

17. See St. German, *Doctor and Student*, Dialogue I, Chaps. 1, 3; and John Perkins, *A Profitable Book, treating of the Laws of England*, "Proemium Johannis Perkins." Perkins was a jurist, educated at Oxford, and practicing at the bar of the Inner Temple. The above-mentioned book was a popular textbook for law students, first printed in Anglo-Norman in 1530.

18. See Bishop Tunstal's oration delivered before the parliament of 1523 (*Rolls of Parliament, 1513–1533*, p. lxxv; summary in Hall's *Chronicle*, p. 652; also summary by the Venetian ambassador, Surian, in *Venetian Calendar*, III, no. 663).

19. Starkey, for example, appealed to the law of nature in his attack on the English laws concerning primogeniture and the rights of wardship (*Dialogue between Pole and Lupset*, pp. 108–114).

by reference to the political controversies of the day. Here its importance can scarcely be overestimated, for it constituted the backbone of all the salient arguments both for and against the Reformation. In Henry VIII's divorce case, in the controversy with Rome and the Church, in the arguments for and against non-resistance, neither political expediency nor weighty reason were cited as justification for men's actions, but the word of God made manifest to the human mind by natural law.

In Henry VIII's great matter, for example, both sides saw that the really vital issue was to determine whether or not the king's marriage to his brother's wife was permissable by the laws of God and nature. Thomas Abell, Catherine of Aragon's chaplain, argued that the prohibition of marriage to one in the first degree of lateral affinity was only the law of the Church, not the law of nature, and that therefore the pope had every right to override it.[20] Henry VIII's supporters, on the other hand, averred that the marriage was contrary to the Levitical law which "is rooted in the law of nature,"[21] and that accordingly it was beyond the pope's power to suspend. At a later date William Thomas, seeking to justify the king's divorce, saw fit simply to state that Henry's first marriage had been

20. *Invicta veritas. An answere, That by no maner of lawe it maye be lawfull for the moste noble Kinge of englande Kinge Henry the ayght to be diuorsed fro the quenes grace his lawful and very wyfe* (allegedly Lüneberg, 1532), p. Bii. To prove that marriage between a man and his brother's wife was not illegal by the laws of God and nature, Abell cited Moses' commandment that every Jewish man should marry his brother's widow. See also on this point, Cochlaeus' (Johannis Dobneck's) *De Matrimonio serenissimi Regis Angliae, Henrici Octaui, Congratulatio disputatoria Iohannis Cochlei Germani, Ad Pavlvm Tertium* (1535), Parts 4, 5. Cochlaeus' point was the same as Abell's. Since the prohibition of such a marriage is only by Church law, and not by divine law, "proinde Papa super eo facile dispensare possit, cum sit tantum humano iure prohibitum."

21. According to Leviticus 18:16, "Thou shalt not uncover the nakedness of thy brother's wife." For references to the Levitical law in justification of Henry VIII's divorce, see Starkey's letter to Cardinal Pole, Feb. 15, 1535, printed in *England in the Reign of King Henry the Eighth*, edited by S.J.Herrtage, p. xvi; Gardiner, *De vera obedientia*, p. 86; *A Glass of the Truth*, Pocock's *Records of the Reformation*, II, 401. The author of the latter argues that the Levitical law is definitely a precept of natural and divine law.

contrary to the law of God.[22] Presumably further explanation was superfluous.

During the controversy over the Church, both sides
again pleaded their case in terms of the natural-law idiom.
The Henrician reformers' most effective argument against
the papal power, as indeed it was the most effective argument used by the continental reformers as well, was to contrast men's traditions and God's laws. To propagandists
like Bishops Gardiner and Bonner "the false pretensed
power of the Bishop of Rome" was "utterly repugnant
against the truth of God's law," and for that reason un-
tenable.[23] Both the privileges of the clergy and the invoca-
tion of a general council under the aegis of the pope were
denounced in similar fashion.[24] Conversely, the conservatives sought justification for the *status quo* in terms of divine law. The stand taken by the Abbot of Winchcombe
and Cardinal Wolsey on the liberties of the Church in
1515 is typical. Both maintained that the said liberties
were inviolable because sanctioned expressly by the law of
God.[25]

An even more amazing use of the natural-law idiom was
made apropos of the subject of non-resistance. As noted
above, the Henrician radical Protestants maintained that
implicit obedience to kings is enjoined by natural and
divine law, as did the supporters of the government,
whether moderates under Henry VIII, radicals under Ed-

22. *The Pilgrim*, edited by J.A.Froude (London, 1861), pp. 16–17. This book
is the record of a discussion which Thomas had with some Italian gentlemen
regarding the policy of Henry VIII.

23. See Gardiner, *De vera obedientia*, p. 92; also Bonner's preface to the Hamburg edition of Gardiner's *De vera obedientia*, printed in *The Royal Supremacy
in Matters Ecclesiastical in Pre-Reformation Times*, edited by B.A.Heywood
(London, 1870), p. 31.

24. The author of the *Treatise proving by the king's laws* describes the exact
powers which, in his opinion, the clergy has the right to exercise by the law of
God (Chap. 2). A general council, "where alonly those men are harde, whiche
are determyned for euer, in all poyntes, to defende the popysshe parte," is
against the law of nature, says the author of *An Epistle of the moste myghty &
redouted Prince Henry the viii . . . to the Emperours maiestie* (London, 1538),
p. Aiii[b].

25. Keilwey's *Reports*, pp. 181, 184[b].

ward VI, or Catholics under Mary.[26] Moreover, while the
Catholic Bishop Christopherson was writing that by the
example of the bees nature teaches all subjects to obey
their prince implicitly throughout life,[27] the Protestant
refugees were thundering from the continent that rebellion, nay, even tyrannicide are justified by the laws of God
and nature![28]

From the evidence cited, it cannot be doubted that the
natural-law concept was still very much alive in the sixteenth century, and that, indeed, it represented the idiom
of Tudor political expression. Had the Tudor political
writer woven his argument around some other medium, he
would have been just as unintelligible to his readers as the
American statesman who today argues about the Supreme
Court without reference to the Constitution. Granted its
ubiquity, however, what precisely did natural law mean?
Did it have specific implications? And, more pertinent to
our purposes, did its precepts apply to the king as well as
to ordinary people?

The sixteenth-century answers to these questions did
not differ much from those supplied by Fortescue and the
preceding century. The important thing to notice is that
however generally, and hence vaguely, the Tudor political
writers defined natural law, they always conceived of it,
as Fortescue had done before them, as having a specific
connotation, applicable to the practical circumstances of
life, and legally binding on all human beings. Fortescue
had defined natural law in the somewhat platitudinous
phrases of the middle ages, but he had gone farther and
had applied it as a working hypothesis to the question of
the Yorkist claim to the throne.[29] The sixteenth century
followed suit and, as already noted above, frequently
applied natural law to the specific problems of the day.
Indeed, Tudor political writers sometimes envisaged nat-

26. See above, pp. 95–99.
27. *Exhortation to all men*, p. Ovii.
28. See above, p. 112.
29. See above, p. 10, n. 17.

ural law as a kind of bill of rights, in this respect anticipating the seventeenth century.

That this was actually the case is evident from the clas-
sic accounts of natural law supplied by the three greatest
political writers of the first half of the century, Christopher St. German, Thomas Starkey, and John Ponet. All
three were interested in the philosophical implications of
natural law, but all three were equally interested in its
specific application. To them natural law connoted something tangible as well as intangible, something of importance in the everyday lives of people as well as in the
mind of the philosopher. St. German, for example, devoted the first chapters of his *Doctor and Student* to defining the theoretical terms of natural law, but he was careful
to give them practical significance. The law of reason,[30]
he said, is derived from the law eternal, and is written in
the heart of every man, teaching him what is to be done,
and what is to be fled. It teaches, among other things, that
one should do unto others as one would be done unto, and
that justice must be accorded to every man.[31] Specifically,
however, St. German, like Fortescue before him, saw in
natural law a principle enjoining the sanctity of personal
rights and private property. By the law of reason primary, "it is lawful for a man," he maintained, "to defend
himself against an unjust power, so he keep due circumstance." By the law of reason secondary general, "satis-
faction must be made for a trespass, and restitution must
be made of such goods as one man hath that belong to
another man; the debts must be paid, covenants fulfilled,
and such other."[32]

30. Note that St. German used the expression "law of reason" in lieu of "law
of nature." As McIlwain points out (*High Court of Parliament*, p. 105), the
common lawyers rejected the term "law of nature" used by the civil lawyers,
and therefore unquestionably their "law of reason" had a somewhat different
connotation from the old "law of nature." "The English 'law of reason,' " says
McIlwain, "seems to have had the same close relation to custom that the old
law of nature had formerly borne to the *jus gentium*."

31. *Doctor and Student*, Dialogue I, Chaps. 1, 2.

32. *Ibid.*, pp. 12, 13. Fortescue had also protected private property by the
law of nature (see above, Chap. I, note 16). John Perkins, St. German's con-

In his *Dialogue between Pole and Lupset,* Starkey described natural law similarly as the spark of divinity rooted in men's hearts which inclines them toward the social life.[33] It consists, he asserted, of the honor to be done to the divine nature, reverence to one's parents, and the repelling of injury.[34] But from that famous passage in the *Dialogue* in which he advocated a reception of Roman law into England, it is evident that Starkey, like St. German, was interested in something more than mere theory. For in the aforesaid passage he practically identified natural law with the *jus civile* and all its technical ramifications.[35] In another place he applied the law of nature to the English rules governing primogeniture and the rights of wardship, and found these rules to be unreasonable.[36]

Ponet, writing from exile during the reign of Mary, was even more insistent than St. German and Starkey on the practical application of natural law. He, too, delineated natural law in general terms as that divine rule implanted in the human mind by God as a principle of government to counteract the effects of original sin.[37] But he went on further to say that natural law is the touchstone by which every man's actions, whether king's or beggar's, should be tried.[38] Identifying it with the Decalogue, he maintained that its general purport "is so plain and easy to under-

temporary, espoused, however, the patristic rather than the Roman civil-law theory of property. He maintained that natural law had ordained all things to be held in common ("istud praeceptum legis naturae, de habendo omnia communia"), but that this rule had been revoked after the Fall ("revocatum est post lapsum"). Ergo, the institution of private property is by human law only ("lege ergo humana, quae et positiva dicitur, haec domus mea est, etc."). See Perkins, *A Profitable Book, treating of the Laws of England,* "Proemium Johannis Perkins."

33. *Dialogue between Pole and Lupset,* p. 14.

34. *Exhortation to Christian Unity,* pp. 41b–42.

35. *Dialogue between Pole and Lupset,* p. 194. The Roman civil law, says Starkey, is "wryte wyth such grauyte, that yf Nature schold hyrselfe prescrybe partycular meanys wherby mankynd schold obserue hyr lawys, I thynke sche wold admyt the same. . . ."

36. *Ibid.,* pp. 108–114.

37. *Short treatise of politic power,* p. Aijb.

38. *Ibid.,* p. Aiii.

stand that no ignorance can or will excuse him that therein offendeth." [39] It is perfectly clear, he said, that a king may not commit idolatry any more than a private man, that he may not kill any person contrary to the laws, and that he may not covet another man's wife.[40] Nor may the members of parliament remit the king's debts for fear of incurring the royal displeasure, for in that case they would not be doing as they would be done unto.[41]

The sixteenth-century political writers followed Fortescue in still another respect. They not only maintained that natural law had specific as well as general implications; they held that those specific implications applied, to use Ponet's expression, to kings as well as to beggars. There can be no doubt whatever that Reformation England followed the medieval tradition which taught that the monarch, whatever his relation to positive law, was subordinate to, and in fact the executive of, natural and divine law. Neither in his capacity as legislator by prerogative, nor as legislator with parliament, was he held to be above that eternal law whose general and specific implications the political theorists had so little trouble in expounding.[42] True, the theorists could not always agree as to the precise meaning of natural law; St. German, Starkey, and Ponet, each had his particular version as to how it was to be applied in practice. But the fact that everyone could agree that there was an eternal law, and that kings as well as beggars were subject to its dictates, constitutes a political principle of no little importance. Certainly, with such a

39. *Ibid.*
40. *Ibid.*, pp. Cij–Cij[b].
41. *Ibid.*, p. Aiii[b].
42. It will be the function of that section of the present chapter entitled the "King in Parliament" to show that statute law, of which the king was in part the promulgator, was also held to be derivative of, and inferior to, natural law. The present section deals only with the subordination of the specifically "king's law" (Fortescue's *Jus Regis*) to the higher law. It must be confessed, however, that there is very often some doubt as to just what the political writers meant when they referred to the "king's law" in relation to divine law. It is to be regretted that they made no such clear-cut distinction as Fortescue's *dominium regale* and *dominium politicum et regale*.

feeling prevailing, there could be no talk of royal absolutism or unlimited royal sovereignty.

A very useful analogy to the Tudor political writers' attitude toward the king and natural law is to be found in their delimitation of the papal power of dispensation. During the divorce case Henry VIII's representatives maintained consistently—at least after Lautrec's death in 1528[43]—that the Levitical law forbidding a man to marry his brother's wife was a provision of divine law, and that it could not therefore be suspended by any human being, even by the pope. This statement, reiterated over and over during the crucial years, 1528–1533, constituted the main argument on which Henry VIII's divorce case was based.[44] The author of the pamphlet, *A Glass of the Truth*, stated the case against the pope clearly. If the pope might dispense with God's law, he asked, "then what folly were it to observe God's law, or any other, but only investigate and search to know the Pope's will in everything, and that to follow accordingly."[45] The first Act of Succession justified the king's divorce precisely on the same ground, that

43. Odet de Foix, Sieur de Lautrec, commander of Francis I's forces in Italy, died before Naples, August 17, 1528. Had his campaign against the imperial forces been successful, Clement VII would have been delivered from Charles V's yoke, and would have been free in consequence to grant Henry VIII's request for a nullification of his marriage. Had this occurred, the king's apologists would not have been driven to draw a distinction between divine and papal law.

44. Henry VIII's instructions to Gardiner and his colleagues in Italy in 1529 are typical. The king urged his envoys to retain some excellent divine who would stick to the principle, "quod pontifex ex jure divino non potest dispensare" (*Letters and Papers of Henry VIII*, IV(3), 5427). As late as November 1529, however, Henry VIII was wondering whether, if the queen were induced to enter a nunnery, the pope could "ex plenitudine potestatis," permit him to proceed to a second marriage; and whether, although this was a thing which perhaps the pope could not do in accordance with divine and human laws already written, he might do it of his absolute power, as a thing with which he might dispense above the law (*Letters and Papers*, IV(2), 4977).

45. Pocock, *Records of the Reformation*, II, 389; cf. also *ibid.*, II, 152. The Henrician position is very neatly summarized in two sentences of this second tract. "Ducere uxorem fratris mortui sine liberis est jure divino et naturali prohibitum. Contra prohibitiones divinas invalida ac prorsus nulla est Romani Pontificis aut alterius cujuscunque dispensatio." See also Starkey's letter to Pole (1535?), printed in *England in the Reign of King Henry the Eighth*, edited by S.J.Herrtage, p. xxix.

"no man what estate, degree, or condition so ever he be
hath power to dispense with God's law."[46] Even Catherine
of Aragon's champions admitted that the pope could not
dispense with divine law. They took their stand rather
on the technical problem of whether Leviticus 18:16 was
actually the law of God or not.[47]

Now it is true, of course, that the Tudor political writers were far more interested in repudiating papal absolutism than in limiting the power of the king whom they
regarded as necessary to the welfare of the state. Nevertheless, they frequently drew the same contrast between
God's law and the king's law that they had drawn between
God's law and the pope's dispensatory power during the
divorce case. Not too frequently, since after all there was
no controversy between king and parliament, but frequently enough to indicate how they really felt about the
matter. Sir William Forrest's lines,

> "What king soever his reign doth subject
> unto the laws prescribed of God,
> worthy he is to rule in full effect:
> with Diadem, Crown, and the Scepter rod
> in peaceable wise: else God forbid.
> And who contemneth God's service and Law:
> he shall (of men) be had in small awe,"[48]

are typical of an attitude of mind which conceived of pope
or king, however arbitrary their power in other respects,
as being subject to an ultimate tribunal.

46. 25 Hen. VIII, c. 22.
47. See above, Chap. V, note 20. It is interesting to note, however, that occasionally the imperialists asserted the omnipotence of the pope's dispensatory
power even over the *jus divinum*. Rodrigo Davalos, writing to Charles V in 1533,
reported, for example, that Dr. Ortiz had informed the French cardinals that
the impediment to the queen's marriage was not *jure divino*, but only *jure
canonico*, with which the pope could dispense, and that even if it were *jure divino*,
the pope could dispense with good cause (*Letters and Papers*, VI, 773).
48. British Museum, Royal MSS., 17 D III, f. 33. This poem, which was dedicated to the Duke of Somerset in 1548, is entitled the *Pleasaunt Poesye of
Princelie Practise*. For a fuller description of the poem and its author, see below, pp. 200–201, n. 27; pp. 202–204.

It was only natural that Sir Thomas More, a staunch Catholic, should, in his hour of need, have reminded the king of the advice which the latter had once given him, "willing him first to look unto God, and after God, to him."[49] But that the moderate reformers and extreme Protestants—men who more or less agreed with Henry VIII—should have echoed the same refrain, is less natural. The assertion that for all his divinity, the king is still "but a servant, to execute the law of God, and not to rule after his own imagination" becomes in the mouth of Tyndale, who in 1528 had everything to gain by flattering the king, an immensely important political principle.[50] Henry Brinkelow, another of the extreme religious reformers, was even more vehement about the king's subordination to divine law. He waxed fairly indignant at the mere thought of a man working for the king on Sunday. "As though it were lawful," he ejaculated, "for the king to break God's commandment! . . . What king or emperor . . . can dispense with God's Word, which he either biddeth or forbiddeth?"[51] The fiery Latimer, too, in his first sermon before Edward VI, asserted that every king is subject unto God, as all other men are subject unto the king.[52] Some years later Ponet wrote that inasmuch as kings and princes had nothing to do with the making of God's laws, so they have no authority to dispense with them.[53] Kings are, after all, but executors of God's laws, he declared, and like everyone else, are "bound to be subject and obedient unto them."[54]

Even when the Henrician political writers were emphasizing the divinity which hedges a king and the importance of non-resistance, they enunciated concomitantly the prin-

49. Roper, *Life of More*, p. 50.
50. See *Obedience of a Christian Man*, p. 334.
51. *Complaynt of Roderyck Mors*, edited by J.M.Cowper (E.E.T.Soc., London, 1874), p. 63.
52. *Sermons by Hugh Latimer*, edited by Rev. G.E.Corrie (Parker Soc., Cambridge, 1844), p. 93.
53. *Short treatise of politic power*, pp. Biij^b–Biiij.
54. *Ibid.*, p. Cvi.

ciple of the king's subordination to divine law. Implicit obedience to the prince is a religious duty, they preached, *with one exception*. If the king orders anything directly contrary to God's law, he is to be obeyed under no circumstances, but is to be resisted passively. This one exception to the general rule the political pamphleteers stipulated, even in their most ecstatic moments. Let the subject for God's sake obey even ungentle masters and comply with their laws, wrote the moderate reformer Gardiner, "in so far as they do not stand against God's precepts."[55] If the powers that be command anything against right and law, they are to be suffered, asserted the radical reformer Barnes, "always provided that it repugn not against the Gospel, nor destroy our faith."[56] Even the official *Homilies of 1547* asserted that kings and magistrates are not to be obeyed "if they command us to do anything contrary to God's commandments."[57]

St. German was too much in favor of Henry VIII's ecclesiastical reforms ever to become involved in a discussion of the king and natural law. However, there can be no doubt that if he had been asked for a candid opinion, he would have had to answer, as Fortescue had done before him, that the *Jus Regis* can no more be compared to the law of nature than a fly to an eagle.[58] Had St. German lived a hundred years later, he would have turned his law of reason protecting private rights and property to no little advantage against James and Charles Stuart. Here was unquestionably a potential Sir Edward Coke.

2. THE KING AND PARLIAMENT

BUT what had St. German and his contemporaries to say about the king and parliament?

55. "Contemptum humanae legis," printed in Janelle, *Obedience in Church and State*, p. 177. See also Sampson, *Oratio*, Strype, *Eccles. Mem.*, I (2), 164. Sampson says that the prince must be obeyed implicitly in everything, "modo nihil mandet contra Deum."
56. *The whole workes of W.Tyndall, Iohn Frith, and Doct. Barnes*, p. 292.
57. *Homilies of 1547*, p. Sj[b].
58. See above, p. 9.

The evidence already cited shows clearly that the early Tudor political writers did not break with the medieval tradition of the subordination of the king to natural or fundamental law. Like Fortescue, they held that the *Jus Regis* could on no account run counter to the fundamental precepts prescribed by God in the Scriptures and the code of nature. There was, however, one serious drawback to this scheme as a limitation on the royal prerogative. As we have already seen, political theorists differed widely in their understanding of the specific meaning of natural law. St. German might safeguard private property by the law of nature, but Perkins might with equal reason take the patristic view that natural law prescribes communism.[59] Likewise, it was possible for Marian Catholics to deduce from the Scriptures that non-resistance is a divine injunction, while at the same time Marian exiles were proclaiming that resistance and even tyrannicide are justifiable in the eyes of God. Natural law was perhaps what the sceptical Halifax later said "fundamental principles" were, "a nail everybody would use to fix that which is good for them."[60] Certainly there was no code or constitution in the sixteenth century defining the specific meaning of natural law, nor was there a supreme court to enforce its decrees.

This general vagueness surrounding the idea of natural law was, of course, to the king's advantage. For he could always insist that his interpretation of the Decalogue and the precepts of nature was the correct one, while admitting in a general way the "fundamental" limitations on the *Jus Regis*. Despite the natural-law concept, the Tudor theorists might still claim for their master an *almost* absolute power within the state by asserting that positive law,

59. See above, Chap. V, note 32.

60. Quoted in Sabine, *History of Political Theory*, p. 519. Cardinal Pole was of the same opinion as Halifax. In his *De ecclesiasticae unitatis defensione* he made the sneering remark that if Henry VIII had taken the other side in the divorce case, he could have just as easily justified his position by the law of God. In a letter to the Earl of Wiltshire, June 13, 1531, Cranmer remarks on Pole's sceptical attitude toward the law of God (*Letters and Papers*, V, App., no. 10).

and particularly statute law, was the prerogative of the king *solus*, rather than of the king in parliament, and that what privileges the members of parliament enjoyed were delegated by the king. This was precisely what Bodin claimed in the *Republic*. He maintained that the king cannot transgress natural law or violate the *leges imperii*,[61] but that in all other respects he is an absolute sovereign with the right to legislate without interference from any assembly within the state.

Before going on to the relation between natural law and statute law it is therefore important to determine what the early Tudor theorists had to say about positive legislation. Whom did they consider to be the supreme promulgator of law within the state, the king *solus* or the king in parliament? In other words, how far was the king's legislative prerogative out of parliament held to extend, and in what sense can the king be said to have been the promulgator of statute law? Did St. German and his contemporaries adhere to Fortescue's belief that in really *fundamental* matters, *e.g.*, the alteration of the common law and extraordinary taxation, the king must rule "politically" rather than "regally"?[62] Or did they incline to James I's dictum in the *True Law of Free Monarchies*, that kings existed before laws ever were made, and that therefore the king may, if he list, legislate without any reference to parliament whatever?[63]

Two observations on the subject of the king and parliament can be made at the outset. First, that a complete analysis is impossible because of the dearth of material available on the theme for the early sixteenth century; and second, that most of the existing material reflects the growing authority of parliament. The dearth of material means that the early Tudors had no absorbing interest in

61. Under natural law, Bodin, like Fortescue and St. German, protected private property. The *leges imperii*, according to Bodin, prevented the king from altering the succession, or alienating the royal domain.

62. For Fortescue's distinction between the *dominium regale* and the *dominium politicum et regale*, see above, pp. 10–11.

63. See *The Political Works of James I*, p. 62.

the general subject of the king and parliament, and that in a time of religious change the political theorists were more concerned with attacking the Church than in weighing the respective merits of proclamation and statute. As stated before, there was no deep-seated quarrel between king and parliament in the early sixteenth century. The pope was the national enemy, and for the time being the king's legal position in the state was left undefined. Therefore, it is in *obiter dicta* that most references to the subject of royal and parliamentary legislation are to be found.

However, isolated passages show that Englishmen were coming more and more to associate parliament with the king in their phraseology, and to speak of legislation as the joint production of crown and people. The Tudors were thus perpetuating the fifteenth-century tradition, yet adding something to it. They believed with Fortescue, rather than with James I, that in fundamental matters the king and parliament must legislate in conjunction. But they went farther and adumbrated, if only vaguely, the view advanced in the ensuing century by parliamentarians like Whitelocke and Pym, that the king has no legislative power outside of parliament except by courtesy.[64]

In point of fact, the early Tudor political writers were in this respect reflecting an actual change in legislative psychology for which the Reformation and its radical implications were directly responsible. The revolutionary nature of Henry VIII's anti-papal and anti-ecclesiastical measures created in the king the desire to identify his policy with the will of the people, and the easiest way to do this was, obviously, to associate parliament with him in all his undertakings. This shifting of responsibility accomplished Henry's immediate purpose of molding a favorable public opinion, but it also presaged the future controversy between royal prerogative and parliament. Henry exalted a House of Commons, which under his father had been a mere cipher in the constitutional picture, into a body

64. See Allen, *English Political Thought, 1603–1660*, I, 33.

144 EARLY TUDOR THEORY OF KINGSHIP

whose consent was through habit becoming necessary for
the validity of all legislation. It was not that actual parliamentary practice was any different under Henry VIII
from what it had been under Henry VII. Henry VIII was
still entitled to use the time-honored devices of proclamation, proviso, and veto. It was simply that the emphasis
was now placed on king *and* parliament working in conjunction, rather than on the king *solus*—an emphasis
which was only natural, considering that for seven long
years, from 1529 to 1536, king and parliament had been
forced to coöperate as never before, and to work hand in
glove to overthrow the old order.

Actually, of course, the king's right to legislate by his
own authority out of parliament was still admitted. A
survey of Henry VIII's statutes reveals the fact that legislation by proclamation and proviso was unquestionably
legal, and that, in fact, the royal prerogative fell heir to
new legislative powers in consequence of the Reformation.
The Act of Proclamations asserted, for example, that
people who had obstinately contemned the king's proclamations had never considered "what a king by his royal
power may do," and that therefore in the future all proclamations made by the king's highness with the advice of
his council should be obeyed as though they were acts of
parliament.[65] The Act of Succession of 1544 provided that
in the event of the failure of heirs to the king, the latter

65. 31 Hen. VIII, c. 8. Pollard is undoubtedly right, however, when he points
out (*Evolution of Parliament*, pp. 267-268) that the Act of Proclamations was
not calculated to be used as an instrument for repealing existing laws and customs, but merely as a means of putting the Act of Supremacy into practice.
The reservations at the end of the statute about the invalidity of proclamations
in violation of old customs (see below, pp. 167-168), and its language at the beginning specifying proclamations made "concerning diverse and sundry articles of
Christ's Religion" (see above, p. 31), point conclusively in that direction. I
would make just one addition to Pollard's remark; namely that the act was intended as well to provide against the exigencies of rebellion when parliament
should not be in session. The act says that occasions fortune many times which
require speedy remedy, and which might cause great prejudice to the realm if
action depended on a parliament (see below, pp 146-147). The landowners and
merchants under Henry VIII had had enough experience with rebellion, and it
seems likely that they took this means of providing a remedy against it.

might by letters patent fix the crown on any person he so
desired—a prerogative, it is safe to say, which none of his
predecessors had even approached.[66] Then, too, the king,
like his father before him, frequently tacked onto the various statutes provisos which never received the assent of
parliament.[67] Moreover, the Royal Supremacy obviously
gave the king extra-parliamentary legislative powers in
the ecclesiastical realm which he had never before possessed. By the Act for the Submission of the Clergy, it will
be remembered, it was provided that the clergy should not
presume to promulgate any "new canons, constitutions,
and ordinances, provincial or otherwise" without the
king's license.[68] Negatively speaking, the statute book
gave the king's heirs on arriving of age the right to repeal
by letters patent any act of parliament which had been
passed during their minority.[69] And the Act of Annates
empowered the king to determine by letters patent, within
a given period of time, whether its provisions should be
executed or not.[70]

Nor is the statute book the only evidence that the idea
of royal legislation out of parliament was still flourishing
during the early Tudor era. Steele's *Bibliography of*

66. 35 Hen. VIII, c. 1.
67. Edward IV and Henry VII had constantly qualified bills by provisos as
is evident from the fifth and sixth volumes of the *Rotuli Parliamentorum*. In
Henry VII's Act of Resumption of 1485, for example, the commons' general
petition fills one column of the printed *Rotuli*, the commons' own provisos five,
and those of the king over ninety (*Rot. Parl.*, VI, 336-384). See also the provisos
at the conclusion of 6 Hen. VIII, c. 25. The proviso for the Earl of Shrewsbury
(XI) was, according to the note, written on a separate piece of parchment,
tacked to the rolls in chancery, and signed at the top "Henry R."
68. 25 Hen. VIII, c. 19. See also 31 Hen. VIII, c. 9, which provides that the
king may appoint new bishops to take care of the religious duties left uncared
for in consequence of the dissolution of the monasteries, and that he may make
regulations for the same which shall have the same authority as an act of parliament.
69. 28 Hen. VIII, c. 17.
70. 23 Hen. VIII, c. 20. The act 26 Hen. VIII, c. 10 also provides that the
king may by proclamation repeal 23 Hen. VIII, c. 7, which had to do with the
importation of French wines at a certain season. And 27 Hen. VIII, c. 26, by
which Wales was made a corporate part of England, was passed with the understanding that the king might suspend or revoke it within three years.

Royal Proclamations of the Tudor and Stuart Sovereigns
reveals the fact that the king in council, or the king *solus*,
was promulgating a vast number of edicts on a wide variety of subjects throughout the sixteenth century. No less
than two hundred proclamations were issued in Henry
VIII's reign alone, regulating prices, coinage, religion,
printing, enclosures, vagabondage, trade, war and peace,
even the clothing to be worn by the bourgeoisie. Indeed,
one of the reasons why Wolsey was so cordially hated by
the squirearchy was because of his proclamations, issued
as lord chancellor, against enclosures.[71] During Elizabeth's reign, Sir Thomas Smith attempted in his *De Republica Anglorum* to sum up the various things which a
monarch might do of his own authority. He may declare
war or contract alliances "at his pleasure or the advice
only of his privy council." In time of war his power is
absolute. And he may, among other things, decree by
proclamation the form and weight of the coinage of the
realm.[72]

It seems probable, however, that during the early
Reformation the right of the crown to legislate independently of parliament was regarded for the most part as
a prerogative reserved for emergencies, and not as part
of the normal routine of government. The Tudor opinion
of the royal prerogative represents an approximation of
the stand later to be taken by the crown lawyers under
James I and Charles I; namely, that under ordinary conditions the royal government must proceed *secundum
leges regni*, but that in the face of an emergency the king
may "do what is necessary without consulting parliament."[73] Thus, according to the Act of Proclamations, the
king must be permitted to legislate out of parliament,

71. See Pollard, *Wolsey*, pp. 85–86; also *Select Cases before the King's Council
in the Star Chamber*, II (Selden Soc., London, 1911), lxix–lxxi.
72. *De Republica Anglorum*, edited by L. Alston (Cambridge, 1906), Book II,
Chap. 3. The *De Republica Anglorum*, first published at London in 1583, is a
description of the English government under the Tudors.
73. See the opinion of Sir Robert Berkeley in Hampden's case, quoted in
Allen, *English Political Thought, 1603–1660*, pp. 18–19.

"considering that sudden causes and occasions fortune many times which do require speedy remedies, and that by abiding for a parliament in the meantime might happen great prejudice to ensue to the Realm." Moreover, the statute 26 Hen. VIII, c. 10, empowering the king to repeal a previous act which had forbidden the importation of French wines at certain seasons, was passed because of the league which had lately been concluded between the king's majesty "and other foreign kings and princes." Sir Thomas Smith observed that absolute administration, which in time of peace "is very dangerous," is most necessary in time of war when the normal machinery of government is topsy-turvy.[74] Even Cromwell, in a letter to the Duke of Norfolk, implied that the king might issue proclamations against the conveying of coin out of the realm only if the situation were acutely dangerous.[75]

However that may be, the remarkable thing about the early Tudor theorists was not that they admitted the king's right to legislate out of parliament, nor that they occasionally qualified that right by implying that it was to be used only under extraordinary circumstances. It was their habit of discussing legislation as the joint product of king *and* parliament that was new. Seven years of the Reformation Parliament had accustomed men to think in terms of parliament, and though they had no doubts about the king's legislative prerogative out of parliament, they had words only for the new phenomenon rising in their midst. Sir Thomas Smith's statement in the early years of Elizabeth that parliament is "the most high and absolute power of the realm of England," consisting of barons, knights, commons, and bishops, as well as king,

74. *De Republica Anglorum*, pp. 16–17.
75. Merriman, *Life and Letters of Thomas Cromwell*, I, 409–410. Cromwell, writing to Norfolk, says that a statute of 5 Richard II has been found which would allow the king to issue proclamations against the conveying of coin out of the realm. But even if there were no statute, he says, the king might make proclamations anyway, providing the danger were as great "as your Grace alleged at my being with you." For the statute, 5 Richard II, to which Cromwell refers, see *Rotuli Parliamentorum*, III, 102ᵇ, 120ᵃ.

and that what is done by the consent of all these is taken for law,[76] represents a state of mind toward which the whole previous thirty years had been tending.

Probably the most outstanding exponent of the new attitude was Thomas Starkey, that precocious writer who at times thought in terms of Stuart rather than Tudor problems. Without dissembling his words, he alone of the early Reformation political writers attacked the king's prerogative directly as an authority which through the centuries had grown into a "manifest injury." To moderate its effects, he advocated a permanent council of fourteen which should retain at London the authority of the Great Parliament during the latter's dissolution. This "little parliament" should then assign to the king a council of ten by whose authority, together with that of the king as president of the council, all matters pertaining to the realm should be decided, including the problems of war and peace.[77] Had Starkey's suggestions been put into practice, the king would thus have been unable to legislate at all without parliamentary interference, direct or indirect. He would have been deprived of his power to levy extra-parliamentary impositions a hundred years before the Civil War, and he would have lost his control over foreign affairs long before the nineteenth century.

But Starkey was a radical among conservatives, and if his *Dialogue between Pole and Lupset* were the only example of an exalted view of parliament, the subject might be dismissed without further ado. In point of fact, however, there were many such opinions in the early sixteenth century, which, while not so revolutionary as Starkey's,[78]

76. *De Republica Anglorum*, pp. 48–49. Smith does, however, devote a separate section of the *De Republica Anglorum* to a discussion of the king's prerogative.

77. *Dialogue between Pole and Lupset*, pp. 169–170, 180–184.

78. Actually, Starkey's views were unique for the early sixteenth century. He probably derived some of his ideas from Marsilius of Padua's *Defensor Pacis*. In my article, "Thomas Starkey and Marsilius of Padua," *Politica*, II, 200, I have pointed out the analogy between Starkey's parliamentary government checking the king, and Marsilius' conciliar government limiting the papal power.

are nevertheless significant.[79] Henry VIII himself was wont in his public statements to identify his actions as closely as possible with the will of parliament, undoubtedly as a device to shift responsibility to other shoulders. In the famous Ferrers case, for example, he said to the lord chancellor and judges "that we at no time stand so highly in our estate royal as in the time of Parliament, wherein we as head, and you as members, are conjoined and knit together in one body politic."[80] And in his answer to the Lincolnshire rebels of 1536, he asserted that the suppression of the monasteries and the Statute of Uses had been granted to the crown by all the nobles and commons in parliament, and had not been set forth by any councillors "upon their mere will and fantasy."[81] There is, moreover, an interesting passage in Sir John Cheke's *Lamentation* in which the celebrated Greek scholar asks rhetorically why the king's grace by the counsel of lords and commons gathered together in parliament cannot do all the things formerly done by the monks' "Roman god."[82] And William Thomas, justifying Henry VIII's actions to a group of Italians, sought a similar refuge in parliamentarianism. Before extirpating the papal authority from England, he said, Henry VIII had called together the parliament "without which he determined no great matter."[83]

79. It is perhaps significant that St. German, in discussing the six grounds upon which the law of England is based, should have neglected to say anything whatever about the king's legislative prerogative. According to the student in the *Doctor and Student* (Dialogue I, Chaps. 5–11), the law of England is based upon the law of reason, the law of God, divers general customs, maxims, particular customs, and statutes "made by our sovereign lord the king and his progenitors, and by the lords spiritual and temporal, and the commons in divers parliaments. . . ." St. German knew perfectly well that the king possessed a legislative prerogative, but the fact remains that he ignored it altogether in his discussion.

80. See Tanner, *Tudor Constitutional Documents*, p. 582.

81. See Hall, *Chronicle*, p. 821.

82. *Lamentation*, p. Biii.

83. *The Pilgrim*, p. 30. In Thomas' *The historie of Italie* (London, 1549), there is also an interesting passage in which he compares the great council of Venice to the English Parliament. "This foresaied great counsaile," he writes, "maie be lykened to our parliament: For vnto it manie mattiers of importaunce are ap-

Other writers, too, who were less directly concerned with defending the king's actions to the general public, were referring to legislation as though it were always by king *and* parliament. These writers knew perfectly well, of course, that such was not actually the case. But the fact that they wrote frequently as though it were so, was of no little significance for the future. In a remarkable passage in a letter to Somerset in 1547, Bishop Gardiner, for example, asserted that the question of whether faith can exclude charity in justification is like the making of laws in parliament "where the acts be passed by three estates . . . wherein we may not say that any one estate only made the law, or that any one estate excludeth the other in the office of making the law." The law has both a body and a soul, Gardiner asserted. The two houses of parliament constitute, as it were, the body, which lies like dead matter "such as is not apt to take life till the King's Majesty hath, by the breath of his mouth, saying, *le Roy le veult,* breathed a full life into it in the conclusion. . . . And as the King's Majesty, in this similitude of making laws, excludeth not in office of the whole the other two estates, no more do the estates, because they devise and frame laws, exclude the King's Majesty in the office of making laws."[84]

There is an equally striking statement in one of St. German's controversial tracts, *An Answer to a Letter.* The lawyer draws a contrast between the *jus regale* and the *jus regale politicum* which he almost certainly got from Fortescue's famous distinction between the *dominium regale* and the *dominium politicum et regale.* The *jus regale,* says St. German, is the rule whereby the king may make laws without his subjects' consent; the *jus regale politicum* that whereby the subjects' consent is necessary to legislation. The *jus regale politicum* is the rule which the king's grace has in this realm, "where he by assent of his lords spiritual

pealed, and that that it dooeth, is vnreformable. By it all offices are geuen" (p. * ii[b]).

84. *Letters of Stephen Gardiner,* pp. 420–421.

and temporal; and of his commons gathered together by his commandment in his parliament may make laws to bind the people."[85] It is significant, too, that wherever St. German speaks of legislation in his other writings, he invariably refers to the "king in parliament," and not to the king alone. In the Additions to the *Doctor and Student*, he is always alluding to the "king in parliament" when specific acts of legislation are discussed. And he says roundly in Dialogue II that "there is no statute made in this realm but by the assent of the lords spiritual and temporal, and of all the commons, that is to say, by the knights of the shire, citizens and burgesses, that be chosen by assent of the commons which in the parliament represent that estate of the whole commons."[86]

Ponet must have had something similar in mind when he wrote in Mary's reign that just as there is a diet in Germany to defend the people against the Emperor, so in France and England there are parliaments which preserve the rule that nothing can be done without the consent of all.[87] Is it not important, moreover, that Henry Brinkelow should have addressed his *Complaint of Roderick Mors* to parliament, which he referred to as "the head council of all realms," rather than to the king, or to the king's council?[88] And though too much cannot be made of a fanciful description, it will be remembered that the government of More's *Utopia* was actually republican. The prince in each city was obliged to share his rule with the representatives of the people, the "Syphograntes" and "Tranibores." "And that is provided that nothing touching the commonwealth shall be confirmed and ratified, unless it has been reasoned of and debated three days in the council, before it be decreed."[89]

There were others, of course, like Wolsey who ignored parliament altogether as a legislative body, or like Crom-

85. *Answer*, pp. Gv^b–Gvi^b.
86. *Doctor and Student*, p. 249.
87. *Short treatise of politic power*, p. Avi^b.
88. *Complaynt of Roderyck Mors*, p. 5.
89. *Utopia*, pp. 135–138.

well who saw in it only a means of executing the royal will. Evidently, Wolsey was distrustful of parliament, for during his régime no parliamentary sessions were held between 1515 and 1529, except for one abortive meeting in 1523. Had he been incautious enough to express an opinion, Wolsey unquestionably would have spoken out for conciliar as opposed to parliamentary or "mixed" government. Cromwell, too, as early as 1523 was expressing his contempt for the dilatory methods of a legislative body which never got anything done.[90] On the whole, however, the men of the early Reformation were speaking of parliament as they had never done before. While not questioning the king's right to legislate out of parliament, they tended in their language to refer always to the king and parliament together as the supreme legislator. The Reformation Parliament was not enough to cause men to change their traditional views about prerogative, especially seeing that crown and parliament were for the moment in alliance. But its extraordinary duration and the momentous problems with which it dealt, definitely enhanced parliament's prestige as a legislative body, and doubtless prepared the way for more radical thinking at the turn of the century. Once the threat of foreign invasion had been removed and the middle class had begun to feel its strength, it would not be long before Englishmen would begin to challenge the specific prerogatives of the king, and to believe with Prynne that the king has no power whatever over "bills of common right."[91] The Reformation Parliament gave the king an increased power in the ecclesiastical sphere, but in the secular realm it unwittingly sowed the seeds of his future humiliation.

90. Cromwell to John Creke, Aug. 17, 1523, printed in Merriman, *Life and Letters of Thomas Cromwell*, I, 313–314. Cromwell tells his friend Creke how he has "indured" a parliament for seventeen weeks during which such questions as war, peace, strife, contention, proverty, riches, justice, equity, how a commonwealth may be edified, etc., were discussed. In conclusion, he says, we have done as our predecessors, "lefte wher we begann."

91. See Allen, *English Political Thought, 1603–1660*, p. 440. The quotation is from Prynne's *Soveraigne Power of Parliamente and Kingdomes*.

3. KING IN PARLIAMENT

So far it has been determined that the king's power was held to be strictly limited (1) by natural law, and (2) by parliament. It is already evident that the Tudor theorists were not prepared to ascribe to the king *solus* an unlimited supremacy. They advocated "the older constitutional conception of a harmony of powers" by which king, parliament, and the other courts shared the political power of the realm, each possessing certain inherent rights based on customary law, and not on delegation.[92] But what of the king *in* parliament? Did the political writers assign to the king, lords, and commons working in conjunction, if not to the king *solus*, an absolute power of legislation, superior to all other vested corporations or groups within the state, and free of the restrictions of fundamental law? Did the Reformation pamphleteers, in other words, enlarge the powers of the king in parliament and ascribe to him the capacity to create a substantially "new" law? Was the revolution of the thirties productive of a theory of the unlimited sovereignty of the king in parliament?

The fifteenth century, it will be remembered, had returned the medieval verdict that there is no such thing as an unlimited power within the realm; that the king in parliament, no less than the king *solus*, is limited—on the one hand, by the jurisdiction of Church, town corporation, gild; on the other, by natural law. The king in parliament, Fortescue had written, is legally bound to derive his enactments from the higher law. Moreover, "what things soever are either recorded in customs or comprehended in writings, if they be adverse to natural law, are to be held null and void."[93]

The seventeenth-century royalist and parliamentarian theorists repudiated this doctrine in large part. Driven by the heat of the conflict between king and parliament, they enunciated a theory of unlimited sovereignty on the behalf of their respective masters. James I, Thomas

92. See Sabine, *History of Political Theory*, pp. 448–449.
93. See above, p. 9.

Hobbes, Henry Parker, William Prynne—these men abandoned the medieval conception of the law and the "harmony of powers" and asserted the absolute legislative
supremacy of king or parliament in the state.[94] Hobbes,
whose ideas in this respect were not much different from
those expressed by Machiavelli in the *Prince*, advanced
a ruthlessly logical theory of unlimited royal sovereignty.
If society is to avoid anarchy, he stated in the *Leviathan*,
the power of the king must be absolutely unlimited by
either rival jurisdictions, law, or morals. True, civil law
must be in accordance with the law of nature, but this is no
real restriction on the king's power, for it is, after all,
civil law which defines the law of nature. Parker and
Prynne also expounded a philosophy of unlimited sovereignty, but on behalf of parliament rather than the king.
Up to a point, the theory propounded by these two men
was identical. Ultimately, they argued, all power resides
in the people, and therefore in parliament, which is "the
very people itself, artificially congregated." Since parliament is fully sovereign, all powers possessed by the king
are manifestly delegated. To put it in Prynne's words,
"The Parliament is the absolute sovereign power within
the realm, not subject to or obliged by the letter or intend-
ment of any laws, being in truth the sole law-maker and
having an absolute authority over the laws themselves, yea
over Magna Carta . . . to repeal, alter, determine and
suspend them when there is cause."[95]

Now at first glance, it would seem that the Tudor
theorists taught a doctrine of unlimited sovereignty in
respect to king and parliament combined, and that they
were therefore closer in spirit to Hobbes and Prynne than
to Fortescue. At times, men like St. German come very
near to proclaiming the sovereignty of the king in parliament. Pollard has remarked that in Tudor England the
crown in parliament "was emancipated from the control

94. See McIlwain, *High Court of Parliament*, Chap. 5.
95. Quoted in Allen, *English Political Thought, 1603–1660*, p. 443.

of fundamental law."[96] We have already had occasion to note that this was unquestionably the case in actual practice. Under the first two Tudors, medieval liberties were almost entirely absorbed by the central government, and the king in parliament was in fact fast becoming the sole legislative organ of the state. The statute book is ample witness to the thoroughness with which the government wiped out all rival sovereignties. Under Henry VII, acts were passed interfering with borough elections,[97] abolishing franchises,[98] and subordinating corporations to the will of the state.[99] Under Henry VIII, the process was largely completed whereby independent jurisdictions were subordinated to the king in parliament.[100] The expanding statute book under Henry VIII, which comprises 1032 pages as contrasted to 1092 for the whole period from Henry I's Charter to 1509, is a strong indication of the fact that the king in parliament had become the principal legislative authority of the state.[101]

This movement toward centralization was, moreover, reflected occasionally by contemporary writers. The ability of statute law to override custom and previous enactments was affirmed in bolder terms than in the late fifteenth century. Sir Thomas Smith's assertion that parliament "abrogateth old laws, maketh new," and changes the rights and possessions of private men,[102] is typical of the

96. *Evolution of Parliament*, p. 226.

97. For example, the acts restricting the franchise and regulating the elections of Northampton, Leicester, and Exeter. See Pollard, *Henry VII*, II, 181 f, and Pickthorn, *Tudor Government, Henry VII*, p. 141.

98. North and South Tynedale, for example, lost their franchises and were absorbed into the county of Northumberland. See Pickthorn, *Tudor Government, Henry VII*, p. 137.

99. See above, p. 123.

100. By the act 27 Hen. VIII, c. 24, which, among other things, abolished the separate jurisdiction of the palatinate of Durham, and by the anti-ecclesiastical legislation of the Reformation Parliament.

101. See Pollard, *Wolsey*, p. 218, note. Pollard also points out that most of the medieval statutes are given in two languages, while only the single English text is recorded for Henry VIII's statutes.

102. *De Republica Anglorum*, p. 49.

new trend in political thought. The act 25 Hen. VIII, c.
21, for example, declares in its preamble that His Majesty, together with the lords and commons, has full power
and authority to dispense with any laws introduced into
England by the Bishop of Rome, "and all other human
laws of this your Realm." Ponet wrote in a similar vein
that evil customs, "be they never so old," are not to be
tolerated, thereby admitting parliament's right to upset
custom.[103] But St. German surpassed all his contemporaries in eulogizing the powers of parliament. What St. German preached was no less than the doctrine of the infallibility of the king in parliament.[104] In his pamphlet, the
Spirituality and Temporality, he affirmed in the course of
a discussion on mortuaries that, according to those learned
in the law, "the parliament hath an absolute power as to
the possession of all temporal things within this realm, in
whose hands soever they be, spiritual or temporal, to take
them from one man, and give them to another without
any cause or consideration."[105] And in another place, he
stated peremptorily that a statute made against general
customs ought to be observed, and that the law courts
themselves could be changed, and their names altered, by
parliament.[106]

It cannot be doubted that the majority of the early
Tudor political writers believed that the king in parliament constituted the highest political authority of the
realm. What powers they were unwilling to ascribe to
either the king or parliament alone, they bestowed freely
on the king in parliament. Statute law they believed to
be superior to canon law, custom, and "all other human
laws." In this respect, they departed radically from the

103. *Short treatise of politic power*, p. Bvi[b]. Ponet is here repudiating the
idea that a prince, despite the sanction of long custom, may dispense with
positive law.
104. See my article, "Christopher St. German," *Amer.Hist.Rev.*, XLII, p. 646.
105. *Spirituality and Temporality*, p. 228.
106. *Doctor and Student*, pp. 19, 25. On the other hand, it is interesting to
note that in More's opinion, laws could sometimes be abrogated by custom. Let
the king, More says, "not be to hastie in callynge agayne lawes, whyche a
custome hathe abrogated" (*Utopia*, p. 95).

medieval theory of independent jurisdictions, though not so radically, perhaps, from the theory of the late fifteenth century. The king in parliament, they asserted, may promulgate laws in any sphere whatever, spiritual or temporal, free of interference from foreign potentate, convocation, feudal lord, town corporation, or gild.[107] That king and parliament might clash seems seldom to have entered their heads. What they perceived clearly was that king and parliament working in conjunction were supreme within the English state.

But did the political writers mean to imply thereby a theory of unlimited sovereignty such as that propounded later by Hobbes? Did they ascribe to the king in parliament, if not to either king or parliament alone, the power *to legislate* omnipotently, *jus dare?* I think not. In this respect, they spoke the same language as Fortescue, adhering almost entirely to the medieval theory of law. To them, just as to the medieval publicists, law was a thing to be "interpreted," rather than "made," by the rulers of the people. They were not of the opinion that Henry VIII and the Reformation Parliament had enacted anything "new." They had merely "restored" the good old times when the laws of the realm had been more nearly in accord with natural and divine law, and when the king's prerogative had been what it ought to be. To be sure, they believed that statute law was superior to canon and customary law, but this was because they thought (or said so at any rate) that canon and customary law had in many cases run counter to natural law, and thus perverted the order obtaining in the England of yesterday. It was still the universal conviction in the sixteenth century that statute law was derivative of, and subordinate to, that higher law which God had made manifest to man through his reason. Thus, parliament, of which the king was the head, was not primarily a legislative assembly at all, but

---

107. The king *solus* could, of course, promulgate laws for the administration of the Church (see above, Chaps. II, III). If parliament assisted the king in this function, it was by royal delegation.

a court which "interpreted" and promulgated, but did not "make," law.[108]

That the framers of the Henrician statutes were not conscious of changing fundamental law, or of enacting anything new, is revealed by the phraseology of the acts themselves. The description of the laws of England in one act as being "of old antiquity taking commencement founded in the point of right reason according to Justice and Equity"[109] is typical of the spirit of the whole statute book. Some acts were simply intended to be corroborative of former statutes.[110] Others, for example the act concerning artificers and laborers,[111] were passed because of the insufficiency of former statutes dealing with the same problems. And the most important secular laws, those levelled against corporations and franchises, were professedly intended not to create anything new, but to restore the ancient prestige of the king's prerogative. The act 19 Hen. VII, c. 7, for example, was necessitated, according to the reading of the text, because corporations had been making ordinances "contrary to the King's prerogative, his Laws, and the Commonweal of his Subjects." The famous statute 27 Hen. VIII, c. 24, was enacted, according to its preamble, to restore to the "imperial" crown of England "divers of the most ancient prerogatives and authorities of Justice" which it had once enjoyed. The

108. See McIlwain, *High Court of Parliament*, Chaps. 3, 4. Allen questions whether as late as James I any absolute power of lawmaking was recognized. "It may fairly be said," he writes (*English Political Thought, 1603–1660*, p. 12), "that until the difference between an act of legislation and a judgment as to what actually is law was generally recognized, no claim to absolutism could have been, generally, even understood." Sir Edward Coke was entirely medieval in this respect. In Bonham's case, he utterly repudiated the idea of unlimited parliamentary sovereignty. "In many cases," he wrote, "the common law will control acts of Parliament and sometimes adjudge them to be utterly void: for when an act of Parliament is against common right and reason, or repugnant, or impossible to be performed, the common law will control it and adjudge such acts to be void" (quoted in Allen, *ibid.*, p. 37).

109. 7 Hen. VIII, c. 11.

110. See, for example, the act, 1 Hen. VIII, c. 14, against the wearing of costly apparel, and the act, 3 Hen. VIII, c. 13, against the shooting of crossbows.

111. 6 Hen. VIII, c. 3.

alleged purpose of still other acts was to introduce into England an order more in keeping with the laws of God.[112]

That the anti-ecclesiastical statutes of the Reformation Parliament, as well as those laws aimed at secular abuses, were not intended to usher in a "new" order, nor to be subversive of fundamental law, is also apparent from their preambles. To begin with, the preambles denied that the laws of the Church were divine. According to 25 Hen. VIII, c. 14, which provided for a change in the heresy laws, the power of the "Bishop of Rome" is "pretensed," and his laws and decrees "never commonly accepted or confirmed to be any law of God or man within this Realm."[113] It follows that the statutes passed against the privileges of the medieval Church were in no sense directed against divine or natural law. The argument was, in fact, the contrary. The anti-clerical legislation of the Reformation Parliament purported rather to be restoring the realm to a condition more nearly in attune with the dictates of the higher law. Thus, the first Act of Annates was justified on the ground that annates were demanded by Rome only for lucre "against all right and conscience."[114] It was stated in the heresy act that the conviction of any person for heresy except by due accusation did not stand "with the right order of justice or good equity." The anti-clerical laws claimed, moreover, to be reëstablishing a utopian state which had existed in very early times. Illustrative of this claim is the statement in the Act of Appeals that "by divers old authentic histories and chronicles" the realm of England is declared an "empire," sufficient unto itself without the intermeddling of any exterior persons.[115] Where a modern legislative body

112. See, for example, 6 Hen. VIII, c. 5. The decay of market towns, the statute reads, makes the price of food high and the people "sore mynysshed in the realme, whereby the power and defence therof ys feoblyd and empayryd to the hygh dyspleasure of God and agenst hys lawes. . . ."

113. In this connection, see also the act, 28 Hen. VIII, c. 10, whereby the authority of the Bishop of Rome was formally abolished.

114. 24 Hen. VIII, c. 20.

115. 24 Hen. VIII, c. 12.

would cite utility as at least one of the reasons for a radical change of policy, the members of the Reformation Parliament felt that they had to square their proceedings with the fundamental law of nature.

That statute law was held to be strictly subordinate to fundamental law is even more conclusively proven by the statements of the political writers. Following the medieval doctrine, they maintained, first of all, that positive law is in its final analysis an emanation from the laws of nature and God. According to St. German, "a law of man hath not only the strength of man's law, but also the law of reason or of the law of God, whereof it is derived. For laws made by men, which have received of God power to make laws, be made by God."[116] Starkey was of a similar mind. "All good civil laws," he wrote, "spring and issue out of the law of nature, as brooks and rivers out of fountains and wells."[117] Others like Sir Richard Morison were no less emphatic as to the ultimate source of positive law.[118] It is important to notice in this connection, moreover, that to men like Morison and John Rastell,[119] the justification for codifying or abridging the English common law was seen in the fact that positive law expresses the will of God. Morison petitioned the king to have the common laws of the realm codified in the Latin tongue on the ground that "law is the ordinance of God, a rule whereunto every man ought to frame his living," and that at present it is not

116. *Doctor and Student*, p. 52.
117. *Dialogue between Pole and Lupset*, p. 16.
118. Morison said that one must think like the divine Plato, that "all laws, that are made for the wealth and safeguard of man, come of God, albeit they be constituted by men" (P.R.O., St.P. 6: 13, 4, f. 49; cf. *Letters and Papers*, XI, 1409). This manuscript is a treatise against Aske's rebellion. See also the anonymous pamphlet, *Remedy for sedition*, p. Aii, which says that "all those lawes, that are made for the welth and safegarde of mankynde . . . be of God, albeit they be constituted by manne. . . ."
119. John Rastell, printer and barrister, is noted mostly for his publication of various legal works, and for writing *The Pastyme of the People, or the Chronicles of Divers Realms and most especially of the Realm of England*. He was cast into prison, probably because of his relationship to Sir Thomas More (he was More's brother-in-law), and died there in 1536.

available to the people.[120] And Rastell, in one of his pro-
logues to legal works, maintained that man cannot attain
to the *summum bonum* except through the medium of laws,
"which reasonable ordinances and laws proceed and come
principally of God, to the which the providence and will of
God is ever assistant and present."[121]

The political writers asserted, in the second place, that
not only is positive law a derivative of natural and divine
law, but that it is also essentially an "interpretation" or
legitimate extension of the latter. In answer to Martin
Bucer's declaration that there is nothing left for princes
to legislate about, since everything is contained in divine
law, Gardiner rejoined that everything is contained in the
Scriptures "implicitly," but not "explicitly." Whatever
is good or bad, he said, is prescribed in general by divine
law, but human law, taking its example from the Scriptures, may prescribe specific things "according as they
appear good or bad in their very use and performance."[122]
St. German, too, had this idea of interpretation or extension in mind when he said that positive law is "superadded"
to the laws of reason and God "for the better ordering of
the commonwealth."[123] The sixth ground of the law of
England, he affirmed, stands in divers statutes, which were
deemed necessary in such cases where the laws of reason
and God did not seem sufficient to punish the evil and
reward the good.[124]

Thirdly, the political writers emphasized the fact that
in no case must positive law go against the precepts of

120. British Museum, Cotton MSS., Faustina C II, f. 7; cf. *Letters and Papers*,
XVII, App., no. 2. This manuscript is apparently the original draft of the contemporary copy preserved in the Royal MSS., 18 AL. The latter was evidently
the presentation copy sent to the king, for its binding displays the royal arms
with the initials "H.R." (Henricus Rex).

121. *La Liver des Assises et plees del Corone* (London, 1561), "Prologus
Iohannis Rastel in laudem legum."

122. "Contemptum humanae legis," Janelle, *Obedience in Church and State*,
p. 201.

123. *Doctor and Student*, p. 52.

124. *Ibid.*, pp. 35–36.

natural and divine law. Human interpretation, they said, must never be carried to such an extent as to change God's intent. In St. German's words, neither prescription, statute, nor custom may prevail against the law of nature. "And if any be brought in against it, they be not prescriptions, statutes, nor customs, but things void and against justice."[125] Or, stated in Starkey's language, the law of nature is the ground of all civil laws, to which the latter must ever be referred, "none otherwise than the conclusions of arts mathematical are ever referred to their principles."[126]

Sir Thomas More was also an exponent of this conception of law. In the *Utopia* he directed a bitter attack against the law of parliament by which thieves were made punishable by hanging. God has commanded us that we should not kill, he stated, and yet in this instance man's constitutions have ordained killing to be lawful. If this sort of thing should continue, "shall it not then by this reason follow, that the power of God's commandment shall extend no further, than man's law doth define, and permit?"[127] In 1535 the famous martyr was to take his stand against the Act of Supremacy on precisely the same principle. After the jury had found him guilty at Westminster Hall, he stepped forth and denounced his indictment as being grounded on an act of parliament "directly repugnant to the laws of God and his holy Church" and hence as insufficient to charge any man.[128]

The Henrician reformers, men like St. German and Fox, would not have agreed with More that an act against canon law was, in fact, an act against divine law. In the *Doctor and Student* St. German writes that "all the laws canon be not the laws of God."[129] And Fox makes a neat distinction in the *De vera differentia* between "canon" law and "private" law, asserting that in the event of clash

125. *Ibid.*, p. 5.
126. *Dialogue between Pole and Lupset*, p. 16.
127. *Utopia*, pp. 61–62.
128. Roper, *Life of More*, pp. 92–93.
129. *Doctor and Student*, p. 8.

between the two, the bishops' commandments "giveth place unto the private law."[130] But men of all creeds would have agreed in principle, if not in interpretation, that in no case could statute law stand against God's law. In the final analysis, any kind of positive law was held to be derivative of God, not man, the function of the latter being to "interpret," and not to "make," law. And if the interpretation should by any chance run counter to the manifest intent of divine law, it was to be held void.

Thus, the Reformation political writers were no more advocates of unlimited sovereignty than their fifteenth-century predecessors. The king in parliament, no less than the king in council, they held to be strictly limited. They attributed to king and parliament together vaster powers than they had ever wielded before—they might now promulgate laws against custom, corporation, and priest. But the king in parliament was still understood to be rendering judicial decisions according to a fundamental law. His was not the omnipotent power of the twentieth-century legislator by whose authority alone a new order can be enacted into being overnight. His was the more humble prerogative of the law court which has no right—in theory —to create anything "new." It was not until the seventeenth century that a theory of unlimited sovereignty saw the light of day—in the writings of royalists and parliamentarians, provoked by each other into saying more than they perhaps believed.

4. THE KING AND POSITIVE LAW

THE political writers of the English Reformation not only held that the king, in both council and parliament, was subordinate to natural law. They maintained that he was under positive law as well, whether promulgated in the form of statute or custom. This they were logically forced to do, since, as we have already seen, positive law was understood to be natural law rendered explicit. As St.

130. *De vera differentia*, p. 37. By "private" law Fox means, of course, natural law.

German said, "the law of man (the which sometime is called the law positive) is derived by reason, as a thing which is necessary, and probably following of the law of reason and of the law of God."[131] If the king was subordinate to natural law, he had also to be under positive law, since in the final analysis the two were identical. Thus, in still another instance the early Tudor theorists preferred Fortescue and the fifteenth-century tradition to the contemporary continental doctrine. James I's statement that "the King is above the law," and that laws made in parliament may be suspended by the king "upon causes only known to him"[132] was wholly alien to the early sixteenth-century point of view.

On the continent political theory was reflecting practical politics more faithfully than in England. Machiavelli had the same disrespect for law *per se* as the Italian princes whose method of ruling he depicted so vividly in the *Prince*. In France, in proportion as the French monarchy increased in power, at least one group of civil lawyers proclaimed the unconditional authority of the king in relation to positive law. In his *Commentary on the Digest*, Jason de Mayno cited Baldus as having said that the prince has *plenitudo potestatis*, and that he therefore can do anything "supra jus et contra jus, et extra jus."[133] Guillaume Budé, one of the most celebrated of all French civilians, likewise maintained that the prince is *legibus solutus*. The *Princeps*, he said, cannot be treated as the equal of others, for he is a god among men. It is therefore absurd to impose law on him, since he is a law unto himself.[134] True, there was another group of civilians, headed by Alciatus of Milan and the famous Cujas, which denounced the "adulation" of jurists, and repudiated the

---

131. *Doctor and Student*, pp. 9–10.
132. *The Political Works of James I*, p. 63.
133. R. W. and A. J. Carlyle, *History of Mediaeval Political Theory in the West*, VI, 149. Jason did, however, make the reservation that the prince is bound to observe any contracts he has made with his subjects. For contracts, he maintained, are founded on natural law and the *jus gentium* (see *ibid.*, VI, 154–156).
134. *Ibid.*, VI, 294–295.

notion that the prince is above positive law.[135] But the
French monarchy was at least not entirely wanting for
theoretical justification.

In England, on the other hand, political theory was
slow to reflect the growth of monarchical power. Despite
the sometimes arbitrary rule of ministers like Wolsey and
Cromwell, the enhancement of the king's prerogative in
consequence of the Reformation, and the increasing power
of the royal courts of equity, the Henrician attitude
toward the king and positive law remained fundamentally
conservative. Fortescue had said that in England the
dominium politicum et regale, rather than the *dominium
regale*, prevailed, and that therefore the king of England
could be said to be under positive law. This view the early
Tudor theorists accepted without alteration. Like their
medieval predecessors, they conceded that the king, in
some instances *prescribed by law and custom*, might stand
outside the law, or dispense with the law in particular
cases. But this was a different thing from saying, like
Budé, that the king is *legibus solutus*, or, like James I, that
the king may suspend laws "upon causes only known to
him." In point of fact, the principles of the coronation
oath constituted the norm by which the king's actions were
theoretically measured in the sixteenth century, and the
royal prerogative was defined for the most part in traditional fashion. That this was the case is evident from the
careful way in which the king's spiritual prerogative,
inherited from the Act of Supremacy, was restricted to
the spiritual realm, and held to be inoperative in secular
affairs. The evidence also indicates that the threat of the
prerogative courts to the common law was not nearly so
terrifying to contemporaries as has been generally supposed. As we have already noted in another connection,
it was not until the monarchy had begun to decline in the

135. *Ibid.*, VI, 298–301. To these men the term *legibus solutus* meant something entirely different from what it signified to Jason and Budé. They understood it to mean simply that the prince can remit penalties which he himself has
imposed; certainly not that the prince can suspend laws at his pleasure.

seventeenth century that a full-fledged theory of royal absolutism made its appearance in England.

If this was the case, how then, it might fairly be asked,
is one to interpret the radical assertions of a Tyndale or
a Gardiner? What does Tyndale mean when he says "that
the king is, in this world, without law; and may at his lust
do right or wrong, and shall give accounts to God only"?
Does not Gardiner imply that the king is *legibus solutus*
when he says that God has enjoined implicit obedience to
kings without so much as "one syllable of exception"?
That these statements cannot be taken at their face value
is, I think, beyond question. As noted above, the royal
eulogists were over-stating their case, either to save their
own skins, or to set up an antidote to the papacy.[136] The
repudiation of papal power in England could be effected
only by singing the extravagant praises of the king. Certain letters of Gardiner's, written years after the publication of his *De vera obedientia*, indicate clearly that in a
calmer mood, the Bishop of Winchester did not for a min-
ute believe in the superiority of the king to positive law.[137]
In any event, the objective of Tyndale and Gardiner in
the passages quoted above is hardly germane to the present investigation. These reformers were interested in proving, not that the king is above positive law, but rather that
in case the law should perchance be broken, subjects must
not rebel. They did not stop to consider the obligations of
the king to his people, at least in the legal sense. They were
interested only in stating the obligations of the people to
their king, who, in their opinion, whether ruling rightly or
wrongly, must be suffered.

On the whole, it is clear that the early Tudor political
writers were defining the king's relationship to positive
law in terms of the coronation oath. In this they were
simply following Fortescue and their fifteenth-century
forbears. The language of the king's oath, "to hold and
keep the laws and rightful customs of this realm," is to be

136. See above, pp. 125–126.
137. See below, pp. 172–173.

found in the words of the king himself, in the statute books, and in most of the contemporary political treatises. True, Henry VIII caused a new coronation oath to be drafted, the saving clauses of which would have enabled the king to behave toward the law as he saw fit.[138] But the oath thus revised was never administered either to himself or to Edward VI,[139] and in 1533 Henry was writing to Rome that he could not submit his marriage cause to a foreign jurisdiction without the consent of the realm, the laws of which he was bound by oath to observe.[140] St. German was of a similar mind. By the coronation oath, he said, the king is sworn to maintain the customs of the realm, and to see that they are faithfully observed.[141] The king must administer justice to his people according to the laws of the realm,[142] and under no circumstances can he make arbitrary changes or grants. For example, the various courts of the realm, which are established by the common law, "may not be altered, nor their names changed, without parliament."[143] If the king's grace were to make a grant to the bishops of the realm to hold plea of temporal things, as the Emperor Theodosius once stipulated, "the grant were void, for it were against his laws."[144]

The Henrician statutes, despite their exaltation of the royal prerogative in other respects, were no less emphatic in stating the principles of the coronation oath. The Act of Proclamations is a beautiful case in point. It starts out by asserting that henceforth royal proclamations are to be obeyed as of equal validity with acts of parliament. It ends with an all-important saving clause calculated to prevent arbitrary action on the king's part. The words of this

138. In Henry's draft, the king swears to uphold the laws and customs of the realm "*not prejudicial to his crown or Imperial Jurisdiction* [italics mine]." See *English Coronation Records*, edited by L. G. W. Legg, p. 241.

139. *Ibid.*, p. 240.
140. Pocock, *Records of the Reformation*, II, 438–439.
141. *Doctor and Student*, p. 18.
142. *Answer*, p. Av.
143. *Doctor and Student*, p. 19.
144. *Power of the Clergy*, p. Gvii.

act, the statute concludes, shall not be understood in such a way that the king's liege people "should have any of . . . their inheritances, lawful possessions, offices, liberties, privileges, franchises, goods, or cattle taken from them, . . . nor by virtue of the said act suffer any pains of death, other than shall be hereafter in this act declared, nor that by any proclamation to be made by virtue of this act, any acts, common laws standing at this present time in strength and force, nor yet any lawful or laudable customs of this realm . . . shall be infringed, broken, or subverted."[145] The second Act of Succession, following the same line, states that the king can best provide a successor for the realm by choosing one who will "follow in the just and right track of all [his] proceedings, and maintain, keep, and defend the same, and all the laws and ordinances established in [his] gracious time for the wealth of this realm."[146] The statutes also had something to say about the limitations of the king's spiritual prerogative, but this subject will be examined in another connection.

Cromwell, of course, has always been cited as evidence of a different point of view. Tradition would have it that here was a statesman of a new cast of thought, a believer in absolute monarchy, a man who had only contempt for the tenets of the coronation oath. According to his biographer, Cromwell was a man who had drunk deep of the spirit of the Renaissance, who "read and studied his Machiavelli, so that it was a guide to his future political career."[147] Now no doubt something of the sort was true. As we have already seen, Cromwell expressed his exasperation at the dilatory methods of the parliament of 1523.[148] And no doubt he was contemptuous of all merely legal restrictions when the use of the royal prerogative might work a change for the good of the state. Cromwell's motto was probably not unlike Strafford's "Thorough" a hun-

145. 31 Hen. VIII, c. 8.
146. 28 Hen. VIII, c. 7.
147. Merriman, *Life and Letters of Thomas Cromwell,* I, 85.
148. See above, p. 152, n. 90.

dred years later, or James I's belief that in times of stress and danger the king alone can save the state.

It is well to point out, however, that Cromwell was no political theorist, and that therefore he probably had no theoretical views whatever about the relation of the king to the law.[149] Moreover, it is not without significance that the evidence representing Cromwell as a student of Machiavelli and of the political principles of the *Corpus Juris Civilis* is culled almost entirely from the statements of his political enemies. Eustace Chapuys, Cardinal Pole, and Stephen Gardiner, they were the men who testified that Cromwell's political views were revolutionary and subversive. According to Chapuys, Cromwell had boasted that he would make his master the wealthiest prince in Christendom, and had said that the Turk might well be called king or prince for the absolute authority he wields over his subjects.[150] As the agent of the Holy Roman Emperor, however, Chapuys may well have been prejudiced against the man who, more than any other, was responsible for the success of the English Reformation. Cardinal Pole wrote of Cromwell with an even more obvious bias. In his *Apologia ad Carolum Quintum*, written in 1539, Pole says that some years before, Cromwell had suggested that a king is above all laws, since he has the power to change them. A prudent councillor should therefore study first the inclination of his prince, and afterwards his honor. On the occasion of which Pole speaks, Cromwell had allegedly recommended the study of Machiavelli's *Prince* for anyone who did not pursue a dream like Plato, and who was interested in the practical art of government.[151] But the *Apologia ad Carolum Quintum* was written at a time when its author was embittered at his failure to organize a continental crusade against Henry VIII.[152] This failure he associated in

---

149. Merriman notes (*Thomas Cromwell*, I, 86) that Cromwell sought after the practical and useful only, and had little time for men who indulged in idle theorizing.

150. *Letters and Papers*, VII, 1554.

151. *Ibid.*, XIV(1), 200, pp. 82–83.

152. On this point, see Paul Van Dyke, *Renascence Portraits*, pp. 388–389.

his mind with the king's minister, and it was only natural therefore for Pole to refer to Cromwell as *Nuncius Satanae*, the follower of Machiavelli, the evil genius who from a high mountain had tempted his royal master with world dominion. In the enthusiasm of the moment, Pole was led to say things about Cromwell which had no foundation in fact, and which have stigmatized the latter's name ever since.[153] Nor can Gardiner be regarded as a more reliable source for Cromwell's political views. For Gardiner, it must be remembered, was Cromwell's most formidable political opponent in 1538 and 1539, and Cromwell's execution had been immediately followed by the Bishop of Winchester's return to royal favor.[154] How, therefore, is one to evaluate Gardiner's story of how once at Hampton Court, in the presence of the king, Cromwell had turned to him and said, "Come on, my lord of Winchester, answer the king here, but speak plainly and directly, and shrink not, man! Is not that that pleaseth the king a law? Have you not there in the civil law *quod principi placuit*, and so forth?"[155]

153. For the authenticity of Pole's evidence against Cromwell, see *ibid.*, App., "Reginald Pole and Thomas Cromwell." Van Dyke makes the point that Pole did not regard Cromwell as "possessed by the devil" until 1539 when he was unduly embittered by the turn of events. Van Dyke points out that the correspondence between Pole and Cromwell before 1539 had been entirely amicable, and that Pole's book, the *Pro ecclesiasticae unitatis defensione*, written in 1536, had not so much as mentioned Cromwell, although it had bitterly attacked Sampson's *Oratio*.

Moreover, the view that Cromwell "read and studied his Machiavelli, so that it was a guide to his future political career," Van Dyke also disproves beyond any reasonable doubt (pp. 413–414). He shows that this belief is based entirely on Pole's testimony in the *Apologia ad Carolum Quintum*, and that it ignores a letter written by Harry, Lord Morley, to Cromwell on February 13, 1539. In this letter (calendared in *Letters and Papers*, XIV(1), 285; printed in full in *Original Letters*, edited by Sir Henry Ellis, London, 1846, Third Series, III, 63–67), Morley writes to Cromwell that he is sending him Machiavelli's *de Principe*, as though it were a novelty being called to the minister's attention for the first time. As Van Dyke says, the strong probability is that Morley knew more than Pole about Cromwell's knowledge of Machiavelli, for Morley had often talked to Cromwell on political and literary subjects, whereas Pole had conversed with him only once in his life.

154. See Pickthorn, *Early Tudor Government, Henry VIII*, pp. 421–422, 447.

155. Letter to Somerset, October 14, 1547, printed in *Letters of Stephen Gardiner*, p. 399.

Whatever may be the truth about Cromwell's political views, one thing is certain. If Cromwell's motto was really the famous civil-law phrase, *quod principi placuit legis habet vigorem*, he surely did not want for opponents in sixteenth-century England. Did not Sir Thomas More write a *carmen gratulatorium* in honor of Henry VIII's accession to the throne, because the laws, "which had no strength before, nay were forced to do wrong" under the king's father, were now to regain their strength under the new king?[156] Starkey advocated a reception of Roman law into England,[157] but his writings show that he was stoutly opposed to the political principle implied therein. In his *Dialogue between Pole and Lupset*, Starkey affirms in no uncertain terms that "the laws, which be sincere and pure reason, without any spot or blot of affection, must have chief authority; they must rule and govern the state, and not the prince after his own authority and will."[158] Very judiciously, Starkey makes an exception of Henry VIII whose wisdom, he says, is so great "that he may right well and justly be subject to no law." But Starkey takes care to add that after Henry dies, the assembled parliament should choose a successor "which should not rule and govern all at his own pleasure and liberty, but ever be subject to the order of his laws."[159] During such time as the parliament is dissolved, he adds, its authority should be vested in a permanent council of fourteen whose function it should be to defend the liberty of the people, and to see to it that the king does nothing against the ordinance of his laws and good policy.[160]

Taverner and Gardiner were no less vehement in repudiating the civil-law phrase. In Tavener's case, denunciation of the *quod principi placuit* maxim is especially sig-

---

156. *Epigrammata*, p. 19. The Latin is as follows:

"Leges invalidae prius, imò nocere coactae,
Nunc vires gaudent obtinuisse suas."

157. *Dialogue between Pole and Lupset*, p. 194.
158. *Ibid.*, p. 181.
159. *Ibid.*, p. 168.
160. *Ibid.*, pp. 169–170.

nificant, for Taverner was in Cromwell's pay, and might therefore have been reasonably expected to mirror his master's political views. But in the *Garden of Wisdom*, Taverner does not mince his words. Did not Antigonus, king of Macedonia, he asks, reprove the flatterer who averred that all things are honest and just to kings? Did not Antigonus himself say that the king is the minister, not the rule, of honesty and justice? "Would God the ears of Christian rulers were not tickled with like tales, and if they be, that they would with like severity reject them. For what other thing say they, which sing them this note, *Quod principi placuit legis habet vigorem:* that is to say: That liketh the prince hath the strength of law? Which say that the prince is not bound to laws, which give him two manner powers, an ordinary power, and an absolute power, whereof the one can do what the laws, pacts and leagues demand, the other whatsoever it lusteth."[161]

Gardiner's letters to Somerset and the Privy Council in 1547 were almost equally vehement on this score. True, these letters were primarily concerned with limiting the king's spiritual prerogative, but they contain as well immensely important statements of a more general character. In the letter to Somerset quoted above,[162] Gardiner says he answered Cromwell's insolent query at Hampton Court by rejoining to the king that although he had heard of monarchs whose will had been received for a law, he nevertheless opined that it was surer and quieter for kings to make the laws their will. "By this form of government you be established, and it is agreeable with the nature of your people."[163] In other letters, Gardiner cites precedents to show that the king's will has always been held to be subordinate to statute and common law. Chancellor Audley once said, he writes to the Privy Council, that he had never heard of any act of parliament being broken, until the

161. *Garden of Wisdom,* Book I, pp. Cvii^b–Cviii.
162. See above, p. 170.
163. *Letters of Stephen Gardiner,* p. 399.

same had by like authority of parliament been repealed.[164] Judges and lawyers have consistently maintained that the king may not command against an act of parliament, and that subjects may not break the law even with the king's consent. For example, Cardinal Wolsey obtained his legacy from Rome at Henry VIII's request, but he was nevertheless convicted of *praemunire* by the judges because his action was against the laws of the realm.[165] Moreover, one article of indictment which weighed heavily against Wolsey was his grant of injunctions to stay the common laws in the name of the king. "And upon that occasion *Magna Charta* was spoken of, and it was made a great matter, the stay of the Common Law."[166] Chancellor Tiptoft suffered on Tower Hill for likewise offending the laws of the realm, although in so doing he was merely executing the king's commission.[167] And although those who spoke against Queen Anne in parliament did so at the king's special behest, they were obliged to sue for a pardon "because that speaking was against an act of parliament."[168]

Denunciation of the civil-law principle was no less fashionable among the radical Protestants during the reigns of Edward VI and Mary. Hooper wrote in 1551 that men are bound to obey the king "as the king himself is bound to be obedient unto the law, . . . where the laws be not contrary to the law of God and the law of nature."[169] Ponet thundered from Strassburg that kings are but executors of God's and men's laws, and are therefore not exempt from their dictates. "For good and just laws of

164. *Ibid.*, pp. 369–370.
165. *Ibid.*, p. 390.
166. *Ibid.*, p. 391.
167. *Ibid.*, pp. 390–391. John Tiptoft, Earl of Worcester, had aided Edward IV in wreaking vengeance on the Lancastrian party. He was executed for his "butchery" in 1470, despite the fact that Edward was ultimately responsible for his actions.
168. *Ibid.*, p. 377. The act of parliament referred to is the first Act of Succession (25 Hen. VIII, c. 22). By this act the crown was entailed upon Henry's children by Anne Boleyn, and it was made high treason "by writing, print, deed, or act" to do anything to the prejudice of the Boleyn marriage.
169. "Annotations on Romans 13," *Later Writings of Bishop Hooper*, p. 101.

man be God's power and ordinance, and they [kings] are but ministers of the laws, and not the laws self."[170] William Kethe's lines censuring tyrants reveal a similar attitude toward the king and the law. Tyrants, he said, care not how they kill in their cruel rage,

"Respecting their will more, than law, oath, or charge.
Whose fury long fostered by sufferance and awe,
Have right rule subverted, and made will their law."[171]

An even stronger case in point was the attitude of Sir James Hales, judge of the common pleas, toward the accession of Mary. Though a Protestant who must have anticipated with dismay the rule of a Catholic queen, Hales obstinately refused to sign the document whereby Mary was to be excluded from the throne in favor of Lady Jane Grey, on the ground that the succession could only be legally altered by act of parliament, and, by implication, never by a minister acting in the king's name.[172]

This denunciation of the principle implied in the phrase, *quod principi placuit legis habet vigorem*, meant more specifically that the king might not wrest the law to his own advantage through the medium of his judges, and that he might not levy illegal taxes. Tudor Englishmen, it must be confessed, had little to say on these subjects, doubtless because it was the pope, not the king, who was the object of their immediate attack. But what they did say was in line with the opinions expressed by judges and parliamentarians in the succeeding century. In the *Utopia*, for example, More bitterly attacked the New Monarchy, and, among other things, inveighed against the king for trying to influence judges. The manner in which More

170. *Short treatise of politic power*, p. Cvi.
171. "William Kethe to the Reader," printed at the end of Goodman's *How superior powers ought to be obeyed of their subjects*.
172. See article in *D.N.B.*, "Sir James Hales." Hales was in high favor during the reign of Edward VI, and was extremely active in supporting the Reformation. He was created Knight of the Bath at the coronation of Edward VI. In 1549 he was placed on the commission for the extirpation of heresy, and in the same year was appointed judge of the common pleas. He also sat on the commission which deprived Bishops Bonner and Gardiner.

denounced the practice of summoning the judges to argue in the royal presence calls to mind Sir Edward Coke's opinion one hundred years later in the *Commendams* case.[173] The judges, More said, would be thrown into confusion by the royal presence, and would in the end "in every matter dispute and reason for the king's right."[174] In corroboration of More's point of view, Gardiner wrote in 1547 that there were many examples of judges with fines set on their heads for having rendered decisions against the laws of the realm by the royal command.[175]

There was no Petition of Right in the early sixteenth century to denounce extra-parliamentary taxation formally. But there was one significant case in which the king's demand for a benevolence was frustrated. To pay for the war against France without recourse to parliament which was bound to be hostile to ecclesiastical privileges, Wolsey in 1525 demanded an Amicable Loan of unprecedented proportions.[176] When this aroused violent opposition, Wolsey had recourse to a benevolence which was in turn rejected by the mayor and aldermen of the city of London. At a meeting between Wolsey and the city council, one of the councillors averred that the benevolence requested was illegal, because contrary to a statute made in the first year of Richard III.[177] Wolsey insisted that Richard was a usurper, and that therefore his acts were neither good nor honorable. The councillor rejoined that though Richard had done evil, "yet in his time were many good acts made not by him only, but by the consent of the body of the whole realm, which is the parliament." The mayor

173. In this case, decided in 1616, the king's right to make presentations to livings *in commendam* was questioned. James I requested that the judges debate the matter in his presence before they rendered a decision. Coke, alone of all the judges, denounced James' action as constituting an attack on judicial independence. For a discussion of this case, see J.R.Tanner, *English Constitutional Conflicts of the Seventeenth Century* (Cambridge, 1928), pp. 39–40.

174. *Utopia*, pp. 90–91.

175. *Letters of Stephen Gardiner*, pp. 390–391.

176. Wolsey demanded a sixth of lay, and a third of ecclesiastical, property.

177. The statute referred to is 1 Rich. III, c. 2, which made benevolences illegal.

added that the act against benevolences might be revoked by the same common council, that is, parliament, and not otherwise.[178]

But what about the royal prerogative courts? It is a well-known fact that if ever England was in danger of a reception of Roman law, it was during the first half of the sixteenth century,[179] and that in any case, the common law courts were losing business to the courts of chancery, star chamber, and requests. The cessation of the Year Books in 1535 at the height of the Henrician Reformation, the foundation of new lectureships in civil law at Oxford and Cambridge, the use of civil law in the courts of admiralty and the two universities, and the importation of the continental idea that the crown and its servants are outside the ordinary law[180]—do not all these facts convey the impression that the common law was, to use Maitland's expression, "by no means lusty" in the early sixteenth century? And that a certain group around the king was beginning to exalt the royal prerogative above the law?

Holdsworth is of the opinion that the threat to English common law in the reign of Henry VIII has been greatly exaggerated, but he admits that its supremacy "was in serious danger."[181] It is evident that political and economic changes in the fifteenth and sixteenth centuries were creating a new problem with which the common law, with its increasing rigidity of procedure, could not cope. Whether the danger to the common law was threatened by Roman law, or a new royal law, is not so important. The fact remains that under Henry VIII, chancery, star chamber, and requests were interpreting and extending and, indeed, sometimes reversing the decisions of the common

178. For this whole case, see Hall's *Chronicle*, pp. 698–699. For further discussion, see Pickthorn, *Early Tudor Government, Henry VIII*, pp. 67–69; Tanner, *Tudor Constitutional Documents*, pp. 620–624.

179. On this point, see Maitland's essay, *English Law and the Renaissance* (Cambridge, 1901).

180. For a discussion of these points, see Holdsworth, *History of English Law* (London, 5th edition), IV, 217–293.

181. *Ibid.*, IV, 258–285.

law in the interests of strong government and equity.
Chancery was interfering to give landowners a more equitable ownership over their property than they possessed
by common law, to enforce contracts because of the inade-
quacy of the common law on this score, and, among other
things, to issue injunctions where the common law could
not act at all.[182] The star chamber was exercising its jurisdiction in the interests of order against rioting and the corruption of local jurors; and, after the nightmare of civil
strife had passed, in the regulation of economics.[183] The
court of requests was attempting to protect the copyholders and tenants-at-will against the rigors of the enclosure
movement.[184] With the king's writ running everywhere,
were there not publicists at court to expound a philosophy
of *legibus solutus*?

It cannot be doubted that the incompatibility between
the prerogative courts and the common law was keenly
felt by contemporaries. The landowners were particularly
indignant against the "new law" for interfering with their
economic freedom, although, it must be confessed, they
never directly attacked the king's prerogative. Time and
again, enclosing and rack-renting landlords like John
Mulsho[185] and William Frauncys[186] echoed the refrain that
the case in question "is matter determinable at the common law and not in this court [star chamber or re-
quests]."[187] The landowners naturally resented the efforts
of the central government to fix prices, to control food

182. *Ibid.*, I, 454–459.
183. See *Select Cases before the King's Council in the Star Chamber* (Selden
Soc., London, 1903, 1911), II, Introduction by I.S.Leadam. The government
constantly interfered in the interest of the consumer to prevent engrossing,
exportation of foodstuffs, and rise in prices.
184. See *Select Cases in the Court of Requests, A. D. 1497–1569* (Selden Soc.,
London, 1898), Introduction by I.S.Leadam.
185. The case of John Mulsho and his grandson, Thomas Mulsho, *vs.* the
tenants of the manor of Thingden, Northamptonshire, between 1494 and 1538,
is a beautiful illustration of the way in which the prerogative courts interfered
in the interest of copyholders and tenants-at-will. See *Select Cases before the
King's Council in the Star Chamber*, II, lix–xc, 6–67.
186. See *Select Cases in the Court of Requests*, pp. lxvii–lxviii.
187. *Select Cases before the King's Council in the Star Chamber*, II, 22.

distribution, and to protect the small farmer. Their only salvation lay in pleading the adequacy of the common-law courts, where their chances of obtaining a favorable decision were greater. Sometimes they went so far as to denounce the action of the central government as tyrannous. John Mulsho, for example, protested vigorously against Wolsey's arbitrary writ ordering the sheriff of Northamptonshire to destroy his enclosures. This writ, he exclaimed, was sent out "without calling the said John Mulsho by any ordinary process to make answer to the same and without any Inquisition or other matter of Record remaining in the said court of Chancery or elsewhere proving the said Inclosure to be contrary to any laws or statutes of this Realm. . . ."[188]

The indignation of the landowners was shared by the common lawyers. In 1547 they accused Chancellor Wriothesley of having "many times altered and violated" the laws of the realm by reason of decrees made in chancery.[189] Their professional jealousy of the prerogative courts is best illustrated, however, by a tract ostensibly written by a "serjeant at the laws of England" to refute certain passages in St. German's *Doctor and Student.*[190] The author defends the common law vigorously against the encroachments of chancery, which he clearly envisages as an instrument of tyranny which would set all law at naught. If a *subpoena* issued in chancery be allowed to take effect, he says, "the king's subjects shall be ordered by the discretion of the chancellor and by no law."[191] "For these two laws," he continues, "one being contrary to the other, cannot stand together, but one of them must be as void. Wherefore it must needs follow, that, if this law be

188. *Ibid.*, II, 40.
189. *Acts of the Privy Council, 1547–1550*, pp. 48–57.
190. This tract is entitled *A Replication of a Serjaunte at the Lawes of England, to certayne Pointes alleaged by a Student of the said Lawes of England, in a Dialogue in Englishe between a Doctor of Divinity and the said Student.* It is printed in *A Collection of Tracts relative to the Law of England* (Dublin, 1787), edited by Francis Hargrave, pp. 323–331.
191. *Ibid.*, p. 325.

maintained in the chancery by a *subpoena*, the common
law, which is contrary to that, must needs be as void and
of no effect. I marvel much what authority the chancellor
hath to make such a writ in the king's name, and how he
dare presume to make such a writ to let the king's subjects
to sue his laws, the which the king himself cannot do right-
wisely; for he is sworn the contrary and it is said, *hoc possumus quod de jure possumus.*"[192] The serjeant adds that
there is no need for conscience in addition to law, for common law is itself the manifestation of the law of God, and
therefore sufficient. He concludes by quoting a statute of
Edward III which, he says, proves "that my lord chancellor nor none other ought to send any writ or writing to
any justices to let them to proceed according to the common law of the realm, the which law the king is bound to
see maintained, as it appeareth by the said statute."[193]

But did this violent attack on the prerogative courts
by landowner and lawyer alike imply that there was a
strong body of opinion in England advocating that subjects should be ordered "by the discretion of the chancellor
and by no law," and that the king is *legibus solutus?* We
know that Wolsey, in the interest of strong, efficient government, was interested in exalting the king's prerogative
above rival factions, and even the law, if necessary.
Whether it means anything or not that he was indicted in
1529 for reversing common-law decisions may be questioned.[194] But it is certainly true that Wolsey was interested in the reform of the common law,[195] and that he spoke

---

192. *Ibid.*, p. 325.
193. *Ibid.*, pp. 330–331. The statute quoted is 20 Edward III, entitled "Ordinance for the Justices." It was addressed by Edward III to the Sheriff of Stafford,
and, among other things, commanded "all our Justices, that they shall from
henceforth do equal Law and Execution of right to all our Subjects, rich and
poor, without having regard to any Person, and without omitting to do right
for any Letters or Commandment which may come to them from Us, or from
any other, or by any cause. . . ."
194. *Letters and Papers*, IV(3), 6075 (Article 20).
195. *Ibid.*, IV(2), 4937. Rich, writing to Wolsey, begs to have an interview
to discuss the reform of the common law, for which he knows Wolsey has
great zeal.

about the "new law of the star chamber."[196] On one occasion, he stopped a suit brought against him in the common pleas on the ground that a chancellor ought not to be
sued in that court, "for then the Common Pleas should
have superiority upon the chancellor."[197] Nor can one
easily forget the indignant outburst of the poet, Skelton,
against the Cardinal's high-handed proceedings in the star
chamber.[198]

For the most part, however, it is clear that Tudor political writers did not justify the prerogative courts by
reference to the continental theory of absolutism.[199] They
were far from maintaining, as the alarmist "serjeant at
the laws of England" would have it, that the king is *legibus solutus*, and that he might therefore set aside the common law at his pleasure. Theirs was rather the good old
medieval view that equity is sometimes necessary to bring
human law more nearly into accord with natural and divine law.[200] They did not regard the prerogative courts
as a threat to the common law, nor did they directly op-

196. *Ibid.*, II(2), App. 38. Pollard describes Wolsey's "new law of the star
chamber" as "a new dispensation of his own, new as distinct from the letter of
the old testament of the common law, and instinct with the spirit of the new
justice; new also in the vigour with which it was to be administered" (*Wolsey*,
p. 73).

197. *Letters and Papers*, III(1), 751.

198. The Cardinal, Skelton says in his poem "Why Come Ye Nat to Court"
(*Works*, London, 1843, edited by Alexander Dyce, II, 32–33),

> ". is set so hye
> In his ierarchy
> Of frantycke frenesy
> And folysshe fantasy,
> That in the Chambre of Starres
> All maters there he marres;
> Clappyng his rod on the borde,
> No man dare speke a worde,
> For he hathe all the sayenge,
> Without any renayenge;" etc.

199. This was especially the case after the fall of Wolsey, for it was Wolsey
who had been largely responsible for widening the jurisdiction of the prerogative
courts. After Wolsey's fall, the star chamber especially never recovered the prestige it had enjoyed between 1515 and 1529. For Wolsey's activity as chancellor,
see Pollard, *Wolsey*, Chap. 3, and his article, "The Star Chamber under the
Tudors," *Eng. Hist. Rev.*, XXXVII, 516–539.

200. See Holdsworth, *History of English Law*, IV, 279–281.

pose the jurisdiction of the king's council to the ordinary courts. They looked on chancery, star chamber, and requests rather as necessary instruments in softening the rigidity of the common law, and in extending it in the interest of justice. There was, in their opinion, nothing essentially "new" in the "new law of the Star Chamber," and therefore there was accordingly no need to propound a theory of royal absolutism to justify its existence.

St. German's *Doctor and Student* is good evidence on this point. As we have already seen, the "serjeant at the laws of England" attacked St. German for ascribing to king and chancellor powers which would enable them to rule England at their will. But that the good serjeant misunderstood St. German's intent is patent. St. German did not attempt to justify the prerogative courts in terms of royal absolutism for the very good reason that he saw nothing unusual in a writ of *subpoena* issuing from chancery. The equitable jurisdiction exercised by chancery signified to him, not the device of an arbitrary government, but merely a necessary extension of the common law. Equity is necessary, he says, to mitigate the rigor of the law, because it is not possible to make any general rule of the law which shall not fail in some particular case. Equity is, after all, simply "an exception of the law of God, or the law of reason, from the general rules of the law of men, when they by reason of their generality, would in any particular case judge against the law of God or the law of reason; the which exception is secretly understood in every general rule of every positive law." Equity, as exercised in chancery, is thus not subversive of the common law. It merely seeks to reflect the latter's intent rather than its words.[201]

The author of *A little treatise concerning writs of subpoena*, written in St. German's defense against the aforementioned serjeant,[202] similarly advanced the view that the

201. *Doctor and Student*, Dialogue I, Chap. 16.
202. Printed in Hargrave, *Collection of Tracts relative to the Law of England*, pp. 332–355. This treatise may possibly have been written by St. German him-

jurisdiction of chancery is not synonymous with arbitrary government. To begin with, he says, there is no such opposition between the common law and the law of chancery as the serjeant would have us suppose. When in doubt, the chancellor has often asked the advice of the common law judges.[203] The common law does not prohibit chancery jurisdiction,[204] nor does it affirm that its maxims should apply to all courts.[205] Moreover, the chancellor, even when mitigating the rigor of the common law, is not an irresponsible person who hands out decisions according to his will. On the contrary, the chancellor's conscience "is grounded upon the law of God and the law of reason and the law of the realm not contrary to the said law of God and law of reason."[206] Clearly, the chancellor can under no circumstances subvert the law. "There is no *subpoena* directly against a statute, nor directly against the maxims of the law; for if it should lie, then the law should be judged to be void, and that may not be done by no court but by parliament."[207]

There were others besides St. German and his champion who saw nothing incompatible in the jurisdiction of the prerogative courts and the traditional rule of the king. Starkey, for example, actually advocated a reception of Roman law into England, and yet his *Dialogue between Pole and Lupset* was bold in its denunciation of absolute

self, although the evidence depends entirely on an annotation by Sir Edward Saunders in the original MS., to the effect that the author of the tract was "Christopher Seinte Jerman" (see *ibid.*, p. 321, note by Hargrave).

203. *Ibid.*, p. 332. This seems to have been actually the case. According to Holdsworth (*History of English Law*, IV, 277), the relations between the chancellor and the common-law judges and lawyers "had been of the most intimate character," from very early times.

204. *A little treatise concerning writs of subpoena*, p. 334. The author has been discussing the case of a plaintiff who, because he cannot tell the number of deeds or their contents in a declaration made legitimately some time before, is without remedy at common law. "The common lawe doth not prohibite, but that ther shall be remedye in the chauncerie in the said case, and other like. . . ."

205. *Ibid.*, pp. 338–339.

206. *Ibid.*, p. 353.

207. *Ibid.*, pp. 343–344.

monarchy. Sir Thomas More, a common lawyer, vigorously defended his injunctions as lord chancellor on the
ground that to prevent injury to the people, the rigor of
the law must be mitigated.[208] Even Wolsey, who was so
enthusiastic about the "new law of the Star Chamber,"
saw in the jurisdiction of chancery, not a means toward
irresponsible government, but a check on tyranny. His
oft-quoted speech from Cavendish is not evidence that he
had contempt for the common law, but proof that he held
conscience to be superior even to a king. It is true that he
speaks rather eloquently therein of the function of the king
and his chancellor. "The king ought of his royal dignity
and prerogative," he says, "to mitigate the rigor of the
law where conscience hath the most force; therefore,
in his royal place of equal justice, he hath constituted a
chancellor, an office to execute justice with clemency,
where conscience is opposed by the rigor of the law. And
therefore the Court of Chancery hath been heretofore
commonly called the Court of Conscience; because it hath
jurisdiction to command the high ministers of the common law to spare execution and judgment, where conscience hath most effect."[209] But the important thing to
notice about this speech of Wolsey's is not so much the
speech itself, but the occasion on which it was delivered.
Judge Shelley had been ordered by the king to try to get
Wolsey, who had just surrendered the Great Seal, to give
up York Place. Wolsey admits that the king may do this
by the common law, but he demurs that it is not according to conscience. The speech was therefore delivered, not

208. Roper, *Life of More*, p. 45. More, criticized for his injunctions as lord
chancellor, invites all the judges to dine with him, explains his position, and
then suggests an alternative—"if the Iustices of euery courte . . . wold, vppon
resonable considerations, by their owne discretions (as they were, as he thought,
in consciens bound) mitigate and reforme the rigour of the lawe themselves,
there should from thenceforth by him no more Iniunctions be graunted." When
they refuse, he says, "Forasmuch as your selves, my lordes, drive me to that
necessity for awardinge out Iniunctions to releive the peoples iniury, you cannot
hereafter any more iustly blame me."

209. Cavendish, *Life of Cardinal Wolsey* (London, 1827), pp. 282-284.

to assert the majesty of the king's prerogative above the common law, but to show that the king must sometimes go beyond the letter of the law to rule justly.

To further prove the contention that there was no theory of *legibus solutus* in England during the early Reformation, one has only to turn to the legal collections then most familiar to the educated public. In Sir Anthony Fitzherbert's *Great Abridgement* and his other legal collections, in Sir William Stanford's *Exposition of the king's prerogative*, in Sir Robert Brooke's *Great Abridgement*, in St. German's *Doctor and Student*,[210] there is no conception of a royal prerogative outside the law. These lawyers, it is true, attributed to the king powers over and above those enjoyed by a feudal overlord. During the sixteenth century, the conception of the king as a national sovereign, as well as a feudal overlord, was definitely written into the law, after a struggle for recognition extending over two centuries.[211] As we have already seen, the king was now recognized as possessing supreme control over ecclesiastical matters, coinage, foreign policy, "absolute" power during time of war or insurrection.[212] It is equally true, however, that the Tudor lawyers did not attribute to the king the wide, indefinite powers implied in the doctrine of non-resistance. Where Tyndale and Gardiner saw in the king God's vicegerent on earth who must be obeyed "without one syllable of exception," the lawyers soberly

210. That these particular legal collections were widely read in early sixteenth-century England can scarcely be doubted. No less than fourteen editions of St. German's *Doctor and Student*, either in complete or abridged form, were published in England before 1570; four of Rastell's *Expositions of the terms of the laws of England;* three of Fitzherbert's *Great Abridgement;* four of his *New Natura Brevium;* three of Stanford's *Pleas of the crown;* and two of his *Exposition of the king's prerogative*. Both Fitzherbert and Stanford were judges of the common pleas, Fitzherbert being appointed about 1521, Stanford in 1554.

211. See Holdsworth, *History of English Law*, III, 463–469; IV, 200–206. Holdsworth points out, however, that the conception of the king as a national sovereign was by no means new in the sixteenth century. "In England, as in France," he says (*ibid.*, IV, 200), "the idea that the king was superior to any ordinary feudal lord had been, from the thirteenth century onwards, present to the minds of English lawyers."

212. See above, pp. 145–147.

defined the prerogatives which the king might exercise
according to law. Unlike the civil lawyers in contemporary
France, and some of the crown lawyers during the reigns
of James I and Charles I, the Tudor legists restricted the
royal prerogative to the powers prescribed by customary
and statute law. As Holdsworth says, the prerogative
"was limited at all times by the fact that its extent was
defined by the law."[213]

Ample evidence of this fact is to be found in all of the
above-mentioned legal collections. We have already seen
that St. German's *Doctor and Student* scrupulously
avoided ascribing to the king a power above the law.[214]
Fitzherbert and Stanford were no less conservative in their
point of view. In the *Great Abridgement*, Fitzherbert, for
example, cites the Year Books of Henry IV to the effect
that the king can do nothing against the common law.[215]
In his *Pleas of the Crown*, Stanford quotes Bracton as his
authority that the king may pardon a felon providing he
does not violate his coronation oath in so doing.[216] Both
Fitzherbert and Stanford, it is true, present exceptions
according to which the king may set aside common or
statute law, and thus exercise his "absolute" prerogative.[217] But this "absolute" prerogative was to be used only
in exceptional cases, for example, when the realm was in

213. *History of English Law,* IV, 200–201.
214. See above, pp. 163–164, 181.
215. *La Graunde Abridgement* (London, 1565), p. 6ᵇ. Under "Fraunchise"
Fitzherbert refers to a "Nota par Gascun" (Hil. 8, Hen. IV, 19). "Si les Maires
et Bailes de &c. ount vse de tener plee par briefe de temps dount &c. puis le Roy
graunt a eux puis le temps de memore conusauns de ple par chartre cest graunt
est voide. *quar le Roy ne puit oustre le comen ley* [italics mine] et fuit dit entaunt
que lun fuit contrariant a lauter et ils ount accept en court de recorde le fraunchise par chartre de conusauns de ples ils ount pardue lauauntage de tener ple
par briefe de Droit &c. vide de Fraunchise en title de Forfeture 22. libro assi-
sarum."
216. *Les Plees del Coron* (London, 1560), Cap. 55, p. 99. "Barre in Endite-
ment de felonie; est le pardon le Roy. Quel le prince ou soueraigne gouernour,
ascus faitz doit granter a loffendour, ou il y ad espoirance de son amendement,
& ou le gouernour. *sans violacion de la serement, que il fait en son coronement*
[italics mine], le peut fayre."
217. For the Tudor distinction between the king's "absolute" and "ordinary"
prerogative, see Holdsworth, *History of English Law,* IV, 206–207.

danger, and, in any event, its use was sanctioned by the common law. For example, in his *New Natura Brevium* Fitzherbert asserts that despite the common law to the contrary, the king may by writ or proclamation prohibit his subjects from leaving the country without royal license. But this prerogative the king was to use only sparingly and in time of stress. The king, Fitzherbert says, may exercise this prerogative "because that every man is of right for to defend the King and his Realm."[218] Stanford cites Bracton to the effect that the king may pardon a felon, but only where there is hope of amendment.[219] And another of Fitzherbert's examples of the "absolute" prerogative enjoys a good medieval pedigree. If the king's tenant alienates part of the fief he holds from the king, he or his tenant may be distrained by the king's writ for the whole rent—notwithstanding the statute, *Quia emptores terrarum*.[220] For "it seemeth the King is not bound by the Statute, but a common person is."[221]

Stanford's *Exposition of the king's prerogative* is, however, the most remarkable example of the conservative attitude of the Tudor lawyers toward the royal power. Written in 1548, over a decade after the sessions of the Reformation Parliament which had regaled the king with new and unprecedented powers, this book is simply a restatement of the feudal prerogatives of the crown, and, in fact, merely summarizes the medieval statute or treatise, *Praerogativa Regis*.[222] Stanford does not so much as mention therein the king's prerogatives as national sovereign, much less does he attribute to the king a power above the law.[223] True, he describes the royal prerogative

218. *New Natura Brevium* (London, 1687), pp. 188–189.
219. See above, Chap. V, note 216.
220. 18 Edward I, Statute of Westminster III.
221. *New Natura Brevium*, p. 522.
222. See Holdsworth, *History of English Law*, III, 460. According to Maitland, "Praerogativa Regis" (printed in *Statutes of the Realm*, I, 226–227) was a tract written by some lawyer during the reign of Edward I (see *Collected Papers*, Cambridge, 1911, II, 182–189).
223. Of course, Stanford knew perfectly well that there were "an infinite number of prerogatives more, which were too tedious here to recite," but it is

in glowing terms. In the preface dedicated to Nicholas Bacon, he says that he has taken upon himself to collect such titles as pertain unto the king's prerogative, "not as one in any part worthy to treat of a thing so high and precious as that is." And in the first chapter he defines "prerogative" as a pre-eminence which one person has over another, and which is especially permissible in a prince. For the king is not only the most excellent member of the commonwealth, he is also the preserver and defender of the people, who through his efforts are enabled to enjoy their lives and goods in peace and quiet. In return for these inestimable services, "the laws do attribute" unto the king a prerogative extending not only to his person, but to his possessions as well. But Stanford says nothing about the powers attached to the king's office, and when he turns to a discussion of specific prerogatives, his attitude is thoroughly feudal. The king's person, he says, shall be subject to no man's suit, his possessions cannot be taken from him by any violence, his goods and cattle are under no tribute, toll, or custom.[224] Among other things, the king shall have suzerainty over the lands of those who hold from him as chief;[225] he shall have care of the lands of idiots,[226] and by common law he shall have the right to wreckage, including whales and sturgeons cast up on the shore.[227] It is significant that Stanford's only allusion to prerogatives of a more modern nature is in his phrase, which comes as a kind of afterthought, "an infinite number of prerogatives more, which were too tedious here to recite."[228]

That the king was not regarded as *legibus solutus* is even more eloquently illustrated by the care with which

nevertheless significant that the purely feudal powers of the crown should have occupied so much of his attention.

224. *Exposition of the king's prerogative* (London, 1567), p. 5. This collection was first printed by Richard Tottel in 1567, but it was written at least twenty years earlier, for its dedication to Nicholas Bacon is dated 1548.

225. *Ibid.*, p. 5.

226. *Ibid.*, p. 33.

227. *Ibid.*, p. 37.

228. *Ibid.*, p. 5.

Tudor Englishmen restricted the king's spiritual prerogative to its proper sphere. Except during the early stages of the controversy with Rome, few voices were raised against the king's spiritual powers as such. But there was considerable apprehension lest the king use his extraordinary powers as Supreme Head to trample common and statute law under foot. The statute book reveals this tension in the Act of Proclamations and the act 32 Hen. VIII, c. 26. The Act of Proclamations has been quoted above to prove that royal proclamations were not legal if subversive of the statute and common law of the realm.[229] However, as has been noted elsewhere, the main purpose of this act was to give effect to the king's new spiritual powers, to provide the king as Supreme Head with a weapon with which to execute his ecclesiastical decrees.[230] This being the case, the concluding paragraph protecting the fundamental rights of the people under positive law betrays a real fear lest the king use his spiritual prerogative to scale new heights. The act 32 Hen. VIII, c. 26, represents a similar state of mind. All doctrinal decrees made by the clergy and confirmed by royal letters patent, it reads, shall be obeyed as if promulgated specifically in this present act, with the reservation "that nothing shall be done, ordained, defined, or provided by authority of this act, which shall be repugnant or contrary to the laws and statutes of this realm."

As a religious conservative, Gardiner found it convenient to take his stand on a similar principle. In 1547 the council issued royal injunctions enjoining the use of a new book of homilies which contained radical Protestant innovations.[231] Gardiner rejoined that the injunctions were illegal, on the ground that the *King's Book* was still on the statute books, and that the Royal Supremacy could do nothing contrary to common law or act of parliament. In a letter to the Privy Council in August, Gardiner as-

229. See above, pp. 167–168.
230. See above, p. 144, n. 65.
231. See *Letters of Stephen Gardiner*, pp. 252–253.

serted that he had heard the common lawyers say "that if any, although he be deputed by the King, do, in execution of spiritual jurisdiction, extend the same contrary to any Common Law or act of Parliament, it is a *praemunire* both to the judge and the parties, although it be done in the King's Majesty's name: *because they say the King's Majesty's supremacy in visiting and ordering of the Church is reserved to spiritual jurisdiction.*"[232] In another letter written from the Fleet in October, Gardiner again denounced the *Homilies of 1547* because its provisions were contrary to the doctrine established by act of parliament.[233] He recalled the Act of Proclamations, in which, he said, there had been a plain promise that nothing should be done by its authority against statute or common law.[234] He also related a conversation held with Chancellor Audley some years before, in which he (Gardiner) had asked whether it was not strange that a man acting in the king's name should fall into a *praemunire*. According to him, Audley had answered that by the Act of Supremacy, the king's prerogative was limited to a spiritual jurisdiction, and that by another act, "it is provided that no Spiritual Law shall have place contrary to a Common Law or Act of Parliament.[235] And [if] this were not, . . . you bishops would enter in with the King, and, by means of his supremacy, order the laity as you listed. But we will provide . . . that the *praemunire* shall ever hang over your heads, and so we laymen shall be sure to enjoy our inheritance by the Common Law and acts of parliament."[236] Sir James Hales maintained substantially

232. *Ibid.*, p. 370 (italics mine). The council was, of course, entirely within its rights in ordering the use of a new book of homilies. For, by virtue of the Royal Supremacy, the king's spiritual prerogative was absolute, and hence legally free of parliamentary interference. The *King's Book*, a purely doctrinal treatise, could be superseded by the royal authority alone, even though originally it had been passed as an act of parliament.
233. *Letters of Stephen Gardiner*, p. 382.
234. *Ibid.*, p. 391.
235. Audley (if, indeed, Audley actually said what Gardiner here reports) undoubtedly is referring here to the aforementioned act, 32 Hen. VIII, c. 26.
236. *Letters of Stephen Gardiner*, p. 392.

the same principle when, on Mary's accession, he refused to relax the laws against nonconformists in favor of Roman Catholics, even though expressly ordered to do so by the queen. So long as the laws of Henry VIII and Edward VI remained on the statute books, Hales argued, he had no alternative but to enforce them. Questioned by Gardiner at Westminster Hall, he maintained that he had given orders therein "as the law required. For I have professed the law, against which, in cases of justice, will I never (God willing) proceed, nor in any wise dissemble, but with the same show forth my conscience, and if it were to do again, I would do no less than I did."[237]

It may be concluded that the early Tudor political writers were remarkably conservative in their attitude toward the king and the law. They attributed to the king vast powers in the ecclesiastical realm, and they preached a doctrine of absolute non-resistance. But they were not prepared to make the king an unlimited sovereign in the temporal sphere. They taught that the king is subordinate to natural and positive law, that he is in no sense absolute, *legibus solutus*. They also held that he shared his political power with parliament, without which, to use Thomas' phrase, "he determined no great matter." Their ideal was a perfect balance between different branches of government, not an "inorganic" state in which one branch was supreme, the other branches performing their respective functions by delegation. Nor did the political writers ascribe to the king in parliament an unlimited sovereignty. They believed that nowhere was the king so powerful as in his capacity as head of parliament, and, in contrast to their fifteenth-century predecessors, they believed that the king in parliament might promulgate laws for the state as a whole, rival jurisdictions notwithstanding. But they wrote under the spell of the medieval conception of law. They insisted that the king in parliament is no legislator at all, that he merely "interprets" a more fundamental law. As McIlwain says, "It required the shock of

237. Foxe, *Acts and Monuments*, VI, 712–717.

civil war to teach men that the High Court of Parliament had become the Sovereign Legislature of the Kingdom."[238]

Certainly, the Tudor theorists reflected the growing power of the monarchy to a lesser extent than their continental contemporaries. This was because there was no real conflict in Tudor England between king and parliament. King and parliament were temporarily allied in demolishing papal and clerical power.

238. *High Court of Parliament*, p. 137.

VI

THE KING'S MORAL RESPONSIBILITY

For it is God's own office, yea, his chief office, which [kings] bear and abuse. For as Justice is the chief virtue, so is the ministration thereof the chiefest office: and therefore hath God established it with the chiefest name, honoring and calling Kings, and all officers under them by his own name, Gods. You be all Gods, as many as have in you charge and ministration of Justice. What a foul shame were it for any now to take upon them the name and office of God, and in their doings to show themselves devils? God cannot of Justice, but plague such shameless presumption and hypocrisy, and that with shameful death, diseases, or infamy. BALDWIN, *Mirror for Magistrates*, Dedication.

TO guard against arbitrary government, the early Tudor political writers appealed to the king's conscience as well as to the law. When it occurred to them, they asserted that the king's prerogative is limited *legally*—by natural and positive law, by parliament. But they said more than this. They insisted as well that the king, by the very nature of his office, is *morally* responsible to rule for the good of society as a whole. In the fifteenth century, Fortescue, it will be remembered, had simultaneously described the king's subordination to natural and positive law and preached the medieval doctrine of the moral responsibility of the ruler. "*Rex datur propter regnum, et non regnum propter regem,*" he had written, quoting St. Thomas.[1] During the early sixteenth century, and particularly during the years immediately following the convening of the Reformation Parliament, the English political writers carried on this teaching, and in fact, gave it a fresh emphasis. On the one hand, they proclaimed the doctrine of non-resistance and the heinousness of rebellion against the king. On the other, they stated in no uncertain terms that kings have been instituted by God to administer justice in this world, and to lead their subjects back to the rule of natural law. If they shirk their

1. See above, p. 12.

duty, if they work for self-aggrandizement rather than for the good of their subjects, they will be visited at death by a horrible and summary vengeance. By so teaching, the political writers did not impose a legal check on the king's prerogative, but they definitely reminded the king that his office had been created for a moral purpose, that his *raison d'être* was to rule in the interest of the commonwealth as a whole, and not for his own selfish pleasure.

One has not to look far to discover the reasons why the early sixteenth-century political writers, continental as well as English, went out of their way to emphasize the king's moral responsibility. In the first place, the growth of absolute monarchy during the Renaissance and Reformation made men everywhere apprehensive of tyranny.[2] Monarchy they approved of wholeheartedly. Did not Erasmus reflect popular opinion when he wrote that "although there are many types of states, it is the consensus of nearly all wise thinking men, that the best form is monarchy"?[3] Absolute monarchy, too, had its points. Was it not surety against feudal disorder and foreign invasion, and did it not foster commerce and industry? But absolute monarchy also had its dangers. What was there to prevent the absolute monarch from ruling arbitrarily, with regard only for his personal whims and fancies? The political writers knew of only one practicable solution to this dilemma. They reminded kings that, regardless of their relationship to the law, they still had a moral obligation to society. They appealed not so much to the law—such an appeal was more peculiar to the seventeenth century —as to the royal conscience. It was not desirable just then to make an issue of the king's subordination to the law— the pope and feudal nobility had to be disposed of first. Moreover, there was always the chance that kings might

2. As H.H.S.Croft puts it, "The moral and social duties of princes, a topic which in the middle ages had frequently exercised the pens of the schoolmen and theologians, acquired still greater prominence in the fifteenth century, in consequence probably of the steady progress towards absolute monarchy. . . ." (Introduction to Elyot's *The Governour*, I, lxiii).

3. See *The Education of a Christian Prince*, edited by L.K.Born, p. 173.

scorn an appeal to customary law over which they were slowly extending their control. But in a religious age they could scarcely disregard the threat of divine vengeance in the event of misbehavior. The political writers allowed the godliness of benevolent despotism, but they preached the essential sinfulness of tyranny.

There was a second reason why the moral-responsibility theme was especially popular among sixteenth-century political writers. The Renaissance inspired men with a new interest in Greek and Roman political theory, one of the salient characteristics of which had been its insistence on the ruler's service to the state. There was the tradition of the *Corpus Juris Civilis* which taught that the ruler is *legibus solutus—quod principi placuit legis habet vigorem*. But there was also the classical tradition of the perfect prince who, like the good physician, prescribes not for his own welfare, but for that of his patient. From Isocrates and Plato to Marcus Aurelius and St. Augustine one of the dominant themes in political theory had been the moral responsibility of the ruler to society, the subordination of the ruler's individual welfare to the common good. Treatise after treatise had been written describing what the model prince should be like and how he should be educated—*specula principis* they were called.[4] For until philosophers are kings or kings are philosophers, cities will never have rest from their evils. The middle ages had inherited this literary *genre*, the *speculum principis*, and had given it the Christian stamp of approval.[5] The medieval political theorists had transformed Plato's philosopher-king into the Christian prince whom God has instituted especially to secure justice for mankind. St. Thomas' *De Regimine Principum* was thus lineally descended from Plato's *Republic*, with certain peculiarly Christian additions. But it may be thought that the revival of classical

4. See *ibid.*, L.K.Born's introductory chapter, "Ancient Theories of Statecraft," pp. 44–93.
5. *Ibid.*, "The Perfect Prince from the Sixth Century to the Sixteenth Century," pp. 99–124.

political theory during the Renaissance had much to do with the increased popularity of the perfect-prince theme in the sixteenth century.

The Reformation also had something to do with this phenomenon. Interpreted in one light, the Reformation represented a reaction against the moral corruption of the Catholic Church. The English religious reformers, ranging from Erasmians like Dean Colet to radicals like Tyndale and Barnes, demanded, above all, a purification of ecclesiastical morals, and the strict performance of clerical duties. But they flailed the guardians of secular society for moral lassitude as well. Machiavelli, the Renaissance publicist, very largely separated politics from morals in the *Prince*. The religious reformers, on the other hand, made bold to assert the grave moral responsibility of all classes of society alike. They bitterly attacked the ecclesiastical princes, principally the pope, for neglecting their proper duties for temporal pleasures. And on a similar ground they assailed the rapacious capitalists—rack-renters and enclosers—and conscienceless rulers.

For a variety of reasons, then, the doctrine of the king's moral responsibility received a fresh emphasis during the fifteenth and early sixteenth centuries. On the continent, numerous treatises were devoted entirely to this subject, and all of them enjoyed a wide popularity. Egidius Romanus' *De Regimine Principum*, modeled in large part upon St. Thomas' treatise of that name, was published for the first time in 1473. Giovanni Pontano's *De Principe* and Philip Beroaldo's *De Optimo Statu et Principe* also saw the light of day in the fifteenth century. Francesco Patrizi, Bishop of Gaieta, wrote a tract on the same theme entitled *De Regno et Regis Institutione* which was printed for the first time at Paris in 1518 and reprinted many times thereafter in the sixteenth century.[6] Antonio de Guevara, court preacher and historiographer to Charles V and bishop of Guadix and Mondoñedo, wrote an even more famous treatise, *Relox de Principes*, more generally

6. See H.H.S.Croft's Introduction to Elyot's *The Governour*, I, lxiv–lxv.

known as the *Libro aureo* or *Golden Book of Marcus Aurelius*.[7] This book, which is a selection of anecdotes and quotations illustrating how princes ought to rule, enjoyed a tremendous vogue in the sixteenth century. It was first published at Valladolid in 1529 and in one version or another was forthwith translated into many tongues. "Scarce any book except the Bible," remarks one writer, "has been so much translated or so frequently printed."

Erasmus also interested himself in the moral-responsibility theme. Though hardly a political theorist, the famous humanist wrote a number of works exhorting princes to rule well, and to prepare themselves properly for their office.[8] In 1504 he published his *Panegyricus* to Prince Philip on the occasion of the latter's safe return from Spain. "No other way of correcting a prince is as efficacious," Erasmus wrote to a friend, "as offering the pattern of a truly good prince under the guise of flattery to them." In 1530 appeared his *Utilissima consultatio de bello Turcis inferendo* in which he assailed princes for playing with war rather than with seeking to rule for the good of their subjects. In 1531 he issued his *Apophthegmata*, a collection of maxims designed to persuade young princes to virtue. But his most famous political work was the *Institutio principis Christiani*, dedicated in 1516 to Prince Charles, the future Emperor Charles V. The purpose of this work Erasmus stated frankly in the dedicatory epistle—"to set forth the likeness of the perfect prince" to enable the young Charles to rule like a philosopher. The king, Erasmus wrote in succeeding pages, is a *paterfamilias* who rules as God's representative on earth. His virtues make for the common good, but his deficiencies bring on general destruction. Only the king who rules for the good of the state itself, and not for himself, deserves the title of "prince." All other rulers are "tyrants," pos-

7. See José Maria Gálvez, *Guevara in England, nebst neudruck von Lord Berners' "Golden Boke of Marcus Aurelius"* (Berlin, 1916), pp. 1-32.
8. See *The Education of a Christian Prince*, "The Political Theories of Erasmus," pp. 3-25.

sessing the title, but not the soul, of true regality. If Charles would gain the favor of God and merit the reward of every true Christian, "there is no better way . . . than by showing [himself] a beneficial prince for [his] people."[9] That the *Institutio* was a widely popular book in the sixteenth century cannot be doubted. It ran to no less than eighteen editions before Erasmus himself died in 1536.

In England, no less than on the continent, numerous writers propagated the moral-responsibility theme. These writers may be divided into three distinct groups. There were the radical Protestants or Puritans whose inspiration was the Reformation, and who demanded that kings, no less than clerics, bestir themselves from their moral lethargy, on pain of eternal damnation. There were those secular writers whose inspiration was the *speculum principis* tradition, and who devoted entire tracts to the perpetuation of that theme. Lastly, there was a miscellaneous group of writers who clearly believed in the ruler's moral responsibility without, however, devoting undue attention to the subject.

Of the three groups, the Puritan group was the most vehement. Men like Tyndale, Brinkelow, Hooper, Lever, and Latimer were as forthright in addressing kings as in denouncing papists, enclosers, and rackrenters. In pamphlets dedicated to the king, or in sermons preached before the court or in London, these fearless reformers informed the prince of his duty in no uncertain terms. While admitting the king's divine origin and the heinousness of rebellion against God's vicegerent on earth, they thundered *ad nauseam* that the king's office implies duty, not license. The doctrine of non-resistance they used as a double-edged sword to proclaim at one and the same time the virtue of absolute obedience to the prince and the prince's moral responsibility to God and man. "Kings ought . . . to remember," Tyndale wrote, "that they are in God's stead, and ordained of God, not for themselves, but for the

9. *Ibid.*, Chap. 1, *passim.*

wealth of their subjects."[10] And again, "the king is but a servant to execute the law of God, and not to rule after his own imagination."[11] The ruler who consumes his subjects' property in card-playing, unjust wars, and whoring, rather than for the benefit of the commonwealth is, according to Ponet, a "tyrant" and not a king.[12]

In order that kings might not mistake their meaning, the Puritans took care not to speak in vague generalities. They applied the moral-responsibility principle to specific every-day problems. Thus, in his *Complaint of Roderick Mors*, Brinkelow urged Henry VIII to consider that he had been called to the throne by God "to be a defense unto the people, that they be not oppressed nor overyoked, but by all godly and politic means to seek the commonwealth of his people."[13] He went on to say—and here can be heard the voice of a Berkshire farmer's son—that the king must accordingly prevent rackrenting on the newly disposed-of abbey lands. Lever took similar pains to be specific in his powerful sermons delivered in 1550. "Look therefore all you that have power and authority of GOD," he thundered, "that you use it, as you are commanded by God: to correct and punish the evil-doer, and to encourage, reward, and maintain the good."[14] Henry VIII, Lever pointed out, had obeyed God in this respect by extirpating devilish religious ceremonies from the realm.[15] Kings and counsellors should further follow this precept by disposing of lands and benefices for the good of the people.[16]

10. *Obedience of a Christian Man*, p. 239. See also Hooper's statement in his "Annotations on Romans xiii," printed in *Later Writings of Bishop Hooper*, p. 106. The magistrate, Hooper writes, "is appointed to his place to defend, help, and preserve such as be good, and punish such as be naughty and evil. . . . The second part of St. Paul's words commendeth the magistrates for their utility and commodity in the commonwealth, because that by their authority evil-doers among the people are punished and corrected, that honest and true men may live in rest and quietness."

11. *Obedience of a Christian Man*, p. 334.

12. *Short treatise of politic power*, pp. Gij–Giij.

13. *Complaynt of Roderyck Mors*, p. 10.

14. *English Reprints. Thomas Lever. Sermons. 1550*, p. 42.

15. *Ibid.*, pp. 40–41.

16. *Ibid.*, "A Sermon preached ye fourth Sunday in Lent before the Kynges Maiestie, & his honorable Counsell," *passim*.

The Puritans threatened the ruler who misbehaved with a horrible vengeance. Take heed, Barnes exhorted princes, for Christ's example will confound the tyranny of mortal rulers, "which be but stubbles, hay and dust, and in a moment be brought to a lump of stinking carrion."[17] Brinkelow also, though with more delicacy, saw fit to remind Henry VIII of Doomsday when his majesty would stand before God's judgment seat with no more reputation than one of those paupers who die in the streets daily for lack of their due portion "wherewith you and your nobles do reward those gnatonical elbowhangers, your chaplains."[18] Ponet threatened tyrants with hell-fire, warning them that at death they will be committed, not to the Tower or the Fleet, "but unto the Jailor of gehenna (to be chained in the ward of eternal pain) . . ."[19] If, on the other hand, the king performs his duties faithfully and advances the honor of the commonwealth, "his account before God shall be allowed and rewarded."[20]

Not so vehement emotionally, but equally insistent on the king's moral responsibility, was the group of secular writers which sought its inspiration in the *speculum principis* tradition. Sir Thomas Elyot, John Bourchier, Thomas Paynell, Sir William Forrest, William Baldwin, scholars all, devoted entire treatises to the subject of the "perfect prince"—how a prince may be educated properly, what evils he must eschew, how he must rule after ascending the throne. For their materials these writers referred, for the most part, either to contemporary continental treatises, or directly to medieval or classical models. They were perpetuators of an age-old tradition, of a specialized literary *genre*, the *speculum principis*. In fact, as noted above, these writers put new life into the

17. *The whole workes of W. Tyndall, Iohn Frith, and Doct. Barnes*, p. 296.

18. *A Supplication of the Poor Commons*, p. 77.

19. *Short treatise of politic power*, pp. Fvi^b–Fvii. See also in this connection Tyndale's *Practice of Prelates*, printed in *The whole workes of W. Tyndall, Iohn Frith, and Doct. Barnes*, p. 341; and Hooper's "Annotations on Romans xiii," *Later Writings of Bishop Hooper*, p. 102.

20. *Sermons by Hugh Latimer*, pp. 99–100.

tradition and refurbished it for the benefit of the new breed of absolute rulers. Their emphasis was necessarily somewhat different from that of the Puritans. They wrote less of hell-fire and divine vengeance, more of education and earthly fame.

Sir Thomas Elyot was the most famous and the most prolific of these writers. He published three works in the *speculum principis* tradition, all of them widely popular. *The Governour*, which borrowed freely from Patrizi's *De Regno et Regis Institutione* and Erasmus' *Institutio principis Christiani*,[21] was first printed in 1531 and exceeded even More's *Utopia* in popular appeal, running into four editions before the middle of the century.[22] The *Image of Governance*, which purported to be a translation of a book originally written in Greek by the Emperor Alexander Severus' secretary, Encolpius,[23] first appeared in 1540 or 1541 and was reprinted in 1544 and 1549. The *Doctrinal of Princes*, which was a translation of Isocrates' *Ad Nicoclem*,[24] presented to king Nicocles on his accession to the throne of Cyprus in 374 B.C., was published three times before 1550—thrice by Berthelet after 1534.

John Bourchier,[25] Thomas Paynell,[26] Sir William For-

---

21. See *The Governour*, I, lxv–lxvi. Elyot was also influenced to a large extent by classical political treatises. He recommends, for example, that when the prospective ruler has reached the age of seventeen, he shall read, in addition to the Scriptures, Aristotle's *Ethics*, Cicero's *De officiis*, and Plato (*ibid.*, I, 92–93).

22. *The Governour* was printed by Berthelet in 1531, 1537, 1544, and 1546.

23. In the preface to the *Image of Governance*, Elyot says that the book "was fyrst written in the Greke tonge by his [Alexander Severus'] secretarie named Eucolpius, and by good chaunce was lente unto me by a gentill man of Naples called Pudericus." For Elyot's integrity in this matter, see *The Governour*, I, cxlv–clxiv.

24. This was the treatise upon which Erasmus modeled his *Institutio principis Christiani*.

25. John Bourchier (1467–1533), second Baron Berners, was appointed deputy of Calais in 1520. He devoted his leisure time there to literary work, translating, among other things, Froissart's *Chronicles* and Guevara's *Libro aureo*.

26. Thomas Paynell (fl. 1528–1567) was an Austin friar who was pensioned at the dissolution of Merton Abbey in 1531. In 1541 he was made Henry VIII's chaplain.

rest,[27] and William Baldwin[28] also published widely popular books in the *speculum principis* tradition. Bourchier's *Golden Book of Marcus Aurelius*, which was a translation of a pirated version of Guevara's *Relox de Principes*,[29] ran to five editions before the middle of the century.[30] In 1533 or thereabouts Paynell published a translation of Agapetus' treatise presented to the Emperor Justinian on the latter's accession to the imperial throne in 527.[31] He called it *The precepts teaching a prince or a noble estate his duty*. In 1548 Sir William Forrest dedicated to the Duke of Somerset a poem entitled the *Pleasant poesy of princely practice* which was, in reality, a free metrical version of Egidius Romanus' *De Regimine Principum*. Finally, in 1559 there appeared the first edition of the famous *Mirror for Magistrates*, edited by William Baldwin.

The burden of these works was not one whit original. With the exception of occasional contemporary allusions, the arguments advanced differed scarcely at all from the stock phrases of previous books in the *speculum principis*

27. Sir William Forrest (fl. 1581) is believed to have been one of Wolsey's retainers. Later he became Queen Mary's chaplain. In addition to the *Pleasant poesy of princely practice*, he wrote a panegyric on Catherine of Aragon, entitled the *History of Grisild the Second*, which he dedicated to Mary.

28. William Baldwin (fl. 1547) was employed during the reigns of Edward VI and Mary in preparing theatrical exhibitions for the court. In 1559 he superintended the publication of the *Mirror for Magistrates*, to which he made several contributions of his own.

29. As stated above, Guevara's *Relox de Principes* was first published at Valladolid in 1529. Prior to that date, however, Guevara had lent a shorter manuscript version of this work to the emperor. This version, usually entitled the *Libro aureo*, had been surreptitiously copied and printed, and it was from one of the pirated editions that Lord Berners made his translation, the *Golden Book of Marcus Aurelius*. In 1529 Guevara published the longer version, from which Sir Thomas North made an English translation in 1557 (see *The Diall of Princes: by Don Anthony of Guevara. Translated by Sir Thomas North*, edited by K.N.Colvile, London, 1919).

30. Printed by Berthelet in 1535, 1536, 1539, 1542, and 1546.

31. Agapetus was deacon of the church of St. Sophia in Constantinople. His treatise, entitled *Scheda regia sive de officio regis*, was first printed at Basle in 1518.

tradition. This was not surprising in view of the fact that the English tracts either borrowed their inspiration from continental sources, or else represented outright translations.

The purpose for which these works were written is clear. Just as Erasmus' *Institutio principis Christiani* was written to set up a model by which Prince Charles, "born to a splendid kingdom and destined to a still greater one," might rule, so the works of Elyot, Bourchier, Paynell, Forrest, and Baldwin were written to impress upon the English ruling classes their duty toward society, and to outline the means by which that duty could be best executed.[32] Elyot wrote *The Governour* to prescribe a system of education for "them that hereafter may be deemed worthy to be governours of the public weal."[33] The *Image of Governance* he translated to make clear the facts of the life of Alexander Severus, which ought to serve as a "wonderful mirror" to all prospective rulers. Paynell described his *Precepts teaching a prince or a noble estate his duty* as "a book of great wisdom and learning, containing all these precepts by the which not only a prince, but all other estates, may learn to do justice, may learn how by humanity and gentleness to order their subjects. . . ."[34] In his dedication to the 1559 edition of the *Mirror for Magistrates*, Baldwin stated bluntly that kings are called "Gods" only because they occupy God's principal office, the main function of which is to administer justice to the people. In Boccaccio's *Fall of Princes* the ruler may read how God has plagued evil rulers in other nations.

32. This was, of course, not the only purpose for which these works were written. Elyot, for example, intended in *The Governour* not only to write an ethical treatise, but "to augment our Englyshe tongue wherby men shulde . . . expresse more abundantly the thynge that they conceyued in theyr hartis (wherfor language was ordeyned)." Both Elyot and Bourchier were, moreover, classicists and consequently interested in translating classical treatises for their own sake.

33. *The Governour*, I, cxcii.

34. *The preceptes teachyng a prince or a noble estate his duetie* (London, bef. 1534), p. Aiii.

In the *Mirror for Magistrates* he may see "as in a look-ing glass" "how [God] hath dealt with some of our coun-trymen your ancestors" who abused their office.[35]

In his *Pleasant poesy of princely practice*, Forrest em-phasized the king's moral responsibility with a view toward ameliorating England's contemporary economic abuses.[36] The king, he wrote, is God's delegate on earth to see to it that justice is administered, and vice duly pun-ished. That the king's office was created for just this pur-pose, Forrest demonstrated by reference to the symbols of royalty. The sword indicates that the king "must all right defend"; the scepter, that he must administer "to the unrighteous, castigation: and to the good, the rule of pity, the proud: to disperse by due equity"; and the regal robes, that he must maintain law and justice in the land.[37] The king's obligation to administer justice, Forrest particu-larly urged. The king, he asserted, is surrounded by four ladies representing the four cardinal virtues—Prudence, Justice, Fortitude, and Temperance. Prudence shall take her place on his right side, Justice on his left.

> "As when by prudence [the king] doth duly know,
> he may by Justice then order the case,
> Who: of no party respecteth the face,
> for kith or king, friendship, or otherwise:
> but as the beam weigheth, by balance of justice,
> The beam, which showeth by his 'ostencer'
> When the Scales thereunto depending:
> doth evenly weigh, and in no point differ:
> Such is the office of Justice pretending,
> by plain open truth falsehood revenging,

---

35. *Mirror for Magistrates*, edited by Lily B. Campbell, p. 65. All subsequent citations from the *Mirror* are taken from the 1938 edition.

36. The section of the *Pleasant poesy of princely practice* dealing with con-temporary England is printed in *England in the reign of King Henry the Eighth*, edited by S.J.Herrtage, pp. lxxxv–xcix. The treatise in entirety is available in manuscript only (see British Museum, Royal MSS., 17 D III).

37. British Museum, Royal MSS., 17 D III, ff. 13–13b.

in Judgment attending, both end and 'induction'
by Justice to save: or bring to destruction."[38]

Forrest added that the king has nothing to fear if he rules
according to God's wishes, but that he should heed the
time when he himself shall be judged before the ultimate
tribunal.[39]

The authors of the *Mirror for Magistrates* were no less
insistent on the *speculum principis* theme, and, even more
than Forrest, they stressed the horrible end in store for
the irresponsible ruler.

"Happy is the prince that hath in wealth the grace
To follow virtue, keeping vices under,
But woe to him whose will hath wisdom's place:
For whoso renteth right and law asunder
On him at length, lo, all the world shall wonder,
High birth, choice fortune, force, nor Princely mace
Can warrant King or Kaiser from the case,
Shame sueth sin, as rain drops do the thunder."[40]

This was the theme, put into Richard II's mouth, of the
entire book. Thus, Richard himself, after having incurred
his subject's anger by unjust taxes, was defeated on the
battlefield, murdered by order of Henry Bolingbroke, and
reduced in short time to "carrion clay." Edward IV, in
consequence of "his surfeiting and intemperate life," was
returned to worm's meat in the midst of his prosperity.
Richard III, for murdering his brother's children and

38. *Ibid.*, f. 14ᵇ. In his description of the four cardinal virtues and of the dis-
tinction between the king and the tyrant, Forrest is largely following Egidius.
See the latter's *De Regimine Principum*, especially Book I, Part II; and Book
III, Part II.

39. British Museum, Royal MSS., 17 D III, f. 22. The passage in question
reads as follows:

"See, and foresee, that [God] yee [the king] not displease:
See that your owne cause dothe not his preuent.
So maye yee (by vengeaunce) his wrathe uprease.
In woorkinge his weies fynde ye shall moste ease
for thoughe yee as Judge doo reigne heere emonge men:
too bee Judged your selfe: the tyme shall come. . . ."

40. *Mirror for Magistrates*, pp. 111–112.

usurping the crown, aroused God's "great diffidence" and was defeated in short order at Bosworth, and his body

". . . hurried and tugged like a Dog,
On horseback all naked and bare. . . .
[His] head, hands, & feet, down hanging like a Hog,
With dirt and blood 'besprent' . . . ,
Cursing the day that ever [he] was born."[41]

More constructive, and less gory, were the works of Elyot and Bourchier. These writers suggested the manner in which the prince might avoid tyranny, rather than the horrible consequences with which he would be visited in the event of tyranny. Their emphasis was mostly on education. If the ruler is brought up properly, they argued, there need be no fear of irresponsible rule. Alexander Severus, Elyot pointed out in his *Image of Governance*, grew to be a model ruler because of the care bestowed on him during his youth by a virtuous mother and wise counsellors. Through remiss education, Varius Heliogabalus, on the other hand, grew to be a monstrous and loathsome ruler who was eventually slain by his subjects.[42] As Isocrates says in Elyot's *Doctrinal of Princes*, the business of ruling is difficult, indeed, so difficult, that "therefore no wrestler or champion ought so much to travail his body in exercise, as kings ought their minds in study."[43] Evidently, this was Guevara's opinion as well, for in the *Golden Book of Marcus Aurelius* (translated by Bourchier), the education of the great emperor is examined in detail. "What masters Marcus Aurelius had in his youth"; "What sciences Marcus the emperor learned"; "What wise ancient men Marcus chose to instruct his son"; "How the emperor reasoned with the masters that should learn his son"; "How science ought to be in princes"—these were the titles of some of the chapters. The deadly seriousness of a prince's education Guevara eloquently sets forth in

41. *Ibid.*, p. 370.
42. *Image of Governance* (London, 1541), p. Avii.
43. *The Doctrinal of princes made by the noble oratour Isocrates* (London, 1534?), p. 6.

a speech supposedly delivered by the emperor to his son's pedagogues. "To be masters of princes in earth," he warns the latter, "is to have the office of gods that be in heaven. . . . For certain he that hath the charge of a prince, is the governor of the ship, the standard of an army, . . . because they have among their hands him that afterwards ought to govern all the world."[44]

In *The Governour* Elyot devoted even more attention to the subject of the prince's education than Guevara in the *Golden Book of Marcus Aurelius*. Elyot, too, was of the opinion that for a ruler to shoulder the heavy responsibilities of his office, he must first receive a proper education. He should be versed, for example, in the science of music in order to understand the perfect harmony of a public weal.[45] The knowledge of painting and carving will stand him in good stead when he comes to devise engines of war, and to map out the country of his adversary.[46] Tragedies he should read so as to abhor the intolerable career of the tyrant, moral philosophy "to inform him unto virtuous manners," and the laws of the realm especially to be able "to serve honorably . . . the public weal of his country."[47]

In addition to the Puritans and the secular writers of the *speculum principis* tradition, there was a third group of early Tudor writers which also stressed the moral-responsibility theme. This was a miscellaneous group of government servants who, for all their loyalty to the king, nevertheless believed firmly in their master's duty toward society. While spreading the gospel of absolute non-resistance, these men simultaneously made it clear, if only

44. *Golden Book of Marcus Aurelius,* printed in *Guevara in England,* edited by José Maria Gálvez, pp. 137–138. Erasmus was also deeply concerned with the problem of the prince's education, as is indicated by the title of his book, *Institutio principis Christiani.* Education Erasmus believed to be a particularly serious problem in the country where hereditary succession is the rule (*The Education of a Christian Prince,* p. 141).
45. *The Governour,* I, Chap. 7.
46. *Ibid.,* Chap. 8.
47. *Ibid.,* Chap. 14.

in *obiter dicta*, that they were wholeheartedly against irresponsible rule. Among this group were Bishop Gardiner, Richard Taverner, William Thomas, and Bishop Christopherson—all of them, it will be noted, staunch advocates of the cult of royal authority. All these men asserted unequivocally that the king must be obeyed, "yea, though he were an infidel," and "without one syllable of exception." Yet Gardiner was careful, even in his most extreme royalist pamphlet, to point out the moral responsibility of princes. "For their duty is to be so much the more careful in the office that God hath given them . . . as they see themselves the more bounden in yielding accounts. For it is a great talent that God hath put princes in trust withal: that is, that they should not only rule the people, but also rule them rightly. . . ."[48] In the *Garden of Wisdom*, Taverner similarly exhorted princes "to remember their function and office whereunto they be called of God Almighty, and unto whom for the same they shall render just accounts, be they now never so haughty and careless."[49] William Thomas, tutor to Edward VI and the author of *The Pilgrim*, threatened irresponsible princes with loss of earthly fame in the preface to his *History of Italy*. This book, he wrote in the preface, purposes to move the noble prince to maintain peace and justice; and to show the tyrant what plagues follow in the wake of cruelty, "and that though his tyranny pass unplagued in this world (which happeneth seldom), yet shall his name be hated and cursed in all ages and among all nations, as Nero, Heliogabalus, and such other princes be."[50] Christopherson took care likewise to point out that though his mistress, Queen Mary, can justly demand implicit obedience, yet she must remember that God has appointed her,

48. *De vera obedientia*, p. 112. Erasmus was also careful to warn Prince Charles that God will demand a strict account of him. "With Him the only effect of your being a prince will be [the fact] that you will be judged more severely in proportion to the great power entrusted to you" (*The Education of a Christian Prince*, p. 181).

49. *Garden of Wisdom*, Book II, p. Bv.

50. *The historie of Italie*, 1549 edition, pp. A2–A2b.

not to satisfy her own lusts or private gain, but to feed her
people, to promote the good and punish the bad.[51]

Such was also the implication of those writers who advocated the "very and true commonweal." Dudley in his
Tree of Commonwealth, More in his *Utopia*, Starkey in
his *Dialogue between Pole and Lupset*, proclaimed in no
uncertain terms the king's duties, and, indeed, the duties
of all classes of society alike, toward the "commonweal"
as a whole. They taught the medieval ideal of the Christian commonwealth in which the well-being of the whole
takes precedence over the aggrandizement of the parts.
To achieve that end, God has created a number of classes,
each of which has been given its function to perform for
the common good. King, clergy, nobility, commonalty, all
these alike are bound to work for each other rather than
for themselves.[52]

This is certainly the burden of the *Tree of Commonwealth*, that complicated and wearisome allegory which
Dudley presented to the youthful Henry VIII in 1510.
Dudley emphasizes particularly therein the moral responsibility of the king from whom grow out all the sus-
taining roots of the tree of commonwealth. The profit
of every prince, Dudley writes, depends on God's grace
which he can win by exercising liberality.[53] It is the king's
duty, in view of his divine origin, to maintain and support
the tree of commonwealth just as his subjects are bound
to love and obey him.[54] The prince must, above all, administer justice, "for the whole authority thereof is given to
him by God to minister by himself or his deputy by his
subjects."[55] He must therefore defend the people against
oppression by great men,[56] and distribute equity to his

51. *Exhortation to all men*, pp. Pvii–Pvii[b].
52. For a brief discussion of the "very and true commonweal," see Allen,
History of Political Theory in the Sixteenth Century, pp. 134–138.
53. *Tree of Commonwealth*, 1859 edition, p. 6.
54. *Ibid.*, pp. 8–9.
55. *Ibid.*, pp. 10–11.
56. *Ibid.*, p. 12.

subjects.[57] If he faithfully performs all these obligations, he will be anointed by God at his death as a king eternal, and rewarded with the crown of God's own immortal glory.[58]

In the first book of his *Utopia*, More also makes it clear that the "very and true commonweal" can be attained only if the various individuals within the state, king and subjects of all classes alike, perform their proper duties. The troubles from which England suffers today are directly attributable to "the unreasonable covetousness of a few," to the avarice of enclosers, rackrenters, forestallers, and, last but not least, the king. If Raphael Hythlodaye were one of the king's counsellors, he would be obliged to tell the king to his face that the commonalty chooses him for their own sake and not for his, "and that therefore the king ought to take more care for the wealth of his people, than for his own wealth, even as the office and duty of a shepherd is, in that he is a shepherd, to feed his sheep rather than himself."[59] In "The Isle of Nowhere," Utopia itself, the magistrates retain their offices only so long as they foster the "commodity of the commonwealth."[60]

In his *Dialogue between Pole and Lupset*, Starkey asserts that nature has created man for this one purpose— that he might live in civil life, preferring the commonweal to his own selfish pleasures and fantasies.[61] Like More, Starkey believed that England's current misfortunes were due to the upsetting of this principle. Too many people in our own country, he writes, are idle, too few "exercise themselves in doing their office and duty pertaining to the maintenance of the commonweal."[62] The nobles spend their time drinking and playing games, the clergy devote themselves to idle pleasures.[63] But, without doubt, the

57. *Ibid.*, p. 15.
58. *Ibid.*, p. 63.
59. *Utopia*, pp. 92–93.
60. *Ibid.*, Book II, Chap. 3.
61. *Dialogue between Pole and Lupset*, p. 57.
62. *Ibid.*, p. 76.
63. *Ibid.*, p. 77.

greatest destruction to this realm has been the selfish attitude of the kings themselves who have judged "all things
pertaining to the state of our realm to hang only upon
their will and fantasy."[64] By implication, Starkey, no
less than Dudley and More, preached the moral responsibility of the ruler.

To sum up, it may be stated that the political writers of
the English Reformation were far from preaching the
doctrine that the king's will is law. Practical politics—
the growth of the monarchy under Henry VII and Henry
VIII and the Reformation—influenced them, it is true, to
ascribe to the king new powers in both the spiritual and
temporal spheres. In propounding the twin doctrines of
the Royal Supremacy and non-resistance, they departed
radically from the theory of kingship expounded by Sir
John Fortescue in the preceding century. But there they
stopped short. They were willing enough, most of them, to
attribute to the king an unlimited power in the ecclesiastical realm, but they were absolutely unwilling to attribute to him a like power in the secular realm. They believed
that the government of England should be a "mixed" government, that the king should rule for the most part in
conjunction with parliament. They made it quite clear,
moreover, that the king, either *solus* or in parliament, is
subordinate to natural and positive law. And, lest the king
become too puffed up with his own importance, they put a
fresh emphasis on the medieval doctrine of the moral responsibility of the ruler toward his subjects. They were
unwilling, in other words, to go as far as James I and
Hobbes. It remained for a later age to propound the doctrine of divine right and unlimited royal sovereignty.

64. *Ibid.*, pp. 100–101.

APPENDIX A

HENRY VIII'S PROPAGANDIST CAMPAIGN[1]

IN his biography of Stephen Gardiner, Janelle remarks that
Henry VIII and his Council suppressed all public opinion
hostile to the Royal Supremacy by "violence faite aux âmes,
c'est-à-dire propagande."[2] There can be little doubt that this
was actually the case. An examination of the Henrician statute
book and royal proclamations, and especially of the kinds of
books published in England during the vital years, 1528–1539,
clearly reveals the fact that Henry VIII understood the value of
propaganda, and used it to make permanent the new order implemented by the Reformation Parliament. He knew that to
make a revolution permanent, one must, above all, change men's
habits of thinking. One must demonstrate to men, by unmis-
takable "proof," how rotten was the *ancien régime*, and how in-
finitely godly and reasonable is the new order. Accordingly, he
launched a far-flung literary campaign to denounce the medieval
scheme of Church and State, and to herald the triumph of
"truth." And he used his prerogative in respect to the printing
press to drive the opposition underground, to prevent the conservatives from using one of the most effective organs for influencing public opinion.

The subject of Henry VIII's literary offensive against the
Roman Church has already been discussed at some length in
chapters III and IV of the text. But to illustrate the extent to
which the king and Cromwell were prepared to go in the formulation of a new political creed, I have drawn up a chart of the
most important pro-royal tracts published in England (with a
few exceptions) between 1528 and 1539. This chart proves beyond any question of doubt the close relationship which then
existed between the government and the English printing press.

1. This is a subject which has heretofore received little attention from Tudor
historians. Janelle is the important exception. In his *L'Angleterre Catholique*, he
has written two stimulating chapters entitled "L'Expression intellectuelle du
Schisme," in which he stresses particularly the part which propaganda played
in the success of the English Reformation.

2. *L'Angleterre Catholique*, p. 185.

PRO-ROYAL BOOKS PUBLISHED, 1528-1539*

Author	Title	Printer
	1528	
Tyndale	Obedience of a Christian Man	"Hans Luft" (Antwerp)
Tyndale	Parable of the Wicked Mammon	"Hans Luft" (Antwerp)
	1529	
Fish	Supplication for the Beggars	?
	1530	
St. German	Doctor and Student, Dialogue II	P. Treveris
Tyndale	Practice of Prelates	"Hans Luft" (Antwerp)
	1531	
St. German	Doctor and Student, Dialogue II	P. Treveris
St. German	Doctor and Student, Dialogue II	R. Redman
St. German	Doctor and Student, Additions to Dialogue II (2 editions)	Berthelet
	1532	
Anonymous	A Glass of the Truth (2 editions)	Berthelet
St. German	Doctor and Student, Dialogues I and II	R. Redman
St. German	Spirituality and Temporality	Berthelet
St. German	Spirituality and Temporality	R. Redman
	1533	
St. German	Salem and Bizance	Berthelet
Sampson	Oratio	Berthelet
Anonymous	Dialogue between a knight and clerk	Berthelet
Anonymous	Articles devised by consent of king and council	Berthelet

* Except where indicated, the books listed in this chart were printed in London. For full titles, the reader is referred to Appendix B. The dates are submitted only on the basis of probability, for where books are printed anonymously without dates, certainty is impossible. Even Pollard and Redgrave's *Short-Title Catalogue* and Duff's *Hand-Lists of Books Printed by London Printers, 1501-1556*, it will be found, disagree radically on many dates. In such cases, I have been forced to use my own judgment, and very often to make a decision on the basis of internal evidence. Moreover, I do not pretend that the chart is entirely complete, although in some instances I have indicated the various editions to which a book ran.

Author	Title	Printer
	1534	
Fox	*De vera differentia*	Berthelet
Swinnerton	*Muster of schismatic bishops of Rome*	J. Byddell
Barnes	*Supplication to Henry VIII*	J. Byddell
	1535	
St. German	*Power of the Clergy*	T. Godfray
St. German	*Constitutions Provincial and Legatine*	T. Godfray
St. German	*Answer to a Letter*	T. Godfray
Gardiner	*De vera obedientia*	Berthelet
Starkey	*Exhortation to Christian Unity*	Berthelet
Simon Matthew	*Sermon at St. Paul's*	Berthelet
Marsilius of Padua	*Defensor Pacis* (English translation)	R. Wyer
Anonymous	*Dialogue between Julius II and St. Peter*	J. Byddell
	1536	
Gardiner	*De vera obedientia*	Franz Rhode (Hamburg)
Gardiner	*De vera obedientia*	Wendelin Rihel (Strassburg)
Cheke	*Lamentation*	Berthelet
Anonymous	*Remedy for Sedition*	Berthelet
Anonymous	*Answer to Rebels in Lincolnshire*	Berthelet
Anonymous	*Answer to Rebels in Yorkshire*	Berthelet
	1537	
John Bekinsau	*De supremo regis imperio*	Berthelet
Official	*Bishops' Book*	Berthelet
Anonymous	*Protestation of pope's council*	Berthelet
Anonymous	*Regis sententia de concilio et bulla*	Berthelet
	1538	
Fox	*De vera differentia*	Berthelet
Anonymous	*Epistle from Henry VIII to Emperor*	Berthelet
Anonymous	*Henrici octavi ad Caesarem epistola*	Berthelet
Anonymous	*Treatise concerning councils*	Berthelet
Anonymous	*Protestation of pope's council*	Berthelet
Anonymous	*Treatise proving by the king's laws*	Berthelet
John Longland	*Sermon before the king*	T. Petyt
	1539	
Morison	*Exhortation to Englishmen*	Berthelet
Morison	*Invective against treason* (3 editions)	Berthelet
Tunstal	*Sermon on Palm Sunday*	Berthelet

The political pamphlets are shown to reflect to an amazing degree the fluctuations of the political barometer.

The chart indicates that, prior to 1532, few respectable books attacking the old ecclesiastical order were published. Henry VIII had not yet broken with the pope, and the government was not therefore confronted with the necessity of fomenting public opinion against Rome. To be sure, Tyndale's works denouncing the papacy and preaching absolute obedience to the secular sovereign were published before 1532. So were Fish's *Supplication for the Beggars* "exposing" the scandalous extent of clerical property and power in England, and several editions of St. German's *Doctor and Student*, including the thirteen Additions to Dialogue II. But Tyndale and Fish were tainted with heresy and could scarcely hope to influence respectable public opinion, and the *Doctor and Student* was more of a theoretical legal treatise than a polemic.

In 1532, however, with the impending failure of the king's divorce and the passage of the first Act of Annates, the government became actively interested in propaganda for the first time. In that year, accordingly, Thomas Berthelet, the royal printer, struck off the anonymous *A Glass of the Truth*, which limited the pope's judicial powers, and St. German's first anticlerical tract, the *Spirituality and Temporality*.[3] During the three years, 1533–1536, when the Reformation Parliament passed its most revolutionary legislation, and Fisher and More were executed, the government, in vital need of propaganda, kept the printing establishments of Berthelet and others working day and night. The banner year was 1535. In that year Thomas Godfray published St. German's three most devastating political tracts, Berthelet issued Gardiner's *De vera obedientia*, and Marsilius of Padua's *Defensor Pacis* appeared in an English translation for the first and only time.[4] In 1536 the peace of the realm was threatened by the Pilgrimage of Grace, and as a result four books were put on sale expounding the sinfulness of rebellion.[5] In 1537 and 1538 any number of tracts denouncing the pope's right to convene a general council were published by Berthelet in response to Paul III's summons to an oecumenical conclave at Mantua.[6] In 1539 another crisis occurred. In June

3. For fuller discussion of these tracts, see above, Chap. III, *passim*.
4. See above, Chap. III, *passim*, especially p. 44 n. 27, 66.
5. See above, Chap. IV, *passim*, especially p. 93.
6. See above, pp. 51–52.

of the previous year a ten years' truce had been negotiated at Nice between Charles V, Francis I, and Paul III, and Cardinal Pole was moving heaven and earth to organize a joint crusade against the English Turk. Accordingly, Berthelet's press once more became active, and in 1539 struck off Tunstal's *Sermon on Palm Sunday*, and Morison's most important works on non-resistance, one of which ran to three editions.[7]

Not all these books, of course, can be proved to have had actual official sponsorship,[8] but the fact that most of them were published by the royal printer removes any reasonable doubt. Unquestionably, the government at least approved their publication, for no printed material could be legally sold without the approval of the Council or its deputies. Moreover, the opportunistic way in which the pamphlets appeared during years of political crisis can scarcely have been accidental.

Furthermore, it is evident that during a revolution some men write against the old régime spontaneously, without the necessity of pressure from the group in power. A propagandist campaign does not mean a campaign conducted entirely by the government. It means a literary offensive sponsored by the government *in alliance with all the sympathetic people of the nation.* Thus, in Henry VIII's reign St. German needed no urging to attack the Catholic Church. He was a common lawyer who had been jealous of ecclesiastical jurisdiction even before 1529. Tyndale and Barnes likewise were willing enough to denounce the "whore of Babylon" on their own initiative. For they saw in the exaltation of the king's prerogative a means of effecting doctrinal innovation, and of saving their own skins from clerical attack. Moreover, there were those who, like Starkey and Morison, naturally wrote for the king's side because they occupied posts in the government service. The government, of course,

7. See above, Chap. IV, *passim*, especially pp. 93–94.

8. A few of them can, however. It is a well-known fact that Gardiner was faced with the alternative of disgrace and even annihilation, or complete capitulation to the king, proof of which was demanded in the form of a written diatribe against the papacy. Hence, the *De vera obedientia*. It is strongly suspected, moreover, that St. German was in the king's pay when in 1532 he published his *Spirituality and Temporality* (see Janelle, *L'Angleterre Catholique*, p. 150). This suspicion is owing to the striking similarity between St. German's treatise and the "Petition of the Commons." In the case of William Marshall's translation of the *Defensor Pacis*, there is evidence of direct subsidization. In Marshall's letter of 1534 to Cromwell, he says that he has already begun to print the *Defensor Pacis*, counting on Cromwell's promise to lend him £12 (*Letters and Papers*, VII, 423).

directly saw to it that books like *A Glass of the Truth* and *Articles devised by consent of the king's council* were produced at the appropriate moment. But probably the only group of people actually bullied into writing in favor of the Royal Supremacy was the episcopacy—men like Fox, Sampson, Gardiner, Tunstal, and Bonner who, though willing from the beginning to acquiesce in the repudiation of the "Bishop of Rome," were more obstinate in defending clerical privileges against royal encroachment.[9] Perhaps it was for this reason that the books written for Henry VIII by the recalcitrant bishops were all published by the royal printer while St. German's three most radical tracts could be entrusted to a private printer, Thomas Godfray.

The various types of material used in the propagandist campaign illustrate how the government tried to reach all classes of public opinion. There were official declarations to startle the timid, translations to satisfy the pedants and historians, Latin works to influence the educated, legal treatises to interest the lawyers, tracts preaching the sinfulness of rebellion to bring the religious into line, scurrilous pamphlets to attract the salacious and sensational-minded, and even poems to lull those musically inclined into obedience. The *Bishops' Book* of 1537 and the *King's Book* of 1543 may be taken as typical examples of official declarations representing the government's precise position in regard to religious doctrine and political thought.[10] As for translations, there were Marsilius of Padua's *Defensor Pacis* and the anonymous *Disputatio inter clericum et militem*, done into English as the *Defence of Peace* and the *Dialogue between a knight and clerk*.[11] As stated above, the government was interested in proving that its ecclesiastical innovations actually boasted a hoary tradition, and for this reason translations were invaluable. However, as Janelle has pointed out, the government ran into a stone wall in its attempt to discover English medieval treatises which did not at least assume the titular supremacy of the pope, and Wiclif was discredited because of his heretical taint.[12] Hence the necessity of translations of continental treatises like the

9. For Gardiner's opposition to royal desires in respect to convocation and the privileges of the clergy, see above, p. 64; p. 64 n. 93. Tunstal was another bishop who was not easily persuaded. He protested against the title of "Supremum Caput," maintaining that it should be qualified to read "in temporalibus, post Christum" (Wilkins, *Concilia*, III, 745).

10. See above, Chap. III, *passim*.

11. See above, Chap. III, *passim*, especially p. 44 n. 27.

12. *L'Angleterre Catholique*, pp. 236–237.

Defensor Pacis, with its questionable chapters carefully deleted, and of the *Disputatio*.

Among the Latin works, the most important were Fox's *De vera differentia*, Sampson's *Oratio*, and Gardiner's *De vera obedientia*, which, because calculated to appeal to the educated public, were circulated abroad as well as in England.[13] St. German's treatises were all written from the legal point of view and were therefore presumably influential in legal circles.[14] And there were any number of tracts on the subject of non-resistance, of which Gardiner, Morison, and Cheke were the outstanding authors.[15]

In the so-called scurrilous pamphlets, the play was on the emotions, and the medium resorted to, abusive language. Several pages of *A Glass of the Truth* are, for example, devoted to an unsavory story about Prince Arthur's and Catherine of Aragon's first night of wedded life, in an attempt to show how ridiculous were those who imagined that the two had never consummated their marriage.[16] Thomas Swinnerton, in his *Muster of schismatic Bishops of Rome*, submits a long list of papal enormities to prove that popes can err, and that in fact they have erred many times in the past. In other pamphlets the pope is frequently referred to as "the Antichrist," the "whore of Babylon," and "the misty angel of Satan."[17] The anonymous *Dialogue between Julius II and St. Peter* employs ridicule in exposing the tyranny of the papacy.[18] It begins with the admonition, "Reader, refrain from laughing," and shows Julius II knocking at the door of heaven after death, and being refused admission by

13. Henry VIII and Cromwell apparently went out of their way to influence foreign as well as English public opinion. Editions of Gardiner's *De vera obedientia* were printed at Hamburg and Strassburg in 1536. Already in 1535 Cromwell had sent Gardiner, then serving as envoy to Francis I, a dozen copies of both his own book and Sampson's *Oratio* for circulation in France. And the same works were forwarded to Cardinal Pole in Italy in order to persuade the latter to accept the Royal Supremacy. On these points, see Janelle, *Obedience in Church and State*, pp. xxvi–xxxiii.

14. See above, Chaps. III, V, *passim*.

15. See above, Chap. IV, *passim*.

16. Pocock, *Records of the Reformation*, II, 414–415.

17. This kind of language was employed chiefly by the minor pamphleteers. See, for example, *Here begynneth a boke, called the faule of the Romyshe churche* (?, 1540?), and *The Sum of the Actes and decrees made by diuerse bisshops of rome* (London, 1540?). For the full titles of these and subsequent books and manuscripts mentioned, see Appendix B.

18. This dialogue has been attributed to Erasmus. See P. Smith's *Erasmus* (New York, 1923), p. 127.

St. Peter. Most interesting of all, perhaps, is Walter Lynne's *Beginning and ending of all popery*[19] which presents a series of woodcuts to illustrate the sins of the papacy. The Church Fathers, according to Lynne, saw well what the papacy was to become in the future, but, not daring to speak openly, they set forth the truth in figures. One such figure, presented in a woodcut, depicts the pope as a deputy receiving orders from a huge lion representing Satan.

In addition, there were a number of sermons which the government saw fit to print from time to time, and a few poems, hardly worthy of the name. Simon Matthew's *Sermon at St. Paul's*, Bishop Longland's *Sermons before the king*, and Tunstal's *Sermon on Palm Sunday* were all published by Berthelet. Peter Moone's *Treatise of things abused in the popish church* and the fragment entitled *A Ballad on the defeat of the Devon and Cornwall rebels of 1548* are examples of poems aimed at the pope and upholding the Royal Supremacy.

The king's literary campaign was not, however, confined to the use of the press. The numerous references in the *Letters and Papers of Henry VIII* to manuscript works defending the Royal Supremacy are evidence enough that manuscripts, as well as printed books, were being circulated to influence public opinion. Although there is no means of knowing how wide a circulation these works enjoyed, their number may be inferred from the numerous citations in the *Letters and Papers*. One citation, for example, includes under one heading no less than eleven such tracts.[20] Some of these are now available in printed form in collections like Pocock's *Records of the Reformation*, and Burnet's *History of the Reformation*, or in individual editions like Gardiner's "Si sedes illa," printed in Janelle's *Obedience in Church and State*.[21] The great majority, however, are still in manuscript form, and can be read only in the British Museum, Public Record Office, or in private collections like Hatfield House. Without a glance at these, the extent and nature of the king's propagandist campaign cannot be fully understood.

The manuscripts, like the printed books, deal with every conceivable phase of the controversy with Rome and the Church.

19. Lynne was a printer, translator, and ardent reformer who enjoyed Cranmer's patronage.

20. *Letters and Papers*, VII, 1602.

21. Thomas' *The Pilgrim* is available in Froude's edition. And the letter written jointly by Tunstal and Stokesley to Pole in 1537 can be read in an edition of 1560 (see Appendix B).

One, for example, consists of a series of articles for unlearned priests concerning the Royal Supremacy and the usurped jurisdiction of the "Bishop of Rome."[22] One is entitled "Against the supremacy of the pope,"[23] and another "The question moved whether these texts ensuing pertain especially to spiritual prelates or to temporal princes."[24] Still another deals with the right of the prince to appoint and depose bishops,[25] and two, including one by Morison, preach the doctrine of non-resistance.[26] Finally, there are three which grapple with the problem of the king's relation to general councils.[27]

The circulation of pro-royal tracts, both in printed and manuscript form, was not sufficient, however, to ensure the complete success of the Henrician schism. The government realized perfectly well that to propagate the new gospel without at the same time stifling the opposition was to leave its task dangerously incomplete. Accordingly, Henry VIII used his undoubted prerogative in respect to the printing press[28] to suppress all books except those countenanced by the government. Proclamations were issued and statutes passed to obtain for the king in council an absolute control of the press.

Prior to 1529, the regulation of the English book trade had been in the hands of the English Church. The "Ex officio" statute of 1410 had empowered the ecclesiastical officials to arrest and to proceed judicially against those who "make or write any book contrary to the catholic faith and determination of the

22. P.R.O., St.P. 6: 5, 5; cf. *Letters and Papers*, VIII, 294. This tract has since been published in Dunham and Pargellis, *Complaint and Reform in England, 1436–1714* (New York, 1938), pp. 130–134.

23. St.P. 1: 88, ff. 13, 14; cf. *Letters and Papers*, VII, 1602 (7).

24. St.P. 6: 2, 9; cf. *Letters and Papers*, V, 1022.

25. St.P. 6: 7, 27; cf. *Letters and Papers*, VII, 1384.

26. Morison's tract is to be found in St.P. 6: 13, 4; cf. *Letters and Papers*, XI, 1409. See also St.P. 1: 99, ff. 213–236; cf. *Letters and Papers*, IX, 1064.

27. The most important of these is the tract at Hatfield House entitled "A Treatise concernyng general Counseilles," calendared in *Letters and Papers*, VII, 691 (2). There are also two tracts among the Cotton MSS. at the B.M.— Cleopatra E. VI, ff. 331–331ᵇ, and ff. 332–335, the first of which is a sermon or exhortation in defense of Henry VIII concerning a general council; and the second of which is entitled "By whatt authorite and whow generall counsayles may be callyd." See above, pp. 50–51, 54.

28. See W.M.Clyde, *Struggle for the Freedom of the Press from Caxton to Cromwell* (Oxford, 1934), Chap. 1, *passim*. As Clyde says (p. 9), "The principle of the freedom of the subject to publish his thoughts had not been formulated. To the sixteenth century Englishman it would have seemed a dangerous and undesirable claim for anyone to make."

Holy Church." In the fifteen-twenties it was Tunstal, Bishop of London, who called the London booksellers together and warned them against importing Lutheran tracts, and it was the ecclesiastical courts which enforced Tunstal's monitions.[29] But in the late twenties the control of the book trade passed into the hands of the Privy Council[30]—one of the most striking instances of the growing power of the monarchy. After 1529 it was the king, not the bishops, who issued proclamations regulating the activities of the London booksellers, and it was the Privy Council, not the ecclesiastical courts, which dealt with press misdemeanors.

The king used his newly-secured prerogative to ensure the success of his propagandist campaign. Many of his proclamations regulating the book trade had as their primary objects, to be sure, the suppression of radical works on religious doctrine—for Henry was a good Catholic—and the protection of native printers against foreign competition.[31] But some of them were also unquestionably designed to supplement the government's current propagandist campaign.

Three proclamations in particular are important in this respect. One, dated January 1, 1536, denounced sundry writings and books, including a sermon by the late Bishop of Rochester containing many errors and slanders. All persons, reads the edict, having in their possession a sermon of the late traitor or any slander on the king and his authority repugnant to the statutes made for the royal succession and abolishing papal authority, must deliver up these books within forty days to the Lord Chancellor or Secretary Cromwell.[32]

A second proclamation, dated November 16, 1538, aimed doubtless at pro-papal as well as heretical works, banned the importation of English books printed abroad. No person, accord-

29. See Arthur W. Reed, "The Regulation of the Book Trade before the Proclamation of 1538," *Transactions* of the Bibliographical Society, XV, 157–184.

30. In March, 1529, the king, not the Bishop of London, issued a proclamation prohibiting certain heretical books (see *Tudor and Stuart Proclamations*, edited by Robert Steele, I, no. 114).

31. These were undoubtedly the main objects of the proclamations of March, 1529, and June, 1530 (summarized in *Tudor and Stuart Proclamations*, I, nos. 114 and 122), and of the statutes, 25 Hen. VIII, c. 15 and 34 Hen. VIII, c. 1. That the device of the Index was not peculiar to the Catholic Church is evident from these two proclamations which include lists of prohibited books, including Tyndale's works and Fish's *Supplication for the Beggars*.

32. *Tudor and Stuart Proclamations*, I, no. 155.

ing to the proclamation, may legally print "any book in the English tongue" except after examination by the Privy Council.[33] In April, 1543, steps were taken against printers for violation of this edict. Publishers were summoned before the Privy Council to answer for printing "such books as were thought to be unlawful." Those released were required to submit a declaration of the number of books they had bought and sold within the last three years, and to name other merchants whom they knew to have imported prohibited books.[34]

A third proclamation, dated July 8, 1546, provided for the regulation of the book trade in the provinces. Printers were expressly forbidden therein to sell copies of their books before "the mayor of the town where [they] dwelleth" had scrutinized them carefully. This regulation, it was calculated, would serve to suppress "such English books as contain pernicious and detestable errors and heresies."[35]

But, it may well be asked, did these proclamations succeed in their purpose? Was Henry VIII successful in suppressing printed diatribes against the Royal Supremacy? At first blush, it would seem not. We know that certain Antwerp publishers—Christoffel and Hans van Ruremund, Hans Luft (Johannes Hoochstraten), and Martinus de Keyser—made their livelihood by smuggling heretical works into England. In 1528 Hans van Ruremund is reported to have abjured in England "for causing fifteen hundred of Tyndale's New Testaments to be printed at Antwerp, and for bringing five hundred into England." We know that similar illegal presses were operated at Strassburg and Cologne.[36] We know, too, that the king was forced to issue one proclamation after another denouncing the works of the English and continental reformers—a tacit admission of the fact that suppression was proving unsuccessful.

However, a close examination of the books actually printed in England and on the continent during the decade, 1528–1539, entitles us to come to a somewhat different conclusion. It will

33. *Ibid.*, no. 176.
34. See E.G.Duff, *A Century of the English Book Trade* (London, 1905), pp. xxiv–xxv.
35. *Tudor and Stuart Proclamations*, I, no. 295.
36. See M.E.Kronenberg, "Notes on English Printing in the Low Countries (Early Sixteenth Century)," *Library*, 4th series, IX, 139–163; and Robert Steele, "Notes on English Books printed abroad, 1525–1548," *Transactions* of the Bibliographical Society, XI, 189–236.

be evident to anyone who has perused Pollard and Redgrave's *Short-Title Catalogue*,[37] Duff's *Hand-Lists of Books Printed by London Printers, 1501–1556*,[38] and Steele's *Tudor and Stuart Proclamations* that, in fact, very few books opposing the king's great matter and the Royal Supremacy were printed during these years. Heretical works by Tyndale, Barlow, Frith, and others there were aplenty, printed in the Low Countries and smuggled into England by London merchants. But tracts opposing the king *politically* there were few. The royal proclamations denounce *ad nauseam* the radical doctrinal works of the Protestants. They mention not at all conservative tracts defending the old order and striking at the Royal Supremacy.[39]

The government, in other words, was thoroughly successful in driving the political opposition underground, if not the radical theologians. The opposition did, of course, occasionally print privately,[40] and smuggle in contraband material from the continent.[41] But not very often, and such works were apt to be ruthlessly suppressed at their inception.[42] In any case, such a press could not hope to vie with the king, supported as he was by all the respectable printers of England, and financed by the royal treasury.

37. *A Short-Title Catalogue of Books Printed in England, Scotland, and Ireland, And of English Books Printed Abroad 1475–1640*, compiled by A.W.Pollard and G.R.Redgrave (London, 1926).

38. London, 1913.

39. See the list of English books prohibited by name during Henry VIII's reign in Steele, "Notes on English Books printed abroad," *Trans.* of Bibl. Soc., XI, 214–217.

40. Fisher's book on Henry VIII's divorce, if ever actually published, must have been the product of a private printing press.

41. Abell's *Invicta veritas*, Cochlaeus' *De Matrimonio*, and Pole's *Pro ecclesiasticae unitatis defensione* were printed abroad and smuggled into England. Abell's book, though marked Lüneberg, was printed at Antwerp by Martinus de Keyser, while Pole's tract was published at Rome. It seems probable that Friar Peto's answer to *A Glass of the Truth* (reviewed in Pocock, *Records of the Reformation*, II, 422–435) was also struck off at Antwerp. Like Abell's book, it claims to have been printed at Lüneberg, but there seems actually to have been no printing press at Lüneberg then.

42. If ever published, Fisher's book on the divorce must have been suppressed in this way, for there is no extant copy of it today. The manner in which hostile books were treated by the government can be inferred from the warm reception accorded to unorthodox Bibles. In the words of Duff (*A Century of the English Book Trade*, p. xxi), "Taking the case of the New Testament it would not be too much to say that of the editions which can from sound evidence be proved to have been printed before 1532, of not one quarter does the slightest trace remain."

To propagate its opinions in manuscript was thus the only alternative left to the opposition. A large number of manuscript tracts were written against the king's ecclesiastical changes, it is true. The *Letters and Papers of Henry VIII* calendar many such treatises, of which Volume V, no. 1020, may serve as a typical example. In this citation there are mentioned two pro-ecclesiastical works, one of which is entitled "That the bishops have immediate authority of Christ to make such laws as they shall think expedient for the weal of men's souls,"[43] and the other "Clerici sunt exempti de jurisdictione laicorum, etiam de jure divino." Bishop Fisher himself wrote two treatises in manuscript opposing the king, one a history of the divorce, and the other defending the rights and dignity of the clergy.[44] And there are references to a book of notes written by the rebel, Sir Francis Bigod, maintaining that the head of the Church of England might be a spiritual man like the Archbishop of Canterbury, but not the king.[45] When all is said and done, however, propaganda by manuscript is ever feeble and ineffectual in comparison to propaganda by the printed word. The sheer physical labor involved in producing a manuscript keeps the number of available copies low, and only a small reading public can accordingly be reached.

The real impotence of the opposition is, I think, most eloquently revealed by the fact that its natural leaders refrained from committing their views to writing for circulation. Sir Thomas More scrupulously avoided penning anything directly against the Royal Supremacy, and his anti-heretical books avoided the issue altogether.[46] Archbishop Warham's opposi-

43. St.P., 6: 1, 8. This tract has since been published in Dunham and Pargellis, *Complaint and Reform in England, 1436–1714*, pp. 125–129.

44. St.P., 6: 11, 15; cf. *Letters and Papers*, VIII, 887 (6).

45. *Letters and Papers*, XII (1), 201 (p. 92); 202 (p. 103); 1087 (p. 499). See above, p. 117.

46. Even after he had been sent to the Tower, More could not be persuaded either to speak or to write against the Royal Supremacy. It was not until the very end of his trial, when he saw that he would inevitably be condemned, that he was moved to "discharge" his conscience. The attitude of Richard Reynolds, one of the inmates of Sion Abbey, was much the same as More's. In his examination before the Lords, Reynolds said that he had hoped he would not be required to speak on the subject of the Supremacy, but that now he feels he must speak out his mind (*Letters and Papers*, VIII, 661). More's *Dialogue, Supplication of Souls, Apology*, etc. were occupied almost exclusively with refuting Lutheran heresies and defending the clergy against scurrilous attacks. They were aimed, therefore, at Tyndale, Frith, St. German, and Fish rather than at the government.

tion to the new order was limited to a formal protest against the legislation of 1529–1532, and to a speech which was never delivered.[47] And Bishop Gardiner, who so vigorously defended the privileges of the Church during the stormy days of the "Petition of the Commons," ended by capitulating to the king unreservedly.

Thus, with the exception of a number of manuscripts written by comparatively obscure men, the opposition was for the most part limited in its protest to isolated statements made by parish priests and rebels. There are references in the *Letters and Papers*, for example, to the curates Sir Richard Crowley and Sir Richard Jacksone, attacking the Royal Supremacy from the pulpit; to Friar Pecock defending the pope's primacy in a sermon at Winchester; to Richard Marshall fleeing for his life in consequence of preaching against the king.[48] But to offset preaching of this sort, Cromwell in 1533 set on foot a thoroughgoing plan for regimenting the pulpit as well as the press.[49] No stone was left unturned in stifling the fomentation of conservative opinion.

Is it any wonder that the English Reformation proceeded so smoothly in its early stages? Between 1532 and 1547 the government alone prescribed the intellectual diet of the English public, and seldom was the latter permitted to partake of forbidden fruit.

47. *Letters and Papers*, V, 818, 1247.
48. *Ibid.*, IX, 46; XI, 1393; VII, 449; X, 594.
49. *Ibid.*, VI, 1087. In "memoranda for the king's council" Cromwell proposes to examine the bishops on their political orthodoxy, to make arrangements with the bishops for preaching the Royal Supremacy, to cause friars, monks, parish priests, and even the mayor of the city of London, to preach the same.

APPENDIX B

BIBLIOGRAPHY OF EARLY TUDOR LITERATURE ON POLITICAL THEORY

TWENTY years ago, McIlwain remarked that Tudor literature on the controversy of Church and State "is of far greater importance for the history of political thought than is generally recognized if we may judge from the attention it has received from the historians." It is with this statement in mind that I submit the following bibliography of early Tudor literature on political theory. For despite its importance, no one has yet attempted to compile such a bibliography.

There exist, of course, a number of short and highly suggestive bibliographies on the subject. In his *Bibliography of British History, Tudor Period* (pp. 93–99), Conyers Read has cited a number of the most important Tudor political tracts, and McIlwain has done likewise in his *Political Works of James I* (pp. lxxi–lxxxvi). Janelle has gone rather more deeply into the subject in his *L'Angleterre Catholique* (pp. 346–349). And Pollard and Redgrave's *Short-Title Catalogue of Works printed in England, 1475–1640*, and the *Letters and Papers of Henry VIII* contain a vast number of references to treatises, both in printed and manuscript form.

But nowhere is there a bibliography in which these references are brought together. It is with the hope of supplying this deficiency, and of thus making available the general *corpus* of early Tudor political literature, that I have compiled the list below. Needless to say, I do not pretend that this list is by any means exhaustive. However, I believe that I have omitted no really important tract, and that I have supplemented former lists by the addition of a number of tracts hitherto unknown.

ABELL, THOMAS. *Invicta veritas. An answere, That by no maner of law it maye be lawfull for the moste noble Kinge of englande, Kinge Henry the ayght, to be diuorsed fro the quenes grace, his lawful and very wyfe* (Antwerp, 1533).[1]
BALDWIN, WILLIAM. *A Myrroure for Magistrates* (London,

1. This date, and every date hereafter, refers to the *first* date of publication.

1559); reprinted under the same title by Lily B. Campbell (Cambridge, 1938).

BARNES, ROBERT. *A supplicatyon made by Robert Barnes doctoure in diuinite unto the most excellent and redoubted prince kinge henrye the eyght* (London, 1534?); reprinted in *The whole workes of W. Tyndall, Iohn Frith, and Doct. Barnes* (London, 1573), pp. 183–205.

BARNES, ROBERT. "That mens constitutions, which are not grounded in Scripture, bynde not the conscience of man vnder the payne of deadly sinne," printed in *The whole workes of W. Tyndall, Iohn Frith, and Doct. Barnes*, pp. 292–300 [not published when first written in ?].

BECON, THOMAS. *The Policy of War wherein is declared how the enemies of the Christian Public Weal may be overcome and subdued* (London, 1542); reprinted in *The Early Works of Thomas Becon*, edited by Rev. John Ayre (Parker Soc., Cambridge, 1843), pp. 230–261.

BECON, THOMAS. *A confortable Epistle too Goddes faythfull people in Englande*, wherein is declared the cause of takynge awaye the true Christen religion from them, & howe it maye be recouered and obtayned agayne, newly made by Thomas Becon (Strassburg, 1553).

BEKINSAU, JOHN. *De Svpremo et absolvto regis imperio* (London, 1547?); reprinted in Melchior Goldast, *Monarchiae S. Romani Imperii Siue Tractatus De Iurisdictione Imperiali*, III (Francofordiae, 1613), 735–756.

BONNER, EDMUND. Preface to Gardiner's *De vera obedientia*, Hamburg edition (1536); reprinted in *The Royal Supremacy in Matters Ecclesiastical in Pre-Reformation Times*, edited by B. A. Heywood (London, 1870).

BOURCHIER, JOHN. *The Golden Boke of Marcus Aurelius* (London, 1535); reprinted in José Maria Gálvez, *Guevara in England, nebst neudruck von Lord Berners' Golden Boke of Marcus Aurelius* (Berlin, 1916).

BRINKELOW, HENRY. *Complaynt of Roderyck Mors . . . unto the parliament howse of Ingland his natural cuntry* (London, 1548?); reprinted under the same title by E. E. T. Soc., edited by J. M. Cowper (London, 1874).

BRINKELOW, HENRY. *The Lamentacyon of a Christen Agaynst the Cytye of London, made by Roderigo Mors* (London, 1542); reprinted under the same title by E. E. T. Soc., edited by J. M. Cowper (London, 1874).

BRINKELOW, HENRY. *A Supplication of the Poore Commons*

(London, 1546); reprinted under the same title by E. E. T. Soc., edited by F. J. Furnivall (London, 1871).

BROOKE, SIR ROBERT. *La Graunde abridgement* (London, 1573).

BULLINGER, HENRY. *A treatise or Sermon of Henry Bullynger, much fruitfull and necessarye for this tyme, concernynge magistrates and obedience of subiectes.* Also concernyng the affayres of warre, and what scryptures make mension thereof. whether christen powers may war against their ennemis. And whither it be laufull for a christyan to beare the office of a magistrate, and of the duety of souldiers with many other holsom instructions for captaynes & souldiers both (London, 1549).

CHEKE, SIR JOHN. *A Lamentation in vvhiche is shevved what Ruyne and destruction cometh of seditious rebellyon* (London, 1536).

CHEKE, SIR JOHN. *The hurt of sedicion howe greueous it is to a Communewelth* (London, 1549).

CHRISTOPHERSON, JOHN. *An exhortation to all menne to take hede and beware of rebellion:* wherein are set forth the causes, that commonlye moue men to rebellion, and that no cause is there, that ought to moue any man therevnto, with a discourse of the miserable effectes, that ensue thereof, and of the wretched ende, that all rebelles comme to, most necessary to be redde in this seditiouse & troublesome tyme, made by John Christoferson (London, 1554).

COCHLAEUS (JOHANNIS DOBNECK). *De Matrimonio serenissimi Regis Angliae, Henrici Octaui, Congratulatio disputatoria Iohannis Cochlei Germani, Ad Pavlvm Tertium Pont. Max.* (?, 1535).

CRANMER, THOMAS. "Notes for a Homily against Rebellion," printed in *Miscellaneous Writings and Letters of Thomas Cranmer*, edited by J. E. Cox, (Parker Soc., Cambridge, 1846), pp. 188–190 [not published when first written in 1549?].

CRANMER, THOMAS. "A Sermon concerning the Time of Rebellion," printed in *Miscellaneous Writings and Letters of Thomas Cranmer*, pp. 190–202 [not published when first written in 1549?].

DUDLEY, EDMUND. "The Tree of Common Wealth," printed under the same title (Manchester, 1859) [not published when first written in 1510].

ELYOT, SIR THOMAS. *The Boke named The Gouernour* (London, 1531); reprinted under the same title by H. H. S. Croft, 2 vols. (London, 1880).

ELYOT, SIR THOMAS. *The Doctrinal of princes made by the noble oratour Isocrates & translated out of Greke in to Englishe by syr Thomas Eliot knight* (London, 1534?).

ELYOT, SIR THOMAS. *The Image of Governance compiled of the actes and sentences notable, of the moste noble Emperour Alexander Seuerus, late translated out of Greke into Englyshe, by syr Thomas Eliot knight, in the fauour of Nobylitie* (London, 1541).

ELYOT, SIR THOMAS. *Of that knowlage, whiche maketh a wise man. A disputacion Platonike* (London, ?).

ERASMUS, DESIDERIUS. *Institutio principis Christiani* (Basle, 1516); translated into English by L. K. Born as *The Education of a Christian Prince* (New York, 1936).

FISH, SIMON. *A Supplicacyon for the Beggars* (?, 1529); reprinted under the same title by E. E. T. Soc., edited by F. J. Furnivall (London, 1871).

FISHER, JOHN. [Treatise in defence of the rights and dignity of the clergy, 1535?], P. R. O., St. P. 6: 11, 15.

FITZHERBERT, SIR ANTHONY. *La Graunde Abridgement* (London, 1516).

FITZHERBERT, SIR ANTHONY. *La novel natura brevium* (London, 1534); translated into English as *The New Natura Brevium of the Most Reverend Judge, Mr. Anthony Fitzherbert* (London, 1687).

FORREST, SIR WILLIAM. Pleasaunt Poesye of Princelie Practise (1548), B. M., Royal MSS., 17 D III; extract printed in *England in the Reign of King Henry the Eighth*, edited by S. J. Herrtage (E. E. T. Soc., London, 1878), pp. lxxxv–xcix.

FOX, EDWARD. *Opus eximium de vera differentia regiae potestatis et ecclesiasticae, et quae sit ipsa veritas ac virtus utriusque* (London, 1534); reprinted in Melchior Goldast, *Monarchiae S. Romani Imperii Siue Tractatus De Iurisdictione Imperiali*, III (Francofordiae, 1613); translated into English by Henry, Lord Stafford, as *The true dyfferens betwen the regall power and the Ecclesiasticall power* (London, 1548).

GARDINER, STEPHEN. "Si sedes illa," printed in Pierre Janelle, *Obedience in Church and State* (Cambridge, 1930), pp. 22–65 [not published when first written in 1535].

GARDINER, STEPHEN. *De vera obedientia* (London, 1535); reprinted in Janelle, *Obedience in Church and State*, pp. 68–171.

GARDINER, STEPHEN. "Contemptum humanae legis," printed in Janelle, *Obedience in Church and State*, pp. 174–211 [not published when first written in 1541].

GOODALE, JOHN. *The Lyberties of the Cleargy Collected out of the*

Lawes of this Realme both necessary for Vycars and Curates (London, 1540?).

GOODMAN, CHRISTOPHER. *How Svperior powers oght to be obeyd of their subiects; and Wherin they may lawfully by Gods Worde be disobeyed and resisted* (Geneva, 1558); reprinted in facsimile by Facsimile Text Soc. (New York, 1931).

HALES, SIR JAMES. *The Commvnication betwene my Lord Chauncelor and iudge Hales, being among other iudges to take his oth in VVestminster hall* (London, 1553); reprinted in Foxe, *Acts and Monuments*, edited by Rev. S. R. Cattley, VI (London, 1838), 712–717.

HENRY VIII. *Assertio Septem Sacramentorum* (London, 1521); reprinted under the same title by Rev. L. O'Donovan (New York, 1908).

HOOPER, JOHN. *Godly and most necessary Annotations in ye xiii Chapyter too the Romaynes* (Worcester, 1551); reprinted in *Later Writings of Bishop Hooper*, edited by Rev. C. Nevinson (Parker Soc., Cambridge, 1852), pp. 93–116.

HUGHE, WILLIAM. *The troubled mans medicine verye profitable to be redde of al men wherein they may learne pacyently to suffer all kyndes of aduersitie* (London, 1546).

JOHNSON, JOHN. *An confortable exhortation: of oure mooste holy Christen faith and her frutes Written (vnto the Christen bretherne in Scotlande) after the poore worde of God* (Parishe, 1535).

KEILWEY, ROBERT. *Reports d'ascuns Cases (Qui ont evenus aux temps du Roy Henry le Septiême de tres heureuse memoire, & du tres illustre Roy Henry le huitiesme, & ne sont comprises deins les livres des Terms & Ans demesmes les Roys). Seligès hors des papieres de Robert Keilwey Esq; par Jean Croke* (London, 1688).

KETHE, WILLIAM. *William Kethe to the Reader*, printed in Goodman's *How Svperior powers oght to be obeyd of their subiects* (Geneva, 1558).

KNOX, JOHN. *The First Blast of the Trumpet against the monstrvovs regiment of women* (Geneva, 1558); reprinted under the same title by Ed. Arber (London, 1878).

LATIMER, HUGH. *Sermons* (London, 1549); reprinted in *Sermons by Hugh Latimer*, edited by Rev. G. E. Corrie (Parker Soc., Cambridge, 1844).

LEVER, THOMAS. *Sermons* (London, 1550); reprinted in *Thomas Lever. Sermons. 1550*, edited by Ed. Arber (London, 1870).

LONGLAND, JOHN. *A Sermonde spoken before the kynge his maiestie at Grenwiche, vppon good fryday* (London, 1536).

LONGLAND, JOHN. *A Sermonde made before the Kynge, his maiestye at grenewiche, vpon good Frydaye* (London, 1538).

LYNNE, WALTER. *The beginnynge and endynge of all poperie* (beinge taken oute of certaine olde prophecies more then .ccc. yeres agone, here faythfully set forth to the amendement of this presente worlde, out of hye Almayne by Gwalter Lynne (London, 1548?).

MARSILIUS OF PADUA. *Opus Insigne cui titulum fecit autor defensorem pacis, quod questionem illam iam olim controuersam, De potestate Papae et imperatoris excussissime tractet* . . . (Basle, 1522); reprinted in *The Defensor Pacis of Marsilius of Padua*, edited by C. W. Previté-Orton (Cambridge, 1928); translated into English by William Marshall as *The defence of peace: lately translated out of laten in to englysshe* (London, 1535).

MATTHEW, SIMON. *A Sermon made in the cathedrall churche of saynt Paule at London* (London, 1535).

MOONE, PETER. *A short treatyse of certayne thinges abused In the Popysh Church*, longe vsed:
But now abolyshed, to our consolation,
And Gods word auaunced, the lyght of our saluation (Ipswich, 1548?).

MORE, SIR THOMAS. *Epigrammata* (Basle, 1520).

MORE, SIR THOMAS. *Utopia* (Louvain, 1516); reprinted under the same title by J. H. Lupton (Oxford, 1895).

MORE, SIR THOMAS. *Dialogue concerning Tyndale* (London, 1528); reprinted under the same title by W. E. Campbell (London, 1927).

MORE, SIR THOMAS. *The supplication of soules* . . . *againste the supplication of beggers* (London, 1529); reprinted in *The vvorkes of Sir Thomas More Knyght* (London, 1557), pp. 288–339.

MORE, SIR THOMAS. *The Apologye of Syr Thomas More, Knyght* (London, 1533); reprinted under the same title by E. E. T. Soc., edited by A. I. Taft (Oxford, 1930).

MORE, SIR THOMAS. *The deballacion of Salem and Bizance* (London, 1533); reprinted in *The vvorkes of Sir Thomas More Knyght*, pp. 929–1034.

MORE, SIR THOMAS. "A Dialogue of Comforte against tribulation," printed in *The vvorkes of Sir Thomas More Knyght*, pp. 1139–1264 [not published when first printed in 1534].

MORISON, SIR RICHARD. [Discourse upon a commonwealth, and denunciation of the Northern Rebellion, 1536], P. R. O., St. P.

6: 13, 4; the original draft is preserved in B. M., Royal MSS. 18 A. L.

MORISON, SIR RICHARD. *An Exhortation to styre all Englyshe men to the defence of theyr countreye, made by Richard Morysine* (London, 1539).

MORISON, SIR RICHARD. *An Invective ayenste the great and detestable vice, treason, wherein the secrete practises, and traiterous workinges of theym, that suffrid of late are disclosed* (London, 1539).

MORISON, SIR RICHARD. [A discourse touching the reformation of the laws of England, 1542], B. M., Cotton MSS., Faustina C II, 5–22.

PAYNELL, THOMAS. *The preceptes teachyng a prynce or a noble estate his duetie*, Written by Agapetus in Greke to the emperour Justinian, and after translated into Latin, and nowe in to Englysshe by Thomas Paynell (London, 1534?).

PAYNELL, THOMAS. *The Conspiracie of Lucius Catiline translated into englishe by Thomas Paynell* (London, 1541).

PERKINS, JOHN. *Incipit perutilis tractatus magistri Johnis Perkins sive explanatio quorundam capitulorum*, etc. (London, 1528); translated into English as *Here beginneth a verie Profitable booke of Master John Perkins . . . treating of the Lawes of this Realme* (London, 1555); reprinted under the same title by R. J. Greening (London, 1827).

POLE, REGINALD. Reginaldi Poli, Cardinalis Britanni, ad Henricum Octauum Britanniae Regem, *pro ecclesiasticae unitatis defensione*, libri quatuor (Rome, 1539).

PONET, JOHN. *A Shorte Treatise of politike pouuer, and of the true Obedience which subiectes owe to kynges and other ciuile Gouernours, with an Exhortacion to all true naturall Englishe men* (Strassburg?, 1556).

RASTELL, JOHN. *Expositiones terminorum legum anglorum.* Et natura breiuium cum diuersis casibus regulis & fundamentis legum tam de libris Magistri Littletoni quam de aliis legum libris collectis et breuiter compilatis pro iuuinibus valde necessarijs (London, 1525?).

RASTELL, JOHN. *The Exposicions of the termes of the lawes of England*, with diuers propre rules & principles of the lawe, as well out of the bookes of maister Litleton, as of other (London, 1567).

ST. GERMAN, CHRISTOPHER. *Dialogus de fundamentis legum Anglie et de conscientia* (London, 1523); reprinted many times in

English as *Doctor and Student*, most recently in the edition of
William Muchall (Cincinnati, 1874).

ST. GERMAN, CHRISTOPHER. *A Treatise concernynge the diuision
betwene the spiritualtie and temporaltie* (London, 1532); reprinted in A. I. Taft, *The Apologye of Syr Thomas More,
Knyght*, Appendix.

ST. GERMAN, CHRISTOPHER. *A Dialogue betwixte two englyshemen, whereof one was called Salem and the other Bizance* (London, 1533).

ST. GERMAN, CHRISTOPHER. *A treatyse concerninge the power of
the clergye and the lawes of the realm* (London, 1535?).

ST. GERMAN, CHRISTOPHER. *A treatise concernynge diuers of the
constitucyons prouynciall and legantines* (London, 1535?).

ST. GERMAN, CHRISTOPHER. *An Answere to a Letter* (London,
1535?).

SAMPSON, RICHARD. Ricardi Sampsonis, Regii Sacelli Decani,
*Oratio, qua docet, hortatur, admonet omnes, potissimum Anglos,
regiae dignitati cum primis ut obediant, quia verbum Dei praecipit, Episcopo Romano ne sint audientes*, qui nullo jure divino,
in eos quicquam potestatis habet, postquam ita jubet Rex, et
illi non obediant. Qui contra fecerint, eos perspicuè docet,
legem divinam contemnere. Non est ergo quod sibi timeant
Angli, de humana quavis potestate Episcopi Rom. qui aliam
quam humanam, hoc est humano consensu, in Anglos non
habet. Obediant igitur Deo, non homini (London, 1534); reprinted in Strype, *Eccles. Mem.* (Oxford, 1822), I(2), 162–175.

SCORY, JOHN. *An Epistle wrytten by John Scory the late bishope
of Chichester unto all the fayfhfull that be in pryson in Englande,
or in any other troble for the defence of Goddes truthe*: wherin
he dothe as well by the promises of mercy as also by then-
samples of diuerse holy martyres, comfort, encorrage &
strenghten them paciently for Christes sake to suffer the
manifolde cruell and moste tyrannous persecutions of ye
Antichristian tormentours: exhorting them to contynue in
faythfull prayers, innocency of lyfe, pacience, and hope, that
God maye the rather deliuer them, restore againe the his
gospell to Englande, and confounde all the proude, beastly,
& deuelishe enterprises of Antichristes garde, that doo im-
agine nothing els but ye subuersion of the gospell of Christ,
and contynually thruste for the bloud of all true Christians
(Southwark, 1555).

SMITH, SIR THOMAS. *De Republica Anglorum: The maner of
Governement or policie of the Realme of England* (London, 1583;

first draft written, however, between 1562 and 1566); reprinted under the same title by L. Alston (Cambridge, 1906).

STANFORD, SIR WILLIAM. *An Exposicion of the kinges prerogatiue* collected out of the great abridgement of Justice Fitzherbert and other olde writers of the lawes of Englande by the right woorshipfull sir William Staunford Knight, lately one of the Justices of the Queenes maiesties court of comon pleas (London, 1567; partly compiled earlier, however, for the preface is dated 1548).

STANFORD, SIR WILLIAM. *Les Plees del Coron diuisees in plusiours* titles & common lieux. Per queux home plus redement et plenairement trouera, quelque chose que il quira, touchant les ditz plees (London, 1560).

STARKEY, THOMAS. "Dialogue between Pole and Lupset," printed in *England in the Reign of King Henry the Eighth*, pp. 1–215 [not published when first written in 1538?].

STARKEY, THOMAS. *An Exhortation to Christian Unity* (London, 1536?).

SWINNERTON, THOMAS. *A mustre of scismatyke bysshoppes of Rome, otherwyse naming them selues popes*, moche necessarye to be redde of al the kynges true subiectes (London, 1534).

TAVERNER, RICHARD. *A Catechisme or institution of the Christen Religion* (London, 1539).

TAVERNER, RICHARD. *The garden of wysdom wherin ye maye gather moste pleasaunt stowres, that is to say, proper wytty & quycke sayenges of princes, philosophers, & dyuers other sortes of men.* Drawen forth of good authours, as well Grekes as Latyns, by Richard Tauerner (London, 1539).

THOMAS, WILLIAM. "A conference between William Thomas and certain Italian gentlemen, touching the actions of King Henry VIII," printed by J. A. Froude under the title *The Pilgrim* (London, 1861) [not published when first written in 1546].

THOMAS, WILLIAM. *The historie of Italie, a boke excedyng profitable to be redde: Because it intreateth of the astate of many and diuers common weales, how thei haue ben, & now be gouerned* (London, 1549).

THOMAS, WILLIAM. "Commonplaces of State: a list of politic questions," printed in Strype, *Eccles. Mem.*, II(1), 156–161 [not published when first written in 1548].

THOMAS, WILLIAM. "Six political discourses," printed in Strype, *Eccles. Mem.*, II(2), 365–393 [not published when first written in 1548].

TUNSTAL, CUTHBERT. *A Sermon of Cvthbert Bysshop of Duresme, made upon Palme sondaye laste past, before the maiestie of our souerayne lorde kynge Henry the. viii* (London, 1539).

TUNSTAL, CUTHBERT. *A letter written by Cuthbert Tunstall late Byshop of Duresme, and John Stokesley somtime Byshop of London, sente unto Reginalde Pole, Cardinall, then beynge at Rome, and late byshop of Canterbury* (London, 1560).

TYNDALE, WILLIAM. *Obedience of a Christian Man* (Antwerp, 1528); reprinted in *Doctrinal treatises by William Tyndale*, edited by Rev. H. Walter (Parker Soc., Cambridge, 1848), pp. 127–344.

TYNDALE, WILLIAM. *The Practise of papisticall Prelates* (Antwerp?, 1530); reprinted in *The whole workes of W. Tyndall, Iohn Frith, and Doct. Barnes*, pp. 340–377.

WALSHE, EDWARD. *The office and duety in fightyng for our countrey.* Set forth with dyuerse stronge argumentes gathered out of the holy scripture prouynge that the affection to the native countrey shulde moche more rule in vs christians then in the Turkes and infidels, who were therein so feruent, as by the hystoriis doth appere (London, 1545).

ANONYMOUS[2]

[A Eulogy of Henry VIII, ?], B.M., Royal MSS., 7 C XVI, 174–181.

[A Eulogy of Henry VIII, ?], B.M., Lansdowne MSS., 97, Plut. E LXXV, 148–153.

"A Replication of a Serjaunte at the Lawes of England, to certayne Pointes alleaged by a Student of the said Lawes of England, in a Dialogue in Englishe between a Doctor of Divinity and the said Student," printed in *A Collection of Tracts relative to the Law of England*, edited by Francis Hargrave (Dublin, 1787), pp. 323–331 [not published when first written in ?].

"A Litel Treatise concerning Writs of Subpoena," printed in Hargrave, *Tracts*, pp. 332–355 [not published when first written in ?].

That the bysshoppys haue immediate autoritie of Christ to make suche lawes as thay shall thynke expedyent for the weale of mens sowles (1532?), P.R.O., St.P. 6: 1, 8.

---

2. The anonymous tracts enumerated below are listed in their probable chronological order. The list begins, however, with four tracts the dates of which it is impossible to determine.

The question moved, whether these texts ensuing pertain especially to spiritual prelates or to temporal princes (1532?), P.R.O., St.P. 6: 2, 9.

Articles devisid by the holle consent of the Kynges moste honourable counsayle . . . to enfourme his louynge subiectis of the trouthe (London, 1533); reprinted in Pocock, *Records of the Reformation* (Oxford, 1870), II, 523–531.

A Dialogue betwene a knyght and a clerke, concernynge the power spiritual & temporall (London, 1533).

"A document of the year 1531 on the subject of the Pope's supremacy," printed in Pocock, *Records of the Reformation*, II, 100–103 [not published when first written in 1533?].

A Glasse of the Truthe (London, 1533); reprinted in Pocock, *Records of the Reformation*, II, 385–421.

Constitutions prouincialles, and of Otho and Octhobone. Translated in to Englyshe (London, 1534).

On the power of a prince (1534?), P.R.O., St.P. 6: 7, 27.

Against the supremacy of the pope (1534?), P.R.O., St.P. 1: 88, 13–14.

A Litel Treatise ageynste the mutterynge of some papistis in corners (London, 1534); reprinted in Pocock, *Records of the Reformation*, II, 539–552.

[A discourse in defence of the Royal Supremacy, intended for the use of unlearned priests, 1535?], P.R.O., St.P. 6: 5, 5.

The dyaloge bytwene Jullius the seconde, Genius, and saynt Peter (London, 1535).

[The Obedience of Christian people to their king, 1535?], P.R.O., St.P. 1: 99, 213–226.

Articles devised by the Kinges Hignes Majestie to stablyshe Christen quietnes and unitie amonge us and to avoyde contentious opinions (London, 1536; otherwise known as the *Ten Articles); re-*printed by Charles Lloyd, *Formularies of Faith put forth by authority during the reign of Henry VIII* (Oxford, 1825).

Of dyuers heresies which haue not ben taken for heresies in tyme paste (1536?), P.R.O., St.P. 6: 1, 24.

A Remedy for sedition, vvherin are conteyned many thynges, concernyng the true and loyall obeysance, that commens owe unto their prince and soueraygne lorde the kinge (London, 1536).

By whatt authorite and whow generall counsayles may be callyd [1537?], B.M., Cotton MSS., Cleopatra E VI, 331–331ᵇ.

The Institution of a Christian Man (London, 1537; otherwise known as the *Bishops' Book); reprinted by Charles Lloyd,

Formularies of Faith put forth by authority during the reign of Henry VIII.

A Protestation made for the moste mighty and mooste redoubted kynge of Englande & his hole counsell and clergie, wherin is declared, that neyther his hyghness, nor his prelates, neyther any other prynce, or prelate, is bounde to come or sende, to the pretended councill, that Paule byshoppe of Rome, first by a bul indicted at Mantua, a citie in Italy, & nowe a late by an other bull, hath proroged to a place, no man can telle where (London, 1537).

A Treatise concernyng general Counseilles [1537?], Hatfield House (see *Calendar of the Manuscripts of the Most Hon. the Marquis of Salisbury*, Part I, London, 1883–1933, no. 47).

An Epistle of the moste myghty & redouted Prince Henry the. viii. by the grace of God Kyng of England and of Fraunce, lorde of Irelande, defender of the Faithe, and supreme heed of the churche of England, nexte vnder Christe, written to the Emperours maiestie, to all Christen Princes, and to all those that trewly and syncerely professe Christes religion (London, 1538).

A treatise provynge by the kynges lawes, that the byshops of Rome, had neuer ryght to any supremitie within this realme (London, 1538).

Here begynneth a boke, called the faule of the Romyshe churche, wyth all the abhominations, wherby euery man may know and perceyue the dyuersitie of it, betwene the primatiue churche, of the whyche our souerayne Lorde and kynge is the supreme head, and the malignant churche a sunder (?, 1540?).

The Sum of the Actes & decrees made by diuerse bisshops of rome. Translated out of Latyn into Englysh (London, 1540?).

A Necessary Doctrine and Erudition for any Christen man set furthe by the kynges maiestie of Englande (London, 1543; otherwise known as the *King's Book*); reprinted by Charles Lloyd, *Formularies of Faith put forth by authority during the reign of Henry VIII.*

A proclamacyon of the hygh emperour Jesu Christe, vnto all his faithfull Christen (London, 1547).

Certayne Sermons, or Homilies, appoynted by the kynges Maiestie, to bee declared and redde, by all persones, Vicars, or Curates, euery Sondaye in their churches, where thei haue cure (London, 1547).

A Ballad on the defeat of the Devon and Cornwall rebels of 1548 (?, 1548).

A Caveat for the Christians agaynst the Archpapist (London, 1548).

The olde Fayth of greate Brittaygne, and the newe learnynge of Inglande, Whervnto is added a symple instruction, concernynge the Kinges Maiesties procedinges in the communyon (London, 1549).

BIBLIOGRAPHICAL NOTE

ORIGINAL SOURCES

THE most important source for a study of the theory of kingship during the early English Reformation is the political pamphlet literature written or translated by Englishmen between
1509 and 1553. For a complete list of the pamphlets, printed and
in manuscript, which the author has consulted, see Appendix B,
"Bibliography of Early Tudor Literature on Political Theory."
It will be noted that this list includes sermons and legal works
as well as controversial political tracts.

In addition to the pamphlet literature there are a number of
other important sources for the subject. As every Tudor scholar
knows, the *Letters and Papers of Henry VIII* (edited by J.S.
Brewer and J.Gairdner, London, 1864 ff.) are a veritable mine
of information on every conceivable topic, political theory included, for the early sixteenth century. Indeed, the majority of
the aforementioned political tracts are either calendared or discussed at some length in their pages. Highly suggestive also are
the preambles of statutes, speeches in parliament, coronation
records, cases in the law courts, records of the proceedings of the
privy council and convocation. For these materials the following
publications may be consulted: *Statutes of the Realm* (London,
1810–1828); *Rotuli Parliamentorum* (London, 1832); *Lords'
Journals, 1509 ff.* (London, 1846); *English Coronation Records*,
edited by L.G.W.Legg (London, 1901); *Concilia Magnae Britanniae et Hiberniae*, edited by David Wilkins (London, 1737); *Acts
of the Privy Council* (London, 1890–1907); the collections of the
Selden Society, principally *Select Cases in Chancery, 1364–1471*,
edited by W.P.Baildon (London, 1896), *Select Cases in the Court
of Requests, 1497–1569*, edited by I.S.Leadam (London, 1898),
and *Select Cases before the King's Council in the Star Chamber,
1477–1544*, edited by I.S.Leadam (London, 1903–1911); and
Les Reports de Cases (Ed. II–27 Hen. VIII), edited by John
Maynard (London, 1678–1680). Shorter collections such as *The
Reign of Henry VII from Contemporary Sources*, edited by A.F.
Pollard (London, 1913–1914); *Tudor Constitutional Documents,
1485–1603*, edited by J.R.Tanner (Cambridge, 1922); *Select
Statutes and Other Documents Illustrative of the Reigns of Elizabeth*

and James I, edited by G.W.Prothero (Oxford, 1898); and *Documents Illustrative of English Church History*, edited by H.Gee and W.J.Hardy (London, 1896), are also useful.

In addition to these official sources, contemporary biographies, chronicles, letters, and poems often contain important hints for the theory of kingship. Particularly suggestive are George Cavendish's *Life of Cardinal Wolsey*, edited by S.W. Singer (London, 1827) and William Roper's *Life of More*, edited by E.V.Hitchcock (E.E.T.Soc., Oxford, 1935); Edward Hall's *Chronicle*, edited by Henry Ellis (London, 1809) and John Foxe's *Acts and Monuments*, edited by S.R.Cattley and G.Townsend (London, 1837–1841); *Original Letters Illustrative of English History*, edited by Henry Ellis (3rd series, London, 1846), R.B. Merriman's *Life and Letters of Thomas Cromwell* (Oxford, 1902), and John Strype's *Ecclesiastical Memorials* (Oxford, 1822); and John Skelton's *Works*, edited by Alexander Dyce (London, 1843).

For the fifteenth-century background, the following publications are indispensable: the aforementioned *Rotuli Parliamentorum* and *The Reign of Henry VII from Contemporary Sources*, edited by Pollard; Fortescue's political treatises, printed in *The Works of Sir John Fortescue, Knight*, edited by Thomas (Fortescue), Lord Clermont (London, 1869), and *The Governance of England*, edited by C.Plummer (Oxford, 1885); Bishop Pecock's *Repressor of over-much Blaming of the Clergy*, edited by C.Babington (London, 1860); the anonymous tract, *Somnium Vigilantis*, "A Defence of the Proscription of the Yorkists in 1459," edited by J.P.Gilson, *Eng.Hist.Rev.*, XXVI, 512–525; *Twenty-Six Political and other Poems*, edited by J.Kail (E.E.T.Soc., London, 1904), and *Political Poems and Songs Relating to English History, Composed during the Period from the Accession of Edw. III to that of Ric. III*, edited by T.Wright (Rolls Series, London, 1859–1861); and the Year Book cases and sermons of Bishop Russell printed in Chrimes' *English Constitutional Ideas in the Fifteenth Century* (Cambridge, 1936), pp. 167–191, 350–394.

Among the most useful tracts for the contemporary continental and later English theory of kingship are Machiavelli's *Prince*, Erasmus' *Institutio principis Christiani*, Bodin's *Republic*, Hooker's *Laws of Ecclesiastical Polity*, James I's political writings, Hobbes' *Leviathan*, and Filmer's *Patriarcha*.

SECONDARY MATERIALS

NOT much has been written on the theory of kingship during the early English Reformation. Historians have tended to neglect the theory of the sixteenth-century political upheaval for the practice. Books dealing with the actual political and legal powers wrested by the Tudor sovereigns from rival jurisdictions are numerous. Studies in the Tudor *theory* of kingship are, however, rare.

J.W.Allen has devoted several chapters to the Tudor theory of kingship in his *History of Political Thought in the Sixteenth Century* (London, 1928). Though somewhat abbreviated, these chapters are highly suggestive and constitute a valuable contribution to the subject. Also useful in a general way are J.N. Figgis' *Divine Right of Kings* (Cambridge, 1896), A.J.Carlyle's *History of Mediaeval Political Theory in the West*, VI (Edinburgh and London, 1936), and C.H.McIlwain's introductory chapters to *The Political Works of James I* (Harvard, 1918).

For more specialized studies, P.Janelle's *L'Angleterre Catholique à la veille du schisme* (Paris, 1935), is valuable for the Henrician theory of Royal Supremacy. A.F.S.Pearson's *Church and State* (Cambridge, 1928) and M.Knappen's *Tudor Puritanism* (Chicago, 1939) are important for the Puritan attitude toward the state. H.H.S.Croft's introduction to Sir Thomas Elyot's *The Governour* (London, 1880) and L.K.Born's introductory chapters to his translation of Erasmus' *Institutio principis Christiani* (Columbia, 1936) contain valuable suggestions for the sixteenth-century theme of the moral responsibility of the ruler. For the theory of the king's relationship to the law, McIlwain's *High Court of Parliament* (New Haven, 1910), L.Alston's introduction to Sir Thomas Smith's *De Republica Anglorum* (Cambridge, 1906), Maitland's *English Law and the Renaissance* (Cambridge, 1901), and W.S.Holdsworth's *History of English Law* (5th ed., London, 1923–1938) are indispensable. The reader is also referred to C.W.Previté-Orton's lecture, "Marsilius of Padua," *Proceedings* of the British Academy, XXI, and to the author's two articles, "Thomas Starkey and Marsilius of Padua," *Politica* (London School of Economics), II, 188–205, and "Christopher St. German. The Political Philosophy of a Tudor Lawyer," *Amer.Hist.Rev.*, XLII, 631–651.

Works of a more general nature are also essential for a study of this kind. Of great value for definitions are the *New English*

Dictionary on Historical Principles, the *Encyclopedia of the Social Sciences*, the *Catholic Encyclopedia*, and the *Dictionnaire de Théologie Catholique*. For medieval political theory, G.H.Sabine's *History of Political Theory* (New York, 1937), R.W. and A.J. Carlyle's *History of Mediaeval Political Theory in the West* (Edinburgh and London, 1928–1936), and McIlwain's *Growth of Political Thought in the West* (New York, 1932) are standard works. For the theory of sovereignty and natural law, H.J.Laski's *Studies in the Problem of Sovereignty* (New Haven, London, and Oxford, 1917), Otto Gierke's *Natural Law and the Theory of Society, 1500 to 1800* (Eng. trans., Cambridge, 1934), and McIlwain's *Constitutionalism and the Changing World* (New York, 1939) are important.

For the general field of English political thought during the fifteenth, sixteenth, and early seventeenth centuries, the following works may be consulted: S.B.Chrimes' *English Constitutional Ideas in the Fifteenth Century*, Allen's *History of Political Thought in the Sixteenth Century* and *English Political Thought, 1603–1660* (London, 1938), Pollard's *Factors in Modern History* (New York, 1907), and F.J.C.Hearnshaw's *Social and Political Ideas of Some Great Thinkers of the Renaissance and Reformation* (London, 1925) and *Social and Political Ideas of Some Great Thinkers of the Sixteenth and Seventeenth Centuries* (London, 1926).

For the general political and institutional background, numerous studies in constitutional and church history, and biographies, might be cited. Obviously, it is possible to mention here only a few of the more important works which the author has found useful. For Tudor constitutional history, Pollard's *Evolution of Parliament* (London, 1920) and *Wolsey* (London, 1929); K.Pickthorn's *Early Tudor Government* (Cambridge, 1934); Holdsworth's *History of English Law;* Tanner's explanatory paragraphs in *Tudor Constitutional Documents, 1485–1603;* Leadam's introductions to *Select Cases before the King's Council in the Star Chamber, 1477–1544* and *Select Cases in the Court of Requests, 1497–1569; Tudor Studies*, edited by R.W.Seton-Watson (London, 1924); and G.T.Lapsley's *The County Palatine of Durham* (New York, 1900) are extremely useful. For church history, the following books are important: R.W.Dixon's *History of the Church of England* (Oxford, 1891–1902); J.Gairdner's *History of the English Church in the Sixteenth Century* (London, 1902) and *Lollardry and the Reformation in England* (London, 1908–1913); F.Makower's *Constitutional History and Constitu-*

tion of the Church of England (Eng. trans., London, 1895); and Z.N.Brooke's *English Church and the Papacy* (Cambridge, 1931). Among the biographies which contain valuable hints for the theory of kingship are Pollard's *Henry VIII* (London, 1902) and *Thomas Cranmer* (London, 1904), R.W.Chambers' *Thomas More* (New York, 1935), J.A.Muller's *Stephen Gardiner and the Tudor Reaction* (London, 1925), Merriman's *Life and Letters of Thomas Cromwell*, C.Sturge's *Cuthbert Tunstal* (London, 1938), J.F.Mozley's *William Tyndale* (London, 1937), Paul Van Dyke's *Renascence Portraits* (New York, 1905)—and, of course, the *Dictionary of National Biography*.

INDEX

ABELL, THOMAS
  Invicta veritas, on legality of Henry VIII's first marriage, 131
Agapetus, 201n
  Scheda regia sive de officio regis, translated into English by Paynell, 201
Alciatus, of Milan, denies that king is above law, 164–165
Allen, William Cardinal, 118
Amicable Loan, demanded by Wolsey, 175
Anabaptists, 90, 101; denounced by English Puritans, 97
Anglo-Catholic Advisory Council, on Church of England and Church Universal, 52n
Annates, Act of. *See* Statutes
Appeals, Act of. *See* Statutes
Aquinas, St. Thomas, 193; on king's moral responsibility, 12
  De Regimine Principum, 194; on king's moral responsibility, 12n
  Summa Theologica, on natural law, 7n; on resisting the king, 13
Articles, Thirty-Nine. *See* Thirty-Nine Articles
Audley, Thomas, lord chancellor, quoted to effect that king is under law, 172–173; quoted on king's spiritual prerogative, 189

BALDWIN, WILLIAM, 201
  Mirror for Magistrates, 201; distinguishes between office and person of king, 116n; purpose for which written, 202–203; threatens irresponsible rulers, 204–205
Barnes, Robert, 41; on non-resistance, 80–90; on passive resistance, 113n, 114n, 140; threatens tyrants, 199
  Supplication to Henry VIII, attacks papacy, 41n, 97
Becon, Thomas
  Policy of War, on Turk as God's instrument, 199
Benevolence, demanded by Wolsey, but declared illegal, 175–176
Berkeley, Sir Robert, on royal prerogative in Hampden's case, 146
Beroaldo, Philip
  De Optimo Statu et Principe, 195
Berthelet, Thomas, 2, 41
Bigod, Sir Francis, denounces Royal Supremacy and participates in rebellion, 117
Bodin, Jean, 87; on royal sovereignty, 124, 142
Bonner, Bishop Edmund, attacks papacy, 132
Bossuet, Bishop Jacques, 87
Bourchier, John, 200
  Golden Book of Marcus Aurelius, a translation of Guevara's *Relox de Principes*, 201; on ruler's education, 205–206
Brinkelow, Henry
  Complaint of Roderick Mors, on king's subordination to divine law, 139; addressed to parliament, 151; on king's moral responsibility, 198
  Supplication of the Poor Commons, on passive resistance, 114n

Brooke, Sir Robert
 Great Abridgement, 184
Bucer, Martin, Gardiner replies to, 161
Budé, Guillaume, 165; holds king is *legibus solutus*, 164

CADE, JACK, 101
Calvin, John, 90, 97; attacks authority of Catholic *sacerdotium* but sets up theoc-
 racy at Geneva, 24
Catherine of Aragon, 39, 88, 131, 138
Cecil, Robert, Lord Burghley, 88n
Chancery, court of, appellate power of, under Act of Appeals, 30; encroaches on
 common-law preserve, 122–123, 177; its decisions denounced, 178–179; its
 jurisdiction upheld, 181–183
 See also Courts, royal prerogative; Prerogative, royal
Chapuys, Eustace, plots "Enterprise of England," 88; accuses Cromwell of
 advocating absolute monarchy, 169
Charles I, 90, 146, 185
Charles V, Emperor, 87, 88, 92, 117, 126, 195; concludes truce with Francis I,
 93; Erasmus dedicates treatise to, 196
Cheke, Sir John
 The hurt of sedition, 94; on doctrine of non-resistance, 107; distinguishes be-
  tween office and person of king, 115
 Lamentation, 93; on doctrine of non-resistance, 107; denounces democracy,
  110; on king in parliament, 149
Christopherson, Bishop John
 Exhortation, 94, 100; appeals to natural law to prove doctrine of non-resist-
  ance, 98, 133; cites failure of Wyatt's rebellion, 101; lauds medieval mar-
  tyrs, 102; on tyrant's benefit to society, 106; denounces democracy, 110; on
  ruler's moral responsibility, 207
Church, medieval definition of, 47–48; Marsilius of Padua's definition of, 48;
 Henrician pamphleteers' definition of, 48; defined by author of "Treatise concerning General Councils," 55
 See also Church, Roman Catholic; *Ecclesia Anglicana*
Church of England. *See Ecclesia Anglicana*
Church, Roman Catholic, fifteenth-century publicists assign spiritual sover-
 eignty to, 5; English kings recognize spiritual authority of, 15–16; its relations
 with English *regnum* during fifteenth century, 16; Henry VII's attitude to-
 ward, 16; Pecock and Fortescue on spiritual power of, 17–18; loses its inde-
 pendent existence in England, 22
 See also Church; *Ecclesia Anglicana;* Papacy; Royal Supremacy; Royal
 Supremacy, theory of
Clement VII, pope, 26, 28, 40; excommunicates Henry VIII, 88
Clergy, benefit of, 15, 16; act restricting, 27; debate of 1515 over, 65, 65n
Clergy, English, fifteenth-century publicists on power of, 16–18; Dudley on, 20;
 declared by Hobbes to derive their authority from king, 25; charged with
 praemunire, 27; Act of Appeals maintains independence of, 28–29; *potestas
 jurisdictionis* of, but not *potestas ordinis*, assigned to king by Reformation
 Parliament and Henrician pamphleteers, 29–34, 65–84; resist royal attacks on
 autonomy, 30, 63–64; power of, to interpret Scripture assigned to king, 74–77
 See also Ecclesia Anglicana; Royal Supremacy; Royal Supremacy, theory of;
 Statutes
Cochlaeus (Johannis Dobneck), on legality of Henry VIII's first marriage, 131n

Coke, Sir Edward, 140; on fundamental law, 129; on parliament and common law, 158n

Colet, Dean John, 195

Commonalty, the, Tudor political writers apprehensive of, 108–111; Goodman on, 111n

Commons, House of, 126; exalted by Henry VIII, 143–144
See also Parliament

Commons, Petition of the, 71n; demands subjection of convocation to royal control, 64; its resemblance to St. German's *Spirituality and Temporality*, 66

Constitution, American, 130, 133

Convocation, to be summoned only by king's writ, 29; to promulgate no new canons without king's license, 29; resists royal attacks on autonomy, 30n; Gardiner champions an independent, 64; said to function only by royal delegation, 70–73
See also Royal Supremacy; Royal Supremacy, theory of

Coronation, unctional character not stressed during sixteenth century, 78

Coronation oath, 12, 13, 165; king's relationship to positive law defined in terms of, 166–168; Henry VIII orders new draft of, 167

Corporations, subordinated to central government, 123

Council of the North, 123

Council of Wales, 123

Council, king's, subservient to king, 122; increased competence of, during early Tudor era, 122–123; extra-parliamentary edicts of, 146
See also Chancery, court of; Courts, royal prerogative; Requests, court of; Star Chamber, court of

Councils, general, king and, 49–56; superiority of, to both pope and king asserted, 50–51; pamphleteers reflect Marsilius of Padua's conciliar theory, 51–56
See also Royal Supremacy, theory of

Counter-Reformation, 112, 118

Courts christian, right of, to judge "temporal" cases denied, 73–74

Courts, common-law; on Gelasian dualism, 17n; determine that parliament cannot make king a priest, 33; prerogative courts encroach on, 122–123, 176; St. German on alteration of, 167
See also Courts, royal prerogative

Courts, royal prerogative, during fifteenth century, 4; gain business at expense of common-law courts, 176–177; jurisdiction of, denounced, 177–178; arouse jealousy of common lawyers, 178–179; not regarded as threat to common law by most Tudor political writers, 180–184
See also Chancery, court of; Council, king's; Requests, court of; Star Chamber, court of

Cranmer, Archbishop Thomas, 28, 94; possible author of "Treatise concerning General Councils," 54; on king and *potestas ordinis*, 81; on doctrine of non-resistance, 99–100, 101, 107–108

Cromwell, Thomas, 22, 61, 81–82, 121, 165; concerned with literary propaganda, 35, 44; on king's power to issue proclamations, 147; his contempt for parliament, 152; on relationship between king and law, 168–170; supposed to have read and studied Machiavelli's *Prince*, 168, 169, 170n

Cujas, Jacques de, denies that king is above law, 164–165

Darcy, Thomas, lord, connives at "Enterprise of England," 117

De Grassaille, Charles, asserts that king is *legibus solutus*, 124

De Mayno, Jason
    Commentary on the Digest, declares king to be above law, 164
Democracy, Tudor political writers apprehensive of, 108–111; Goodman on,
    111n
Divine right of kings, doctrine of, 90, 210; not identical with Tudor doctrine of
    non-resistance, 92
    See also Non-resistance, doctrine of; Sovereignty, unlimited
Dudley, Edmund
    Tree of Commonwealth, 18–20; anticipates theory of Royal Supremacy, 20; on
    functional ideal of society and non-resistance, 104; on king's moral respon-
    sibility, 208–209
Durham, Palatinate of, judicial authority transferred to king, 123

Ecclesia Anglicana, 43; part of Roman Church during middle ages, 15; its pre-
    rogative in spiritual sphere during middle ages, 16; changing connotation of,
    in sixteenth century, 23; king declared to be rightful head of, 25
    See also Convocation; Courts christian; Royal Supremacy; Royal Supremacy,
    theory of
Edgeworth, Dr. Roger, on king and *potestas ordinis,* 79–80
Edward IV, *Mirror for Magistrates* on, 204
Edward VI, 91, 99, 111, 119, 139, 167, 173; instructed by William Thomas on
    art of governing, 109–110
Elizabeth, Queen, 87, 90, 91, 111, 112, 113, 147; orders commons to desist from
    meddling in religious matters, 56
Elyot, Sir Thomas, predicts chaos if social hierarchy is upset, 105; popularity of
    his works, 200; on education of ruler, 205–206
    Doctrinal of Princes, popular in sixteenth century, 200; on ruler's education,
    205
    The Governour, predicts chaos if social hierarchy is upset, 105; on lower classes,
    109; its popularity, 200; purpose for which written, 202, 202n; on ruler's
    education, 206
    Image of Governance, popular in sixteenth century, 200; purpose for which
    written, 202; on ruler's education, 205
"Empire," sixteenth-century definition of, 28n; England declared to be, 28, 41;
    Henrician pamphleteers on theme of, 41, 46
"Enterprise of England," early use of expression, 87n; a live issue during early
    sixteenth century, 87–88
Equity, St. German on, 181; anonymous writer on, 182
Erasmus, Desiderius, his political treatises, 196–197
    Institutio principis Christiani, 200; inveighs against commonalty, 110n; on
    monarchy, 193; on ruler's moral responsibility, 196–197; purpose for which
    written, 202; on ruler's education, 206n
    Paraphrase upon the New Testament, 61

Ferdinand, King of Spain, 122
Ferrault, Jean, asserts that king is *legibus solutus,* 124
Filmer, Sir Robert, 98
Fish, Simon, 65
Fisher, John Cardinal, 64; his treatise defending privileges of clergy, 63
Fitzherbert, Sir Anthony
    Great Abridgement, royal prerogative not above law, 184, 185; king may some-
    times set aside common law, 185

New Natura Brevium, king may prohibit subjects from leaving country, and king not bound by statute, 186

Foix, Odet de, Sieur de Lautrec, 137, 137n

Forrest, Sir William, 201n

Pleasant Poesy of Princely Practice, on king's subjection to divine law, 138; a translation of Egidius' *De Regimine Principum*, 201; on king's moral responsibility, 203–204

Fortescue, Sir John, 37, 41, 46, 67, 121, 125, 141, 142, 143, 157, 164, 210; supreme exponent of natural-law philosophy in fifteenth century, 8; his theory of kingship, 8–12; on property, 10n; distinguishes between *dominium regale* and *dominium politicum et regale*, 10–11, 165; on non-resistance, 14, 14n; on relationship between *regnum* and *sacerdotium*, 17; Henrician publicists advance same legal theories as, 127, 129; on natural law, 133; St. German's debt to, 150; on king in parliament, 153; on king's moral responsibility, 193

Declaration against king's title, on ultramontanism, 17–18

De titulo Edwardi Comitis Marchiae, on ultramontanism, 17–18

Governance of England, distinguishes between *dominium regale* and *dominium politicum et regale*, 10; demands monarchy stronger than any of its parts, 18–19

Fox, Bishop Edward, 41n

De vera differentia, denounces Petrine supremacy, 41–42, 43n, 46–47; sets up king as Supreme Head of Church, 58; denies clergy's right to *potestas jurisdictionis*, 68–69; on convocation, 71–72; on courts christian, 74; on king's power of interpreting Scripture, 75; on king's *potestas ordinis*, 82

Francis I, King of France, 88, 123; concludes truce with Charles V, 93

Frauncys, William, attacks royal prerogative courts, 177

Gallicans, 94

Gardiner, Bishop Stephen, 38, 41n, 84, 93, 125; undermines papal claims to *plenitudo potestatis*, 41–42; recites papal enormities, 45n; asserts Royal Supremacy, 47; on English Church and Church Universal, 52n; sets up king as Supreme Head of Church, 58, 61; refuses to obey *Homilies of 1547*, 61; champions independent convocation, 64; turns king's evidence in *De vera obedientia*, 64; abandons Gelasian dualism, 69; attributes *potestas ordinis* to clergy, 79; on obligation of subject to obey king, 140; on making of laws by king and parliament, 150; on origin of positive law, 161; on king's subjection to law, 166, 172–173, 175, 188–189; accuses Cromwell of advocating absolute monarchy, 170

"Answer of the Ordinaries," upholds independent convocation, 64

De vera obedientia, must be treated with caution, 39; asserts Royal Supremacy, 47; defines Church, 48; on king's power of interpreting Scripture, 75; on pope's power against divine law, 132; on king's moral responsibility, 207

"Si sedes illa," recites papal enormities, 45n; on English Church and Church Universal, 52n; denies right of pope to avenge Fisher's execution, 98

Gelasian dualism, 15, 25, 76, 84; Pecock upholds, 17; fifteenth-century common-law courts on, 17n; denounced by continental reformers, 24; retained by Act of Appeals, 28–29; Marsilius of Padua reinterprets, 46; Gardiner abandons, 47, 69; Henrician pamphleteers redefine, 67; pamphleteers do not abandon altogether, 77–84

Gelasius I, pope, 15n, 67

Gerson, Jean, 50

Godfray, Thomas, 2
Goodman, Christopher
 How superior powers ought to be obeyed of their subjects, on popular government and commonalty, 111n; on validity of rebellion, 112, 114
Government, popular, Tudor political writers apprehensive of, 108–111; Goodman on, 111n
Gregory the Great, 13
Guevara, Bishop Antonio de
 Relox de Principes or *Libro aureo*, enjoys sixteenth-century vogue, 195–196; translated by John Bourchier, 201; on ruler's education, 205–206

HALES, SIR JAMES, refuses to support Mary's exclusion from throne, 174; refuses to relax laws against Catholics, 189–190
Hall, Edward, asserts Royal Supremacy, 59; on king's power of interpreting Scripture, 75–76
Henry VII, 4, 19, 21, 116, 155, 210; his attitude toward Church, 16; his use of provisos, 145, 145n
Henry VIII, 1, 2, 4, 18, 19, 21, 22, 23, 27, 31, 39, 46, 57, 58, 62, 87, 90, 91, 92, 93, 99, 107, 111, 117, 119, 122, 125, 126, 131, 137, 139, 146, 155, 171, 198, 208, 210; uses first Act of Annates to force pope's hand in divorce case, 28; pays attention to printing press, 35, 39; determines to abolish papal authority in England, 40; defends pope against Luther, 40; speech before parliament of 1545, 76; concedes *potestas ordinis* to clergy, 82–83; flattered, 86, 121; shifts responsibility for Reformation to parliament, 126–127; identifies actions with will of parliament, 143, 149; use of provisos, 145; answers Lincolnshire rebels, 149; declares he is bound to observe laws of realm, 167; orders new draft of coronation oath, 167
 Assertio Septem Sacramentorum, defends pope against Luther, 40
Heresy, defined by anonymous pamphleteer, 73
Hobbes, Thomas, 38, 75, 76n, 121, 127, 210
 Leviathan, on Royal Supremacy, 25, 77; on natural law, 129; theory of unlimited royal sovereignty, 154
Hooker, Richard, 38, 49
 Laws of Ecclesiastical Polity, asserts that Royal Supremacy is shared with parliament, 59n; denies clergy's divine right to *potestas jurisdictionis*, 77; on king's superiority to general councils, 55n
Hooper, Bishop John, distinguishes between office and person of king, 115; on king and law, 173; on king's moral responsibility, 198n
Hotman, Francis, 112
Hughe, William
 Troubled Man's Medicine, stresses patience and humility, 101
Hunne, Richard, 65

INNOCENT IV, POPE, 17
Isabella, Queen of Spain, 122
Isocrates, his *Ad Nicoclem* translated by Elyot, 200

JAMES I, 56, 58, 92, 95n, 143, 146, 153, 165, 185, 210; declares that king is above law, 164
 True Law of Free Monarchies, on theory of unlimited royal sovereignty, 126–127; on natural law, 129; asserts that king may legislate without parliament, 142

Jus, medieval concept of, 6
See also Law, natural

KETHE, WILLIAM, proclaims validity of rebellion against king, 112, 114n; asserts king's subordination to law, 174
King. *See* Kingship, theory of; Monarchy, absolute; Parliament, king in; Royal Supremacy, theory of
Kingship, theory of, during fifteenth century, 1–20; effect of Reformation and New Monarchy upon, 3; conservative nature of, in fifteenth century, 4–18; Fortescue on, 8–11, 12, 17–18
See also Councils, general; Law, natural; Law, positive; Moral responsibility; Non-resistance; Parliament, king in; Prerogative; Royal Supremacy, theory of; Sovereignty
Kingsmill, Judge, denies that parliament can make king a priest, 33
Knox, John
First blast of the trumpet, on validity of rebellion, 112

LATIMER, BISHOP HUGH, asserts that king subject to God, 139
Law, common, identified with natural law, 7; subordinate to statute law, 155–157; king subordinate to, 172–173; threatened by Roman Law and royal prerogative courts, 176–184; Wolsey interested in reform of, 179–180
Law, divine, as proof of doctrine of non-resistance, 95–98
See also Law, natural
Law, natural, fifteenth-century conception of, 6–9; identified with divine law, 98n, 128n; as proof of doctrine of non-resistance, 98–99; king's relationship to, during early Tudor era, 128–140; belief in, precludes idea that king's will is law, 128; a living principle during early sixteenth century, 129–133; defined by St. German, Starkey, and Ponet, 134–136; kings declared to be subject to its dictates, 136–140; Hobbes on, 154; superior to statute law, 157–163
Law, positive, king declared to be under, 163–191; continental theorists assert king is *legibus solutus*, 164; king's relationship to, in terms of coronation oath, 166–168; statutes place king under, 167–168; Cromwell on relationship of king to, 168–170; Starkey, Taverner, and Gardiner on relationship of king to, 171–173; king may not influence judges or levy illegal taxes, 174–176; royal prerogative courts as threat to, 176–184; Tudor lawyers recognize no royal prerogative above, 184–187; king's absolute spiritual prerogative confined to spiritual realm, 187–190
See also Law, common; Law, statute
Law, Roman, 123, 127, 169, 171, 182, 194; Starkey advocates reception of, into England, 135, 171, 182; England in danger of reception of, during early Tudor era, 176
Law, statute, absorbs medieval sovereignties during early Tudor era, 125; ability of, to override custom, 155–156; subordination of, to natural law, 157–163
Law of reason, 134
See also Law, natural
Lawyers, common, fear Royal Supremacy may encroach on common law, 56–57
Lee, Archbishop Edward, on king and *potestas ordinis*, 79–81
Lever, Thomas, 94; on doctrine of non-resistance, 99, 107; on king's moral responsibility, 198
Levitical law, 131, 137–138
Locke, John, 129
Lollards, 16, 17

Longland, Bishop John
Sermon before the king, 42n
Louis XI, King of France, 122
Louis XII, King of France, 23, 123
Louis XIV, King of France, 86
Luther, Martin, 89; on Church and State, 24

MACHIAVELLI, NICCOLO, 154; advocates absolute monarchy, 124; ignores natural law, 128–129, 164; influence of, on Cromwell, 168, 169, 170n
Prince, on politics and morals, 195
Magna Carta, 8, 10; Prynne on, 154; Gardiner mentions, 173
Marshall, William, 53; translates *Defensor Pacis*, 44n
Marsilius of Padua, 41, 43, 44n
Defensor Pacis, 41; translation of, 44; denounces papal claims and reinterprets Gelasian dualism, 46; defines Church, 48; on general councils, 53–54; its influence on Henrician political theory, 53n; denies *potestas jurisdictionis* to clergy, 68
Mary, Queen, 91, 112, 113, 173, 207
Middle class, supports Tudor monarchy, 21; profits by early legislation of Reformation Parliament, 27
Monarchomachs, 112
Monarchy, absolute, trend toward, during Renaissance and Reformation, 4, 21, 121–123, 193; no theory of, in fifteenth century, 6, 11, 13, 14; definition of, 6n; Tudor publicists offer no theory of, 120–191
Monarchy, New. See Monarchy, absolute
Moral responsibility, king's, doctrine of, 192–210; why stressed by Tudor publicists, 193–195; its popularity on continent during Renaissance and Reformation, 195–197; English Puritans on, 197–199; secular writers on "perfect prince" theme, 199–206; Forrest on, 202–204; *Mirror for Magistrates* on, 204; Elyot on, 205–206; other Tudor writers stress, 206–209; Dudley on, 208; More on, 208–209; Starkey on, 209
More, Sir Thomas, 45, 64; advises Henry VIII in writing on defense of pope, 40n; his statement about England and Church Universal, 50; defends church tradition, 63; on when king may be deposed, 116; does not advocate rebellion against king, 119n; reminds Henry VIII of his subjection to divine law, 139; on parliament and divine law, 162; defends his injunctions as lord chancellor, 183; on king's moral responsibility, 209
Dialogue concerning Tyndale, upholds church tradition, 63n
Dialogue of comfort, stresses patience and humility, 101, 103
Epigrammata, on deposition of prince, 116; lauds Henry VIII's accession, 171
Utopia, 200; on deposition of prince, 116; its government republican, 151; on human and divine law, 162; attacks king for influencing judges, 174–175; on king's moral responsibility, 209
Morison, Sir Richard, on doctrine of non-resistance, 105–106, 106–107; on democracy, 108–109; on natural and positive law, 160, 160n
Exhortation to defend England, on doctrine of non-resistance, 94, 97, 106–107
Invective against treason, on doctrine of non-resistance, 94, 100, 101
Mortuaries, act fixing mortuary rates, 27; St. German on, 70
Mulsho, John, on jurisdiction of royal prerogative courts, 177, 178

NALSON, JOHN, 98
Non-resistance, doctrine of, medieval publicists on, 13; fifteenth-century publi-

cists on, 13–14; Tudor publicists on, 85–119; reasons for appearance of, during Tudor era, 87–90; not identical with theory of divine right of kings, 92; special body of literature devoted to, 93–94; arguments used to elucidate, 94–95; natural law used to prove, 95–98; pamphleteers assert vengeance is entirely remitted to God, 98–99; pamphleteers on God's use of tyrants, 99; patience and humility stressed, 101–103; functional ideal of society and, 103–106; chaos in event of rebellion depicted, 105–107; danger of foreign invasion stressed, 107–108; fear that rebellion will unleash force of democracy, 108–111; passive resistance advocated in some instances, 113–114; Pole on validity of rebellion, 116–117
Norfolk, Duke of, 147
Novel ley, king in parliament cannot create, 9

OCKHAM, WILLIAM OF, 45, 53
Oldcastle, John, 101

PAPACY, medieval publicists on power of, 15; Henry VII's relations with, 16; Fortescue on power of, 18; encroachment on powers of, 22–23; statute of 1512 upholds authority of, 23; statute of 1536 declares its powers usurped, 23; Reformation Parliament declares England an "empire" free of papal control, 26; payment of annates to, and appeals to, forbidden, 28; its power in England abolished, 29; pamphleteers repudiate its power over ecclesia Anglicana, 39–49; Henry VIII writes in defence of, 40; power "extra suam provinciam" denied, 43; additional arguments against supremacy of, 45; Marsilius denounces its claim to plenitudo potestatis, 46; superiority of general councils to, asserted, 49–56; doctrine of non-resistance set up as counterbalance to, 88; publicists limit its power of dispensation, 137–138
See also, Church, Roman Catholic; Clergy, English; "Empire"; Parliament; Royal Supremacy, theory of
Paris, Matthew, 82
Parker, Henry, 127; on parliamentary sovereignty, 154
Parliament, significance of Lancastrian parliaments, 3; arraigns Richard II, 8; anti-clerical feeling in, during fifteenth century, 16; new powers of, in sixteenth century, 21; confers on king absolute power in spiritual sphere, 31–32; king said to share Royal Supremacy with, 59–62; St. German on its absolute temporal power within realm, 71; no controversy between king and, during early Tudor period, 126; said to share rule with king, 140–153; Henry VIII enhances its importance, 143–144; king's power to legislate outside of, 144–147; Starkey an exponent of parliamentary rule, 148; Henry VIII on, 149; Gardiner on making of laws in, 150; St. German on, 150–151; Wolsey and Cromwell on, 151–152
See also Commons, House of; Parliament, king in
Parliament, king in, power of interpreting Scripture assigned to, 74–77; St. German on infallibility of, 76, 156; absorbs medieval sovereignties, 122–123; Henrician publicists on power of, 153–163; limited sovereignty of, 154–163; constitutes highest political authority in realm, 155–157; subordination of statute law to natural law, 157–163
See also Kingship, theory of; Law, natural; Law, positive; Law, statute; Parliament; Reformation Parliament
Parliament, Reformation. See Reformation Parliament
Patrizi, Bishop Francesco
De Regno et Regis Institutione, 195, 200

Paul III, pope, 87, 92, 126; summons council to Mantua, 51; seeks to avenge Fisher's execution, 88

Paynell, Thomas, 200; translates *Conspiracy of Lucius Catiline*, 100

Precepts teaching a prince his duty, translation of treatise by Agapetus, 201; purpose for which written, 202

Peasants' Rebellion, 87, 100

Pecock, Bishop Reginald

Repressor of over-much Blaming of Clergy, on relationship between *regnum* and *sacerdotium*, 17

Perkins, John, on natural law, 130; on private property, 141

Pilgrimage of Grace, 93; Morison denounces, 105

Pius IV, pope, on reconciliation with English crown, 111

Plato, 194

Pole, Reginald Cardinal, 91, 101; on use to which divine law may be put, 141*n*

Apologia ad Carolum Quintum, accuses Cromwell of advocating absolute monarchy, 169–170

De ecclesiasticae unitatis defensione, on validity of rebellion, 117–118; published at Rome against Pole's wish, 119

Ponet, Bishop John, 113

Short treatise of politic power, on validity of rebellion, 112; states that obedience is owed to God and commonwealth before king, 114*n*; distinguishes between office and person of king, 115–116; on deposition of king for tyranny, 116–117; declares king subject to law, 135–136, 139, 173–174; defines and applies natural law, 135–136; on parliament, 151, 156; on king's moral responsibility, 198; threatens tyrants, 199

Pontano, Giovanni

De Principe, 195

Potestas jurisdictionis, parliament confers on king, 29–32; Henrician pamphleteers do likewise, 62–77

Potestas ordinis, parliament does not confer on king, 32–34; Henrician pamphleteers on king and, 77–84

Praemunire, 23, 189; English clergy charged with, 27; Act of Appeals on, 28; Wolsey convicted of, 173

Prerogative, royal, 15; fifteenth-century lawyers on, 10; canons prejudicial to, submitted to special committee, 29–30; in ecclesiastical sphere augmented by parliament, 31; importance of prerogative courts enhanced, 122–123; its subordination to natural law asserted, 136–140; king's power to legislate by proclamation and proviso, 144–147; Sir Thomas Smith on, 146, 147; defined traditionally during Tudor era, 165; increased business of prerogative courts, 176–177; Fitzherbert on, 184, 185, 186; Stanford on, 184–187; Tudor lawyers conceive none outside of law, 184–187; king's spiritual prerogative confined to spiritual realm, 165, 187–190

See also Chancery, court of; Council, king's; Courts, common-law; Courts, royal prerogative; Proclamations; Requests, court of; Royal Supremacy, theory of; Star Chamber, court of; Sovereignty

Press, censorship of, 111

Proclamations, Act of. *See* Statutes

Proclamations, royal, 144, 146

Propaganda, attention paid to, by Henry VIII and Cromwell, 35, 39, 42

Property, private, Fortescue on, 10*n*; St. German on, 134; Perkins on, 141

Provisos, royal, Henry VII's and Henry VIII's use of, 144–145

Prynne, William, 127, 152; on parliamentary sovereignty, 154

Puritans, English, denounce unlimited royal prerogative in spiritual sphere, 56–57; on doctrine of non-resistance, 89–90; denounce Anabaptists and papists, 97; appeal to natural law to justify rebellion, 133; on king and law, 173–174; on moral responsibility of ruler, 197–199

    See also Barnes, Robert; Brinkelow, Henry; Goodman, Christopher; Kethe, William; Knox, John; Latimer, Hugh; Lever, Thomas; Ponet, Bishop John; Tyndale, William

RASTELL, JOHN, 160*n*; on natural and positive law, 161

Redman, Dr. John, on king and *potestas ordinis*, 79, 80, 81

Reformation Parliament, 2, 22, 25, 39, 40, 49, 62, 65, 159; revolutionary significance of, 23; abandons traditional relationship between *regnum* and *sacerdotium*, 26–27; legislates against clerical abuses, 27; legislates against papacy, 28–29; legislates against English clergy, 29–31; confers on king *potestas jurisdictionis*, 32–34; influences Englishmen to think in terms of parliament, 147, 152

    See also Commons, House of; Parliament; Parliament, king in; Royal Supremacy, theory of

Requests, court of, encroaches on common-law preserve during early Tudor era, 122–123; attempts to protect peasants from rigors of enclosure movement, 177

    See also Courts, common-law; Courts, royal prerogative

Revolution, Glorious, 57

Rich, Sir Richard, flatters Henry VIII, 86

Richard II, arraigned by parliament, 8; terms of his deposition, 13

    Mirror for Magistrates on, 204

Richard III, 101; *Mirror for Magistrates* on, 204

Romanus, Egidius

    De Regimine Principum, 195; translated into English by Forrest, 201

Roses, Wars of the, 3–4, 14, 19, 21, 87, 106

Royal Supremacy, 2, 31–32; statutes enacted by Reformation Parliament on, 22, 28, 29–31; does not include *potestas ordinis*, 32–34; doctrine of non-resistance stressed to safeguard, 89

    See also Reformation Parliament; Royal Supremacy, theory of; Statutes

Royal Supremacy, theory of, 37, 38, 84, 125; Wiclif an early exponent of, 16; Hobbes on, 25; analyzed, 39–84; implies freedom of king from papal control, 39–49; Marsilius, Fox, and Gardiner assert, 46–47; implies practical freedom of king from conciliar control, 49–56; application to king *solus*, or to king in parliament disputed, 56–62; implies subordination of English clergy to king, 62–77; king's power of interpreting Scripture, 74–77; attributes to king ecclesiastical *potestas jurisdictionis*, but not *potestas ordinis*, 77–84

    See also Clergy, English; Councils, general; Papacy; Royal Supremacy; St. German, Christopher; Statutes

Russell, Bishop John, on non-resistance, 13

ST. BARTHOLOMEW'S, MASSACRE OF, 112

St. German, Christopher, 38, 84, 130, 141; ascribes to king in parliament ecclesiastical *potestas jurisdictionis*, 37; his controversial treatises, 37; their probable sincerity, 39*n*; attacks papal abuses, 41*n*; his definition of Church, 48, 59; asserts that Royal Supremacy is shared with parliament, 59–60; leader of anti-clerical campaign, 65–66; on source of clergy's *potestas jurisdictionis*, 68; on tithes, 70; on Church goods, 71; asserts parliament's absolute temporal power within realm, 71; on jurisdiction of courts christian, 73; assigns to king in parliament power of interpreting Scripture, 74–75; on king and *potestas ordinis*, 78–79; asserts infallibility of king in parliament, 76, 156; practically identifies natural and divine law, 128n; defines natural law, 134; on private property, 134; on *Jus Regis* and natural law, 140; on royal prerogative, 149n; on king and parliament, 150–151; contrasts *jus regale* and *jus regale politicum*, 150–151; on natural and positive law, 160, 161, 162, 164; on divine and canon law, 162; declares that king *solus* may not alter common-law courts, 167; declares that king must adhere to coronation oath, 167; upholds equitable jurisdiction of chancery, 181; conceives no royal prerogative above law, 184, 185

Answer to a Letter, ascribes to king in parliament ecclesiastical *potestas jurisdictionis*, 37; defines Church, 48, 59; on jurisdiction of courts christian, 73; assigns to king in parliament power of interpreting Scripture, 74–75; on king and *potestas ordinis*, 78–79

Constitutions provincial and legatine, says convocation functions only by royal sufferance, 70n; on Church goods, 71

Doctor and Student, attacks papal abuses, 41n; asserts authority of "king in parliament" in spiritual realm, 60; on ecclesiastical visitations, 71; on courts christian, 73; on infallibility of king in parliament, 76, 156; practically identifies natural and divine law, 128n; on private property, 134; defines natural law, 134; on royal prerogative, 149n; on king and parliament, 151; on natural and positive law, 160, 161, 162, 164; on divine and canon law, 162; declares that king must adhere to coronation oath, 167; attacked by a common lawyer, 178–179; upholds equitable jurisdiction of chancery, 181; conceives no royal prerogative above law, 184, 185

Power of the Clergy, 38n; asserts that Royal Supremacy is shared with parliament, 60; on tithes, 70n; asserts infallibility of king in parliament, 77n; on king and *potestas ordinis*, 78n

Salem and Bizance, on source of clergy's *potestas jurisdictionis*, 68; denies right of spiritual person to interfere in secular courts, 73, 73n

Spirituality and Temporality, resembles "Petition of the Commons," 60; on clergy's encroachment on secular sphere, 68; on parliament's absolute temporal power within realm, 71; on infallibility of king in parliament, 156

Sampson, Bishop Richard, 42n, 43; sets up king, not king in parliament, as Supreme Head of Church, 58

Oratio, attacks papacy, 42; on St. Peter's primary authority, 43n; urges absolute obedience to king, 96

Sancroft, Archbishop William, 91, 92

Sanders, Dr. Nicholas, 112n, 113, 118

Scory, Bishop John

Epistle to prisoners in England, urges patience and humility, 102

Seymour, Edward, Duke of Somerset, 58, 150, 172

Simon, Matthew

Sermon at St. Paul's, 42n

Sixtus V, pope, 24

Skelton, John, attacks Wolsey for proceedings in star chamber, 180

Smith, Sir Thomas

De Republica Anglorum, on royal prerogative, 146, 147; on parliament, 147; on power of king in parliament, 155

Society, functional ideal of, medieval political theorists teach, 103; Henricians use to prove doctrine of non-resistance, 103–106

Sovereignty, unlimited, defined, 5n; no fifteenth-century theory of, 10, 14, 18; attributed to king or king in parliament within spiritual sphere, 83; Henrician pamphleteers generally avoid discussing, 92; Tudor monarchs almost achieve in practice, 122–123; French and Italian publicists attribute to ruler, 123–124; Tudor publicists propound no theory of, 124–125, 126; why no theory of, advanced during English Reformation, 126–127; Henry VIII not interested in asserting theory of, 126–127; incompatible with natural-law theory, 128–129; royal prerogative held subject to natural law, 136–140; king held to rule with parliament, 140–153; Tudor publicists do not assert unlimited sovereignty of king in parliament, 153–163; Hobbes asserts theory of, 154; Parker and Prynne on, 154

See also Law, natural; Law, statute; Parliament, king in; Prerogative; Royal Supremacy, theory of

Speculum principis. See Moral responsibility, king's, doctrine of

Standish, Dr. Henry, attacks benefit of clergy, 65

Stanford, Sir William
Exposition of the king's prerogative, conceives no royal prerogative above law, 184; defines royal prerogative, 187; restates feudal prerogatives of crown, 186–187
Pleas of Crown, king may pardon a felon, 185, 186

Star Chamber, court of, 122, 181; extends jurisdiction in early Tudor era, 177; Wolsey speaks of "new law of the star chamber," 180
See also Courts, royal prerogative

Starkey, Thomas, 119; an exponent of parliamentary rule, 148
Dialogue between Pole and Lupset, on when king may be deposed, 116; advocates reception of Roman law into England, 135; defines natural law, 135; on natural and positive law, 160, 162; on king's moral responsibility, 209–210

Statutes
20 Ed. III (Ordinance for Justices), 179
1 Rich. III, c. 2 (benevolences), 175
19 Hen. VII, c. 7 (Corporations Act), 123, 158
1 Hen. VIII, c. 14 (costly apparel), 158n
3 Hen. VIII, c. 13 (cross-bows), 158n
4 Hen. VIII, c. 2 (benefit of clergy), 65n
4 Hen. VIII, c. 19 (subsidy), 23
6 Hen. VIII, c. 3 (artificers), 158
6 Hen. VIII, c. 5 (enclosures), 159
21 Hen. VIII, c. 5 (probates of testaments), 27
21 Hen. VIII, c. 6 (mortuary rates), 27
21 Hen. VIII, c. 13 (pluralities), 27
22 Hen. VIII, c. 14 (sanctuary), 27
22 Hen. VIII, c. 15 (*praemunire*), 27
23 Hen. VIII, c. 1 (benefit of clergy), 27
23 Hen. VIII, c. 7 (importation of French wines), 145n
23 Hen. VIII, c. 20 (first Act of Annates), 36, 145, 159
24 Hen. VIII, c. 12 (Act of Appeals), 3, 6, 159; declares England to be an "empire," 40–41
25 Hen. VIII, c. 14 (heresy), 159
25 Hen. VIII, c. 19 (Act for Submission of Clergy), 36, 66n, 145
25 Hen. VIII, c. 20 (second Act of Annates), 30
25 Hen. VIII, c. 21 (Dispensations Act), 30, 156
25 Hen. VIII, c. 22 (Act of Succession), 137–138
26 Hen. VIII, c. 1 (Act of Supremacy), 30, 162, 165; expounded by Audley and Gardiner, 189

26 Hen. VIII, c. 10 (Statute of Uses), 147, 149
27 Hen. VIII, c. 24 (Durham), 123, 158
27 Hen. VIII, c. 26 (Wales), 145n
28 Hen. VIII, c. 7 (Act of Succession), 168
28 Hen. VIII, c. 10 (papacy), 23
28 Hen. VIII, c. 17 (minorities), 145
31 Hen. VIII, c. 8 (Act of Proclamations), 31, 36, 58, 121; intended to put Act
   of Supremacy into practice, 144; implies that king's power to use proclamations is reserved for emergencies, 146–147; forbids king to deprive subjects
   of rights and property, 167–168; betrays fear lest king use spiritual prerogative in secular sphere, 188; cited by Gardiner, 188
31 Hen. VIII, c. 9 (bishoprics), 31, 145n
32 Hen. VIII, c. 26 (interpretation of Scripture), 31, 188
35 Hen. VIII, c. 1 (Act of Succession), 144–145
Straw, Jack, 101
Supremacy, Act of. *See* Statutes
Supremacy, Royal. *See* Royal Supremacy
Supremacy, Royal, theory of. *See* Royal Supremacy, theory of
Supreme Head, king declared to be in lieu of pope, 22, 28, 41
   See also Royal Supremacy; Royal Supremacy, theory of

Taille, 122
Taverner, Richard, 96n
   Garden of Wisdom, on king's divine origin, 96; condemns Anabaptists, 97–98;
      denounces maxim *principi placuit legis habet vigorem*, 172; on king's moral
      responsibility, 207
Thirty-Nine Articles, on diversity of Church ceremonies, 52n; on general coun-
   cils, 55, 56n
Thomas, William, instructs Edward VI on art of governing, 109–110, 109n;
   inveighs against commonalty, 109–110
   The Pilgrim, on Henry VIII's first marriage, 131–132; states that Henry VIII
      determined no great matter without parliament, 149
   History of Italy, on king's moral responsibility, 207
Tiptoft, John, Gardiner on, 173
Tithes, St. German on, 70
Treatises, anonymous, published
   Disputatio inter militem et clericum, 41, 44n, 66–67; Cromwell arranges for
      English translation of, 44
   Glass of the Truth, attacks papacy, 41n; asserts superiority of councils to pope,
      50n; on pope's dispensatory power, 137
   Protestation against Paul III's council, on general councils, 51–52
   Remedy for sedition, 93; on lower classes, 109
   Treatise proving by king's laws, repudiates papal authority in England, 42n,
      44; asserts Royal Supremacy is shared with parliament, 60–61; abandons
      Gelasian dualism, 69–70; on convocation, 72; on courts christian, 74;
      assigns to king in parliament power of interpreting Scripture, 75n; on king
      and *potestas ordinis*, 79, 79n
Treatises, anonymous, unpublished
   "By what authority general councils may be called," 54n
   "Of divers heresies," denies convocation's right to legislate *jure divino*, 73, 73n
   "Replication of a Serjeant at the Laws of England," defends common law and
      attacks *Doctor and Student*, 178–179

"Somnium Vigilantis," 14

"That the bishops have immediate authority of Christ," defends liberties of clergy, 64

"Treatise concerning General Councils," reflects Marsilius' conciliar theory, 54–55; defines Church, 55

"Treatise concerning writs of subpoena," defends St. German and chancery's jurisdiction, 181–182

Treatises, official

Articles of 1536, on Royal Supremacy, 58

Bishops' Book, defines Church, 48*n*; on Royal Supremacy, 58; on king's power of interpreting Scripture, 74; concedes *potestas ordinis* to clergy, 83

Homilies of 1547, 61; on Royal Supremacy, 58; on doctrine of non-resistance, 95, 104–105, 113, 140; on functional ideal of society, 104–105; Gardiner denounces as contrary to act of parliament, 189

King's Book, 61, 79; on Royal Supremacy, 58

Triumphus, Augustinus, 17

Tunstal, Bishop Cuthbert, protests title of *Supremum Caput,* 63*n*; on natural law, 130*n*

Letter to Reginald Pole, Cardinal, 42*n*; on king and *potestas ordinis,* 79

Sermon on Palm Sunday, 42*n*

Two swords, doctrine of, 15

See also Papacy; Royal Supremacy, theory of

Tyndale, William, 41, 65, 93, 125, 126, 166; preaches non-resistance, 89–90

Obedience of a Christian Man, attacks papacy, 41*n*; on doctrine of non-resistance, 98, 102–103, 106; on subordination of king to divine law, 139; on king's moral responsibility, 197–198

ULTRAMONTANISM, 17, 25; Fortescue on, 17

WALES, COUNCIL OF. *See* Council of Wales

Warham, Archbishop William, 64; on freedom of archbishop from royal control, 63

Whittingham, William, on validity of rebellion, 112

Wiclif, John, 13; on source of bishops' power, 16; his political ideas in disrepute, 16–17, 45

William the Conqueror, 7–8

Winchcombe, Abbot of, defends liberties of Church, 65*n*, 132

Wolsey, Thomas Cardinal, 4, 121, 129, 165; defends liberties of Church, 132; his proclamations against enclosures, 146; distrusts parliament, 151–152; Gardiner on arbitrary actions of, 173; demands Amicable Loan and benevolence, 175; his writ against enclosures denounced, 178; indicted for reversing common-law decisions, 179; interested in reform of common law, 179–180; attacked for proceedings in star chamber, 180; and royal prerogative courts, 180*n*; his speech defending chancery, 183

Wriothesley, Thomas, lord chancellor, accused of violating laws of realm, 178

Wyatt, Sir Thomas, 101

ZWINGLI, HULDREICH, views on Church and State, 24